SPANN'S GUIDE TO

1902-1941

by Joseph E. Spann

ISBN 978-1-57424-267-6
SAN 683-8022

P.O. Box 17878 – Anaheim Hills, CA 92817

The Old Canoe—Moonlight
—and Us Two
Isn't it easy to bring to mind the cozy scene? The swish of limpid waters; subdued voices; the seductive harmony of stringed instruments—lilting notes—dreamy—elusive—soothing as a sweetheart's touch—crashing chords and syncopation, the spontaneous expression of the tingling joy of life and youth. Honestly, whether it be in the memory or but half-acknowledged hope, don't you thrill with the sweet intimacy of that cooling, moon-lit, music-caressed solitude?
But listen to a secret: It isn't the canoe—nor the moon, nor the water that plants the thrills in our hearts. It is the MUSIC—the lingering melodies that haunt us with thoughts of happy hours. And 'tis the same in any setting. Summer's shady nooks; snugly evenings of early Fall; Winter's cheery firesides—always and everywhere the music of the good old Gibsons seems to furnish the indefinable "something" that just naturally eliminates formality, makes hearts brighter, friendships more dear, and love the sweeter, and fills memory's storehouse with precious thoughts. This is the secret, but really there is no secret at all, for anyone can own and play a GIBSON.
Gibson
Instruments
GIBSON Instruments are easy to play, and easy to pay for. They bring self-performed music within the reach of everyone. They are the ideal home and companion instruments, bringing into the lives of thousands, pleasure, privileges, cultural and social advantages that would otherwise be inaccessible.
Gibsons have played a part in hundreds of little romances—confidential human histories—about which we shall be glad to tell you. Also the Gibson book and free trial proposition sent for the asking. These will help you to become better acquainted with the Gibson family.
Teacher salesmen wanted; wonderful field; ask for details. Write us!
GIBSON MANDOLIN-GUITAR COMPANY
1185 PARSONS STREET
KALAMAZOO, MICHIGAN
The only exclusive manufacturers of high-grade fretted instruments. Developers of Mandolin Orchestras.

Table of Contents

Acknowledgements

No work of this kind is created in a vacuum. While this book contains much new and original research, it is also based on the work of many Gibson historians and scholars who preceded me. We are all in their debt.

I would like to thank the following people.

Former Gibson employees and their children who were unfailingly generous with their time and memories: John Bergeon, Lewis Blaisdell, Dave Branch, Edward Chittenden, Jack Cook, Jack Curtis, Jack French, Adrian Glerum Jr., Pat Abrams Grossman, Robert Lamb Hart, Dennis Huis, Jim Hutchens, Doug Hutchens, Davis Kennedy, Donald Kievit, Betty Ferris Nolting, William Nolting, Gerald Post, John Post, Greg Rich, Carl Stadler, and Elizabeth Hart Whitaker

Gibson historians and scholars: Julius Bellson, Glen Bettencourt, Tom Biggs, Jim Burlile, Walter Carter, Gerry Clarke, A.R. Duchossoir, Greg Earnest, George Gruhn, John Hedgecoth, Willi Henkes, Steve Huber, Dan Loftin, Jim Mills, Dave Nichols, Bill Porter, Frank Schoepf, Roger Siminoff, John Thomas, Matt Umanov, Buddy Wachter, Lynn Wheelwright, Darryl Wolfe, and Dr. Robert Woody

Also: Rich Berger, Ed Britt, George M. Edgley Jr., Ruth M. Glover, Brian Hoover, Bob Reiser, Tom Schmitt, Jack Straley, Phil Veen, and Karlene V. Vontz

I would especially like to thank Cathy Serra of the Kalamazoo Public Library, Local History Department and all the staff of the many public libraries I contacted. They deserve special mention for providing excellent service in answering my endless questions. Bless you all for your patience with me.

Ron Middlebrook and everyone at Centerstream Publishing.

My wife April Hughes Spann for her love and support.

Joe Spann
Winter Haven, Florida
2011

Introduction

The history of Gibson before World War II can be divided into four distinct periods, clearly differentiated by the leadership of the men who served the company, each in his turn as general manager. This book is not concerned with the history of Orville Gibson or the instruments he manufactured prior to 1902. The subject matter covered herein relates only to the Gibson company from 1902 through the onset of World War II.

This book is not a history of the Gibson company. Other authors have sufficiently covered that ground before me. The first attempt at a cohesive company history was compiled by long-time Gibson employee Julius Bellson and published privately by him as *The Gibson Story* in 1973. Bellson was an eyewitness to events from 1935 forward and as such provided an irreplaceable, invaluable record of that period. Every Gibson scholar owes him a debt of gratitude. Twenty years later Walter Carter updated that history with his own landmark contribution to the canon *Gibson Guitars 100 Years of an American Icon*. With the assistance of other luminaries like Roger H. Siminoff, Michael Holmes, Tom Wheeler and A.R. Duchossoir, his book still stands today as the most detailed, comprehensive look at the company history. The author recommends both of them highly. With the Gibson company as subject matter, this book must necessarily cover some of the same ground. However, as a work of reference my approach will be "more data, less story."

This is a challenging book. It was a challenge to write and it will be a challenge for us to read. It is iconoclastic by nature and could hardly be otherwise. Some of the conclusions are difficult to accept because they destroy our cherished myths.

Future scholars will discover that this book has omissions and contains unintentional errors. The fabric of compiled history is always woven from such cloth. They will no doubt correct the vision presented here and are most welcome to do so.

Most importantly, this book is the result of a lifetime obsession with pre-World War II Gibson instruments, decades of collecting evidence, and four years of detailed analysis. It is my hope that it will be a useful, daily tool for others like me.

Joe Spann
Winter Haven, Florida
2011

List of Tables

Chapter 1 - The Factory

The Parsons Street factory, circa 1941
Kalamazoo Public Library Local History Collection

The First Factories 1902 - 1917

The first instruments produced by the Gibson Mandolin-Guitar Company were constructed in a building which had previously been a bakery. Meeting minutes of the board of directors indicate that this was probably the former Witwer Bakery at 114 East Main Street in Kalamazoo. The company was located there from 1902 through November 1906. Long-time Gibson sales manager Lewis A. Williams would later say, "We stayed in that building until we were driven out, not only because of lack of room, but because the cockroaches became so thick we could hardly prevent using them for bookmarks!"

The second Gibson factory was located at 114 East Exchange Place in Kalamazoo and was in use from November 1906 through 1911. The move from the old bakery didn't take long because the new

location was directly across a nearby alley. Both the bakery site and its immediate successor were situated right in the heart of Kalamazoo's main downtown business district. This allowed no direct access to rail transport for delivering raw materials and shipping finished products. Hot on the heels of the company's initial success came the realization that a better location was a necessity.

The third factory at East Harrison Court, circa 1915
Collection of the author

By 1910 the public appetite for mandolins and mandolin music had reached a fever pitch in the United States, and the demand for Gibson mandolins had clearly exceeded the capacity of the factory at 114 East Exchange Place. In 1911 the company moved about a half mile northeast and leased another pre-existing building at 521-523 East Harrison Court. This would be the home of Gibson from 1911 through 1917 and was a much better site for the company. Photographs and drawings show a two-story brick building with large windows and wooden floors. There was plenty of room to place the various manufacturing processes in separate areas. The building was served by the Michigan Central Railroad on the north side and functioned well enough until the company could build its own plant. The structure was still standing in 1973 but was demolished in the late 20th century. Today, the concrete slab foundation serves as a convenient parking lot for workers in the nearby light industries.

225 Parsons Street (1917-1984)

Gibson actually began planning for a purpose-built factory in 1909 but was not able to start construction on the project until 1916. The new facility was located at 225 Parsons Street, about a half mile northwest of the East Harrison Court location. The building opened for business in July 1917 and still stands as of 2011. It contains three floors, with the lowest floor being partially underground. The building's footprint is rectangular with the long axis pointing north and south. A stairwell on the southern end allowed quick access for employees and visitors to any of the three floors. On the west side a large Otis elevator with manually operated doors allowed the easy transfer of large materials and instruments. The Grand Rapids & Indiana Railway (later Pennsylvania Railroad) ran along the eastern side of the building.

Gibson's Parsons Street factory is the building most associated with the company. It was home to Gibson for 67 years and was the location where most of today's highly prized, collectable "golden-age" instruments were produced. In a 2009 interview Adrian Glerum Jr., son of long-time Gibson employee Adrian Glerum Sr., recalled that the mixture of nitrocellulose lacquer, hot hide glue, and freshly cut lumber created a heady aroma inside the Parsons Street factory. This was particularly true first thing in the morning after the building had been shut up all night. In the late 1930's Adrian Sr. was tasked with getting the glue pots heated up each day before production started. Adrian Jr. would sometimes accompany his father on Saturday mornings and vividly remembered being impressed by the dark, cavernous interior filled with mysterious machines and intoxicating smells.

"Daylight Factory" Style

The design of the structure is in the "daylight factory" style, popular in the early 20th century for its innovative use of concrete, steel, and glass. Architect Ernest Ransome first developed this style in the late nineteenth century, using a system of poured concrete beams strengthened with reinforcing steel rods to form the skeleton of his buildings. The floors and ceilings were sometimes also constructed from reinforced concrete. This method had the advantage of making the building virtually fireproof and allowing more open floor space between the support columns. In his style the exterior walls consisted of large, steel sash windows, with very little other structure. The idea was to allow the most daylight possible into the plant, keeping electrical costs at a minimum. Usually the same pattern was repeated on multiple floors with an elevator to connect the working levels. These buildings were often designed to be easily expandable via the addition of identical floors. Gibson's board of directors considered adding two more floors to the Parsons Street building in 1918 but for unknown reasons did not follow through.

We do not know specifically who designed the Parsons Street factory, but it may have been Albert Kahn (1869-1942), an architect from Detroit, Michigan. He became famous for his work within the "daylight factory" criteria, designing many industrial buildings in Michigan, including several for the Ford Motor Company. Certainly many of the design elements present in the Parsons Street structure are similar to other industrial buildings attributed to him.

A Tour of Parsons Street Before World War II

Over the course of seven decades, the Parsons Street factory was expanded several times and modified considerably. Updated manufacturing techniques, new equipment, and the constantly changing instrument types all required that production areas be repurposed from their original uses. However, with the aid of photographs, published accounts and the memories of former employees, the layout of the Parsons Street facility before World War II can be reconstructed.

THE DAYLIGHT PLANT OF
The Gibson Mandolin-Guitar Company

The First Floor

As stated earlier, the first floor was actually a half-basement. The floors here were polished concrete, and many of the interior walls were covered in ceramic tile. There were large, round support columns spaced evenly throughout the area. The main employee access was through the stairwell on the southern end of the building. The first floor was home to several important functions and activities.

Furnace Room - Smokestack

The coal-burning factory furnace was located in its own structure adjacent to the northwest corner of the factory. The iconic furnace smokestack which is featured in so many photographs was constructed by the M.W. Kellog Company of New York City. The furnace provided heat for the factory, and a place for burning scrap. Through an auxiliary device it also heated water to provide steam for the wood-steamer.

Factory supervisor Ted McHugh and two other unidentified employees inspect some rough cut lumber on the first floor, circa 1928.
Steve Huber Collection

White Wood Shop

Seasoned lumber which was ready for production was brought into this area. There was a very large bandsaw here used in cutting the lumber to rough shape and size. According to the 1937 catalog, rough lumber was stored outside and allowed to air-dry for a period of 5 to 10 years before being used.

Wood Steaming

This area was set up specifically for the purpose of steaming wood so that it could be bent without breaking. Jigs in this area were used to bend, hold and glue up the hot, wet wood into curved shapes. Thin hardwood veneers were bent into the compound curves needed for making the sides of guitars and mandolins here. Banjo rims were constructed in this department by bending and gluing thick plies of maple on a jig especially built for that purpose. Banjo resonators were produced here as well. The steamer was entirely homemade and consisted of a long, large metal tube capable of holding many pieces of lumber at the same time. It had a locking door on the end, which resembled a small safe door or submarine hatch. Once loaded with lumber, the device received steam via a metal pipe which connected with a hot water tank that had been attached to the factory boiler. It was still functional in the early 1960's.

Ted McHugh and Henry T. Reeves in the Engineering Office, circa 1923
Collection of the author

Patternmakers Shop / Engineering Office

Photographs from the 1924 era indicate that the Patternmakers Shop was in a corner of the first floor, probably the southeast corner. The patternmakers' benches were along the eastern wall, next to the windows which opened out onto the railroad tracks. Design work and drafting were carried out in this area. The many master patterns used to accurately reproduce complex shapes were also stored here. Some of these took the form of thin metal templates which could be laid down on a piece of lumber and used as tracing guides for items like pegheads and bridges. Other patterns were three dimensional items, like the tone ring models used by the company machinists to transfer measurements when they turned down raw castings. The long metal rulers used as guides for checking the placement of fret slots were also kept here. Drafting tables were also set up in this area for the purpose of design work. Factory superintendent Ted McHugh and his assistants could be found here. Henry T. Reeves and Theodore J. Cook both served as draftsmen at different times, as their initials are found on many of Gibson's original blueprints.

Lloyd Loar in his Experimental Lab, circa 1923
Collection of the author

Experimental Lab

Lloyd Loar's famous "experimental lab" was located on the first floor, possibly in the northwest corner, but certainly somewhere along the western side of the building.

This photo of the first floor machine shop was taken on December 19th, 1923. The door to the fireproof vault can be seen at left. The celluloid and lacquer were stored there until 1945. Steve Huber Collection

Machine Shop

The Machine Shop was located right next to the Patternmakers Shop on the first floor. This area contained many power tools, including shaper tables, table saws, joiners, and a very large lathe. Former Gibson employee Jim "Hutch" Hutchins described the lathe as being "about five feet long with a four-jaw chuck and gears that were changed manually." "Hutch" came to work at Gibson in 1964, and one of his first jobs was turning down banjo tone rings from the raw castings. The Machine Shop supervisor and pre-war employee Jack Doorenbos taught him how to accomplish this job. "Hutch" indicated that the enormous lathe was "definitely pre-war." The various wooden parts of the instruments were created in the Machine Shop and then sent on to the Assembly Department for gluing up.

Instrument Repair Shop

In the pre-World War II period, the Instrument Repair Shop was located on the first floor. Adrian Glerum Jr. remembered visiting his father there. One of the long-time repair shop employees was Dan DeValk. Dan was remembered by Adrian as an individual who thoroughly enjoyed life. DeValk was particularly fond of the baseball game held during the annual company picnic on the Fourth of July, perhaps not so much purely from a love of the sport, but also because of an attraction to the liquid refreshments provided to the employees on that occasion. He and his wife Willimyja were both natives of the Netherlands, and the couple had no children. DeValk started at Gibson before 1920 and he was still working there at the end of World War II.

Building Maintenance Office
The janitors' office was on the first floor.

Stockroom – First Floor
There was a stockroom at the front of the first floor.

The Second Floor
The second floor was reached via the stairwell on the southern end of the building. It had wooden floors, and extant photos show an extensive sprinkler system for containment of fires.

The Assembly Department on the second floor in 1936
Kalamazoo Public Library Local History Collection

Assembly Department
This area was located on the west side of the second floor. Parts and subassemblies which had been prepared in the White Wood Shop and Machine Shop on the first floor arrived here for basic assembly. Each worker had a station with a workbench which was about waist high. As instruments were assembled, they were placed in rolling racks which would allow them to be moved as a group to the next department.

The Binding and Gluing Department on the second floor in 1936
Kalamazoo Public Library Local History Collection

Binding and Gluing Department
Binding was done on the north end of the second floor. Instruments were received here in rolling racks from the Assembly Department.

Banjo & Electric Hawaiian Guitar Final Assembly Area
Jim "Hutch" Hutchins indicated that there was an area set aside here for the final assembly of banjos and after 1935 for electric Hawaiian guitars. After receiving stain and finish on the third floor, they must have been returned to this area for assembly. For banjos, only the rims, necks, and resonators moved along the production line process. It seems probable that no new banjo was completely assembled until just prior to shipment. The difficulty of keeping the skin heads from breaking (due to changes in temperature and humidity) and strings from going bad would have been problematic otherwise.

Employee Lunchroom
The employee lunchroom was located on the second floor. The continuous presence in the surviving financial records of money owed to local wholesale grocers suggests that Gibson made drinks and food available to employees for purchase here.

Administrative Offices
The administrative offices were located on the southern end of the second floor. The general manager had a separate office in the southeast corner which joined the office of the assistant manager (factory production supervisor). The sales force was housed in offices on the southwest corner. According to John Post, son of Gibson salesman George Post, they always felt this was "a little too close to the boss." There was a general open area for the secretarial and accounting staff. Surviving financial records show supplies purchased for a variety of office equipment, including Addressographs, Dictaphones and typewriters from Remington, Smith-Corona, and Underwood.

Showroom
In 1928 a writer for *Musical Merchandise Magazine* toured the Gibson factory and in a subsequent article gives a tantalizing description of "..a room in which were display cases...here we inspected an immense collection of every type and style of instrument. The walls were crowded with photographs of artists and groups using Gibson products.." This room was located on the second floor of the factory, near the sales office.

Stockroom – Second Floor
There was also a stockroom on this floor, probably for metal parts used in banjos.

The Third Floor

Staining and Finishing Department
Staining and finishing were carried out on the west side of the third floor. Instruments arrived off the elevator in the rolling racks and received their staining, finishing, and buffing here.

The Staining and Finishing Department in 1936
Kalamazoo Public Library Local History Collection

Factory manager Rodney Chittenden holding a bass banjo, circa 1929
Edward Chittenden Collection

Final Inspection - Storage
One pre-war employee stated that completed instruments were stored in permanent racks in an area on the third floor, unstrung and uncased. Only when an instrument was ready to ship did the final inspection occur, a procedure which included placing the paper serial number label inside the instrument, stringing, and casing. The empirical evidence of compiled serial number lists agrees strongly with this testimony. Many pre-war instruments have been observed with factory order numbers which do not agree chronologically with their serial numbers.

According to one eyewitness, since the length of time an instrument might remain in inventory was unknown, Gibson would not string it up until just prior to shipment. This policy reduced waste, since a set of strings could go bad fairly quickly in the factory environment. Similarly, putting an instrument in a case before you knew exactly which case the customer wanted was a waste of labor. For instruments that received a paper label with a serial number, the labels were not attached until just before shipping. Serial numbers basically served a warranty function and if an instrument never left the factory, it would never need a warranty repair. Issuing them before they were needed was unnecessary. Some exceptions to this policy are explained in chapter five.

Shipping Department

The location of the Shipping Department in the pre-World War II period remains somewhat vague. A 1929 photograph of factory superintendent Rodney Chittenden which was taken on the third floor shows many cardboard boxes ready for shipment. It would make sense for the Shipping Department to have been located there, near the storage for newly completed and new-old-stock instruments. One former pre-war employee remembered seeing areas of the third floor used in this way.

Like everyone else at Gibson, the Shipping Department sometimes worked six days a week. It was not unusual for them to send out over 100 instruments in a day and occasionally closer to 150. Any instrument which sold with a hard case could be shipped in a cardboard box stuffed with "excelsior." The company's monthly bill to the Excelsior Wrapper Company of Grand Rapids sometimes approached $300. But many instruments sold without a case. For them, Gibson used special wooden shipping crates built by the Mengel Company of Louisville, Kentucky. This company is perhaps best known for supplying the Coca-Cola Company with their iconic yellow and red bottle-carrying containers.

Working in the Shipping Department was at least a two person job. Many mistakes have been detected in the shipping ledgers which are "sound-related." These errors are easily explained if one employee was calling out the serial numbers while another employee logged them in the ledgers. Letters which sound the same like "D" and "E" are often found to be mis-reported in the records.

Amplifier Repair Shop

Gibson first marketed electric guitar amplifiers in 1936. The original model was built for Gibson at Lyon & Healy in Chicago. In the beginning, warranty repairs were handled by sending the amps back to Chicago. By 1938 Gibson was taking care of this process in-house on the third floor, a process which consisted mainly of switching out parts until the unit began working properly.

Chapter 2 - The Employees

This December 1923 image shows the administrative office staff. First row (left to right): Clarence Havenga (salesman), Rodney Chittenden (accountant), unknown, Harry L. Ferris (general manager), Ted McHugh (factory supervisor), Guy Hart (accountant), unknown, and Lloyd Loar (acoustical engineer). The names of the ladies are lost to history.
Edward Chittenden Collection

Overview

The overwhelming majority of Gibson employees before World War II were of Dutch ancestry. Many of them were born in Holland themselves, and most of the rest had parents who were born there. Several members of the same family often worked for Gibson at the same time. Over the years Gibson employed three successive generations of certain families. The Dutch tended to be rather clannish, sometimes making it difficult for outsiders to obtain and keep jobs. Gibson tried to hire experienced cabinet makers for the woodworking positions. They could do so fairly easily because of the numerous furniture factories in the Kalamazoo area at that time. Except for a brief period 1929-1931, other specialty skills were generally outsourced.

Workforce Size

Thirteen people were employed at Gibson when the company was formed in 1902. The popularity of the mandolin and Gibson's innovative mandolin design had enlarged the workforce to 61 employees

by 1915. The banjo boom of the 1920's swelled the factory force to an all-time high of 130 in 1927. A decline in sales for 1928 and 1929 was mirrored in a slight drop to 108 employees in 1930. A badly timed attempt to bring some formerly outsourced functions into the factory also occurred in 1929. In-house pearl inlaying, case making, and electroplating were all included in this brief but ill-fated experiment. In November of 1931 Gibson still had 116 employees, but the effects of the 1929 stock market collapse were finally catching up with the company. In January 1932 a general purging of employees was necessary in which one out of every four workers was let go. For the next three years, Gibson's workforce continued to shrink, reaching a low of 67 workers in 1934. This trend was reversed by the development of budget-line and off-brand instruments. By 1937 this strategy was paying off, and about 200 employees were working at Gibson.

The entire factory workforce turned out for this photo, taken in 1927 at the southwest corner of the factory.
Kalamazoo Public Library Local History Collection

Working Conditions

Company records reveal that employees sometimes worked six days a week, and often nine hours a day. This work schedule was confirmed in an interview with Adrian Glerum Jr. He stated that his father Adrian Sr. often worked on Saturdays and, being out of school, Adrian Jr. would visit his father at the factory on that day. In April of 1917 the employees petitioned the board of directors to allow them half-days off with full pay, on Saturdays during the summer months. The response from the board was quick and decisive. The minutes of the May 15th 1917 meeting stated: "It is the consensus of this Board that we are opposed to paying employess of the Gibson company for hours of work that they do not perform, and that, therefore the petition of the workmen be denied."

An employee picnic was held each year on the Fourth of July, and two additional holidays were granted on Thanksgiving and Christmas Day. Safety was apparently not of prime concern; old-timers at Gibson could often be identified by their missing fingers. In 1915, wages were as low as 15 cents per hour on the factory floor and averaged 40 cents per hour for supervisors. Design engineer Ted McHugh was the highest paid employee at that time, making about $24 a week. Gibson was not a union shop before World War II, and at least one labor strike occurred there. In a 2009 interview Pat Grossman, daughter of assistant manager Neil Abrams, remembered being driven by the Parsons Street factory in the early 1930's and waving at the striking workers hanging out of the windows. Personnel turnover seems to have been a constant problem. Because Kalamazoo was home to many diverse industries and their support services, a steady supply of jobs was available at all times, and Gibson employees dissatisfied for any reason could move on quickly to other companies.

This photograph was made at the company picnic in 1935 and represents those employees receiving service awards. They are (from left to right): Tom Jaeger, Carl Siebert, Mac Ellerton, Rusty Adams, Joe Curtis, George Altermatt, Gene Weed, James Johnstone, John Kraft, Glenn Cook, Bert Stratton, Pokey Howard (front), Curly Bramble (back), Adrian Glerum, Dorothy Bippes, Dan DeValk, Garrett Bos, Katherine Harris, John Adams, Ernie Stratton, Clarence Havenga, Charlie Best, Red Kuney, Ted McHugh, and Neil DeYoung.
Collection of the author

The Gibson Experience

As might be expected, each person who worked for Gibson before World War II had a unique experience. Some made lasting contributions, even though their tenure was brief. Others spent their entire lives at the company, laboring in obscurity. What follows are some samples of life at Gibson.

Harry Lewis Ferris (1891-1965)

Harry L. Ferris came to work at Gibson as general manager in October of 1923. He replaced long-time Gibson employee Lewis A. Williams, who had allowed the company to fall into financial danger during his last years there. Ferris was a native of Morrison, Illinois and a 1914 graduate of Oberlin College. His father was a successful factory production manager in Portland, Indiana, and the extended Ferris family was one of many distinguished achievements. His mother was an accomplished singer, teacher, and musician. Harry and his brother Paul were partners in the Wisconsin branch of their father's Creamery Package Manufacturing Company at Waukesha by 1920. The factory burned down just prior to Harry's employment at Gibson, suggesting that this was the reason he was available to take a job at Kalamazoo in 1923.

It may seem strange that Ferris would leave the world of manufacturing dairy equipment to lead a musical instrument company 250 miles away in Kalamazoo. His family on his mother's side was a musical one, but as far as we know, Ferris himself did not play an instrument. In all likelihood his connection at Gibson was probably none other than Lloyd A. Loar, the company's resident acoustical engineer genius. Both of them were alumni of Oberlin College in Ohio, and being close in age it is conceivable that they knew each other at school.

Harry L. "Guy" Ferris about 1940
William Nolting Collection

After being hired, Ferris primary task consisted of pulling Gibson back from the brink of financial disaster. Under the leadership of the previous general manager, the company had lost $20,000 in the first part of 1923. Ferris quickly proved his competence. In eleven months he was able to increase sales by 25% and show a profit of $2,000. He accomplished this by instituting production budgeting, increasing procedural efficiency, and using targeted marketing. He brought modern business management to the company.

In a 2010 interview, his daughter Betty remembered that her father was known to his business associates as "Guy" Ferris, a nickname he particularly liked. She remembered him as fearless, straight forward, and headstrong, with a grand sense of humor. Unfortunately, these same characteristics rapidly got him into trouble with Gibson's stodgy board of directors. His candid report to the board concerning their previously poor business decisions, along with a very public information leak about the company's financial problems, resulted in a call for his immediate resignation on September 8, 1924. He obliged the board and left Kalamazoo behind, returning to live at Waukesha. His college mate Lloyd Loar left Gibson in December 1924. Harry L. Ferris went on to live a very successful life and died at Winter Park, Florida in 1965. The family remained unaware of Ferris's connection to Gibson until contacted by this author in 2010. In an ironic twist, one of his grandsons toured the Gibson factory in the 1960's, blissfully ignorant of his own grandfather's role in saving the company.

Guy Hart (1888-1961)

General manager Guy Hart was an outsider at Gibson from the start. Unlike any other Gibson employee, Hart was a true son of the south, with deep family roots in Kentucky and North Carolina. At the age of seven, Guy moved with his parents and siblings from his birthplace at Henshaw, Kentucky across the Ohio River to Carrier Mills Township in Saline County, Illinois. Nothing is known of his early education, but it is assumed that he attended the public schools of Saline County. In 1905 his family moved to Poplar Bluff, Missouri, and it is probable that he went with them. However, his residence in Missouri was not a lengthy one.

By 1910 Guy was rooming at 1613 Oak Street in Chicago Heights, Illinois and working as a clerk in a factory which made wooden handles. His career progressed well, and by 1917 he had moved to Denver, Colorado and was working as a traveling salesman for Hartwell Brothers Company of Chicago Heights. During World War I he served in the US Army, enlisting from Denver. At the conclusion of the conflict, he resumed his career at Hartwell Brothers and was promoted to the position of accountant in their Chicago location.

Guy was married on 11 June 1923 at Trinity Church in Denver to Miss Elva H. Rux. In 1923 Guy and Elva moved to Kalamazoo, Michigan so that he could take a position with Gibson Inc. as an auditor. On September 8, 1924 following a raucous board meeting which resulted in the immediate resignation of general manager Harry L. Ferris, Guy Hart was appointed to replace him. The board acted so precipitously that later they had to backtrack and sell Hart one share of stock in order that he be eligible for the job. Unlike his predecessor, Hart had no real educational qualifications or direct experience for the job of general manager. It has been said that he was hired because of his deferential attitude towards his superiors. He was neither an engineer nor a musician. He was also not well liked by the rank-and-file employees.

Certainly some of the problem was Hart's management style. He would walk around the factory, silently watching the employees and taking notes. When he was upset, his temper usually got the better of him, resulting in unexpected emotional explosions. He was often absent from the factory, though usually with just cause, traveling on sales trips and marketing Gibson products generally. The shipping ledgers show that Hart often took as many samples on his trips as any of Gibson's regular salesmen. However, another explanation for the widespread aversion to Hart's personality may have been cultural in nature. His southern roots may have naturally resulted in poor communication and misunderstanding with the deeply Dutch workforce at Gibson.

Guy Hart in 1923
Edward Chittenden Collection

Regardless of Hart's disadvantages, the term of his leadership at Gibson was one of intense innovation. It is known today as the company's "Golden Period" and produced some of the most revered acoustic instruments in the world. The Super 400 archtop guitar, SJ-200 and J-45 flattop guitars, and Mastertone banjo were all designed and manufactured during his tenure. He traveled extensively for Gibson and expanded markets in England, South Africa, New Zealand, India, and Europe. During World War II he oversaw the factory conversion to war material production and helped earn three Army and Navy "E" awards. He continued as general manager until 1944 when he was elected company president. He retired from Gibson in 1950 but remained on the Board of Directors until his death in 1961.

Neil Kievit (1908-1954)

Neil Kievit came to work at Gibson in 1926 as a commercial artist. One of his first jobs was to design the fingerboard and resonator decorations for the Florentine model banjo. This model used a celluloid material for the fingerboard featuring etched drawings of Italian street scenes.

For some unknown reason, young Mr. Kievit chose street scenes from the city of Venice for his design, not Florence. Perhaps he did this because the buildings of Venice are more iconically Italian for most Americans. His design for the back of the resonator featured a pseudo coat-of-arms which does not at all resemble the original from the city of Florence. However, the work was accepted by Gibson and went forward into production anyway. During the next three years, Neil spent most of his time at Gibson coloring the scenes on Florentine fingerboards and hand-painting Florentine and Bella Voce resonators before they were installed on the instruments. Neil left Gibson in 1930 following a divorce and then worked briefly in the State Hospital at Kalamazoo. He later resumed work as a commercial artist and found employment at various locations in Kalamazoo and Grand Rapids, Michigan. In 1936 Neil moved to Fort Wayne, Indiana where he designed ink pen cases for the Coleman Case Company in nearby New Haven, Indiana. He returned to Kalamazoo in 1938 and worked for the Kalamazoo Stationery Company and later Upjohn Pharmaceutical Company. Neil died in Kalamazoo at the age of 46 in 1954. Kievit did not retain any contact with Gibson after leaving. Today, his designs for the Florentine banjo are known worldwide to Gibson enthusiasts, but Kievit himself is forgotten.

Neil Kievit in his studio at Gibson in 1928
Collection of the author

Rodney Chittenden (1903-1986)
Rodney Chittenden came to work at Gibson in 1923 as an accountant. As an office employee, Rodney came to be close friends with Guy Hart, who started at Gibson in 1923 as an auditor. Hart was fifteen years older than Chittenden and became something of a father figure to him. When Hart was promoted to the position of general manager in 1924, it brought advancement for Chittenden's own career as well. By 1929 he had been promoted to factory superintendent and seemed to have a secure future at the company, even getting his photograph in the 1929 catalog.

In December of 1930 Chittenden was offered a position at the Upjohn Pharmaceutical Company in Kalamazoo. Chittenden agonized over the decision and ultimately decided to resign from his job at Gibson. Within days he regretted this choice and asked Guy Hart for his old job back. Hart was known to be difficult to work for, and was probably very unhappy with Chittenden. However, in this specific case he was amenable and told Chittenden he could come back to Gibson if he liked. Instead, Chittenden decided to stick it out with Upjohn for a few more days and ended up spending the rest of his career there. He remained on good terms with his former co-workers at Gibson, particularly accountant-turned-salesman George Post. Chittenden died in the author's home town of Winter Haven, Florida in 1986.

Rodney Chittenden in 1923
Edward Chittenden Collection

Adrian Glerum Sr. (1889-1956)
In many ways Adrian Glerum Sr. typified the rank-and-file pre-World War II Gibson employee. He was born in Holland and immigrated to the US with his parents in 1901. He came to work at Gibson about 1920 and spent twelve years in the White Wood Shop. He was laid off in the general employee purge of January 1932 but found temporary employment at the Kalamazoo Fire Department and later the State Hospital. He was rehired at Gibson in 1935, working first in the Repair Department and then later in the Finishing Department. Glerum continued to work for Gibson right up to his death in 1956, completing over 50 years with the company, but never rose beyond the level of a skilled laborer.

Lynn J. Blaisdell (1907-1988)
Lynn J. Blaisdell was a native of Arlington, Michigan. His family moved from Van Buren County to Kalamazoo about 1929 where he and his wife Lily and his father Jay all started working for Gibson in 1930. Lynn started in the White Wood Shop as a neck sander in 1930, but left Gibson in 1932. It is likely that he was one of those who were released in a general downsizing of Gibson employees that took place in January of 1932. His wife Lily was also released at that time.

On 1 April 2008 I interviewed Lewis Blaisdell, oldest son of Lynn. According to Lewis, his father was rehired at Gibson in 1937 as a woodworker and machinist. He said that during this second

period Lynn continued working in the White Wood Shop, primarily as a neck builder. Lynn left Gibson for a second time in 1943 and purchased Gates Manufacturing, a small Kalamazoo woodworking company. Almost immediately, Gates Manufacturing became a Gibson vendor, providing them with the wooden casework for their electric guitar amplifiers. In the 1950's and 60's Gates also sporadically provided Gibson with wooden banjo rims. Lewis indicated that his father Lynn retained his contacts at Gibson until he retired in the early 1970's. Lynn J. Blaisdell died at Leesburg, Florida on March 14, 1988.

John Huis (1909-1996)
John Huis came to work at Gibson at the young age of 16 in 1926. Like Adrian Glerum he was born in Holland and immigrated to the US with his parents. But that was where the similarity ended. Huis rose steadily in responsibility from bench hand in 1926, to finisher in 1930, to inspector by 1937. He served a period as plant superintendent as well. He left Gibson in 1943 but returned in 1948 as vice-president. Huis worked another 17 years before leaving for a second time along with company president Ted McCarty to run the Bigsby Company. Huis worked his way through almost every job in the factory and knew the operation inside out.

John Huis posing as the "final inspector," circa 1937
Steve Huber Collection

Henry T. Reeves (1875-1947)
Henry T. Reeves was an anomaly in the Gibson factory. He was born in Richmond, Indiana and came to work at Gibson about 1920 at the advanced age of 45. Prior to his employment at Gibson, he spent at least 10 years working as a machinist for a Kalamazoo enameling company. At Gibson he was the chief draftsman, working every day inside the Engineering Department alongside the venerable Ted McHugh, the company's creative innovater. McHugh is credited with the invention of the coordinator rod system used in Gibson banjo rims, the adjustable bridge for mandolins and guitars, and the truss rod used in Gibson instruments after 1921. Indeed, the period during which Henry Reeves worked with McHugh (1920-1927) was one of furious innovation. The surviving blueprints from that period reveal that Reeves was the man who drew them. How much input did he have in the creative process? His name is the only one appearing on the iconic Gibson "bell truss rod cover" drawing. In 1926 he described his job at Gibson as "experimenter." This is also the period that saw the creation of the world-famous Gibson Mastertone banjo tone rings. As chief draftsman, Reeves might have assisted in their design, but was never credited as such. Henry left Gibson in 1928 and took a job across town as a draftsman at the Shakespeare Company. Reeves died in 1947 as a resident of Galesburg, Michigan. His obituary does not mention Gibson.

Glenn O. Cook (1887-1951)
Glenn Owen Cook came to work at Gibson in 1910 as a 23-year-old and worked there until his death in 1951 at the age of 64. He knew the company's namesake Orville Gibson personally. Glenn spent most of his career in the White Wood Shop and was particularly skilled at bending wood into compound curves and then gluing them up. In 1925 Glenn invented a pressure steamer used to prepare multiple pieces of wood for bending simultaneously and also a banjo rim bending jig. Both of these machines were highly successful, and both were used by Gibson for decades to come. In fact, the steamer was still in place and still functioning in the 1960's. Gibson did not allow production floor employees to patent their inventions but rather paid them a one-time fee for release of their rights and claims. Glenn received $25 for his creativity. He spent his last years at Gibson tending the glue pots.

Lloyd Allayre Loar (1886–1943)
Lloyd Loar was undoubtedly the single most important and influential Gibson employee of the pre-World War II period. His innovative designs kicked open the door to Gibson's "golden era." Loar was an accomplished musician, attending the conservatory at Oberlin College and then receiving a master's degree in 1921 from the American Conservatory of Music in Chicago. During World War I he entertained American troops in Europe while working for the Y.M.C.A. and seized the opportunity to study at the National Conservatory of Music in Paris. His scientific approach to musical instrument construction made him one of the first truly significant acoustical engineers.

Loar officially came to work at Gibson in June of 1919 as a design consultant, but his relationship with the company extended back for more than a decade before that. He had been playing Gibson instruments since at least 1906 and became an endorser in 1911. Gibson began publishing his sheet music in 1913, and by 1914 he was acting as concertmaster for various "Gibsonian" performing ensembles. His early connection with Gibson was severed by the advent of World War I. Upon his return to Gibson in 1919, he was known to the other employees as "Master Loar," a title which may have been the source of the "Master Model" and "Mastertone" labels used to market his new designs. Loar's work schedule at Gibson must have been quite erratic. Besides his experimental

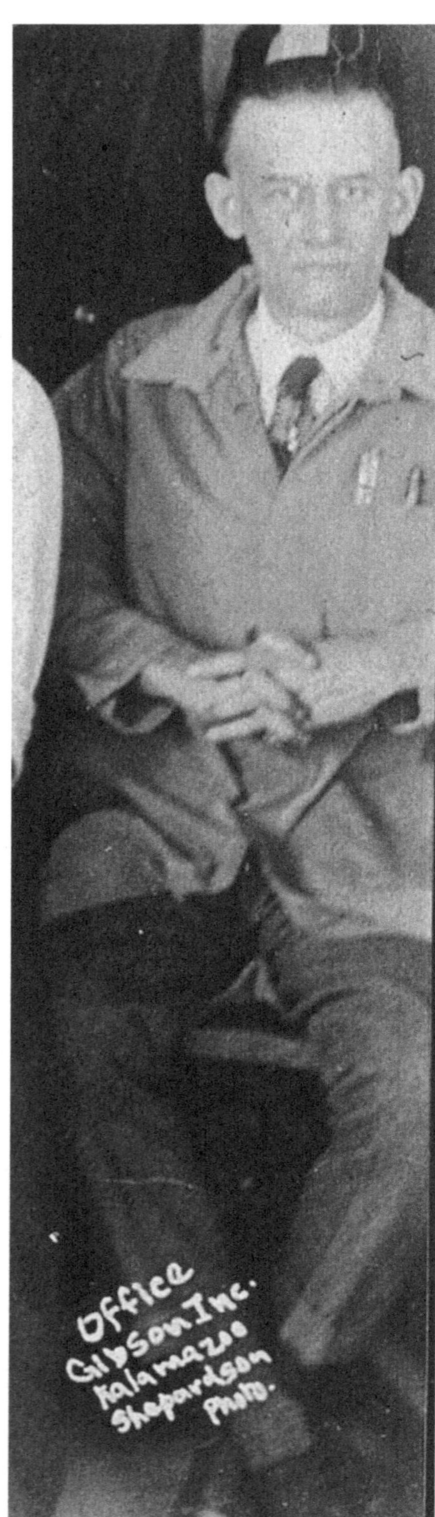

design work, he also served as credit manager, production manager, purchasing officer, and had supervision of the Repair Department. His employment agreement with Gibson included a provision allowing him to take the months of July and August for touring as a concert performer. It was also during this time that he obtained his master's degree from the American Conservatory of Music in Chicago. He simply could not have been at work every day or keeping a regular schedule.

Loar left Gibson permanently in December of 1924. The exact reason for his departure remains a mystery, but several known factors likely played a role. The decline of the mandolin in popular music after World War I made the introduction of his expensive, well-crafted "Master Model" instruments ill-timed. They clearly did not sell well during his time at Gibson or immediately afterwards. The "tap-tuning" manufacturing procedures which rendered these models so superior had to be carried out by hand, and were therefore time consuming and expensive. After two years of waiting for them to begin selling, the board of directors may have simply lost patience with Loar. His erratic work schedule probably caused friction with other department managers. The railroading of his college friend Harry L. Ferris in September of 1924 may have also played a role. Ferris was probably hired at Gibson on Loar's recommendation and thereafter quickly proved his competency and worth to the company by bringing modern business methods to its management. This was not at all unlike what Loar did for the design and manufacturing end of the business. When Ferris was forced to resign over an issue of pride, it may have soured Loar's attitude towards management and the board of directors.

After leaving Gibson, Loar continued his experimental design work, most notably with electrical pickups. In 1933 he co-founded the Vivi-Tone Company with former Gibson general manager Lewis A. Williams for the purpose of manufacturing and developing electric instruments. The company did not prosper, in part due to the advanced nature of the instruments they produced and also because of financial difficulties. In 1925 Loar became a professor of acoustics at Northwestern University in Evanston, Illinois, a position he held at the time of his death on September 14, 1943.

Female Employees

By the mid-1930's women were well established in the Gibson workforce. Indeed women worked in the front office from the early years. Company bookkeeper Kathryn Harris started at Gibson in 1920 and stayed for more than 50 years. By 1930 women were also working on the factory floor. Mildred "Milly" Balch was promoted to the position of repair department supervisor in 1935, and there were females in both the Spraying Department and string-winding areas. A shortage of men during World War II required Gibson to hire more women than ever in the company's history.

The female employees at Gibson in 1944, sitting for a photograph at the south end of the building. Notice the guard shack on left.
Steve Huber Collection

The Salesmen

Gibson employed several "commercial travelers" whose sales efforts were vital to the company's success. General manager Harry L. Ferris had established five regional sales areas in 1924. The Mid-West region covered more than 11 states: Oklahoma, Arkansas, Colorado, Kansas, Missouri, Wyoming, Nebraska, Iowa, North Dakota, South Dakota, Minnesota, and a portion of Texas. It was supervised in 1924 by Frank E. Miller, who lived in Kansas City, Missouri at the time. The Pacific Coast region was initially handled by Mr. A.L. Fram and was perhaps the largest by area, including the balance of western states not covered by the Mid-West region. The remaining three sales territories were the New England region, the Central region and the Southern region.

Each salesman worked on commission, and company records indicate that the salesmen would make at least seven or eight extended trips throughout their specific region, each year. On these trips they carried a dozen or more sample instruments, each dutifully noted in the shipping ledger. Usually these instruments were carried in used or "shop worn" cases. John Post, son of Gibson salesman George H. Post, remembered that general manager Guy Hart was known to make demands upon the salesmen at a moment's notice, sometimes requiring that they leave immediately on long trips. This uncertainty was hard on family life and eventually led many of the salesmen to careers away from Gibson.

Salesman George H. Post
John Post Collection

The dean of the pre-World War II Gibson salesmen was undoubtedly Clarence E. Havenga. He started at Gibson in 1923 and worked the Central region, including that hotbed of "Gibsonites" the state of Ohio. The second-oldest man in seniority, George H. Post, started at Gibson in 1926 as a bookkeeper. When he moved to sales, he was assigned the Pacific Coast region of the country but often worked in other areas as well. Salesmen Lawrence B. "Lanky" Neal and Wallace B. "Doc" Caldwell both joined Gibson in 1935 and spent the next decade on the road for Gibson. The man in charge of the Southern region was Thomas P. Peacock, a Georgia native who never actually relocated to Kalamazoo. He was much older than the other salesmen and worked from his home in Atlanta. Why Peacock went into sales is not clear because before coming to work at Gibson, he had spent his entire career as a bank teller in Rutledge, Georgia.

<u>During World War II</u>

Gibson employed 145 people at the onset of America's entry into World War II in December 1941. General manager Guy Hart lost no time in bidding on government contracts. By March of 1942 the company had already successfully filled two orders for the Quartermaster Department of the Army. However, in the spring of 1942, wartime restrictions on the use of brass, nickel, and copper (and thus by extension the alloy Monel that Gibson used in their strings) and the nationwide curtailing of musical instrument production threatened to shut Gibson down completely. In the face of these difficulties, Hart was able to turn Gibson's woodworking skills and electronics experience into wartime assets. His continual efforts with the Office of Production Management in Washington brought more government subcontracts. During the balance of the war, Gibson was able to ship a few instruments, but the bulk of production was in submachine gun parts, wooden glider skids, and radar assemblies. The factory ran in three shifts, 24 hours a day, until the war was over. Before World War II ended, over 400 people were working at Gibson.

List of Gibson Employees: 1915-1945

The following table lists all Gibson employees from 1915 through 1945 whose identity could be determined. The list is not meant to be all inclusive, and the dates of employment as given are those that could be verified. The data was complied from mostly external sources (e.g., Kalamazoo City Directories, U.S. Federal Census, newspaper articles, obituaries, etc.) Some Gibson seniority lists have survived and were also incorporated into the material. The author is aware of inconsistencies in the job titles as shown. The material is presented in the table as it was found in the original sources. No interpretation, extrapolation, or editorial license was introduced to the data. For persons with more than one job title, the jobs are listed in chronological order.

Last Name	First Name	Job	Known Employment Dates
Abnet	Frank	**Woodworker**	1937-1940
Abnet	Muriel P.	**Assembler**	1943
Abnet	Robert N.	**Woodworker**	1939
Abrams	Archie E.	**Salesman**	1931
Abrams	Neil Bradley	**Bookkeeper, Assistant Manager**	1924-1948
Acton	Foster S.	**Factory Superintendent**	1927
Adams	Hurl George "Rusty"	**Woodworker**	1920-1945
Adams	John	**Finisher, Woodworker**	1920-1939
Adams	Leatrice L.	**Inspector**	1945
Adams	Mary J.	**String Department, Woodworker**	1937-1939
Allers	Ernest P.	**Woodworker**	1939
Allers	Lawrence P.	**Woodworker, Machine Operator, Foreman**	1939-1945
Altermatt	George Henry	**Woodworker, Factory Superintendent**	1908-1948
Alverson	Donna M.	**Inspector**	1945
Anderson	June M.	**Assembler**	1945
Anderson	Robert H.	**Salesman, Sales Manager**	1933-1941
Andres	Lillian B.	**Assembler**	1945
Andrews	Edward W.	**Machine Operator**	1945
Archer	Mrs. Wynn	**Assembler**	1943
Arnold	Byron L.	**Machinist**	1937-1939
Avery	Velma L.	**Assembler**	1945
Babich	Beulah V.	**Solderer**	1945
Bailey	Loretta	**Assembler**	1943
Bailey	Madge L.	**Inspector**	1945
Bailey	Margaret V.	**Assembler**	1945
Baker	Donna	**Radius Former**	1945
Baker	Eugene M.	**Cost Clerk, Production Engineer**	1943-1945
Baker	Tressa	**Parcel Post Department**	1937
Balch	George Bird	**Woodworker**	1926
Balch	Mildred O. "Milly"	**Supervisor Repair Department**	1935
Ballett	Harry	**Woodworker**	1937-1939
Barber	Sherman C.	**Helper**	1945
Barbera	Jennie M.	**Assembler**	1945
Barnes	Dorothy	**Assembler**	1943
Barnes	Estella	**Stenographer**	1926

List of Gibson Employees: 1915-1945 (continued)

Last Name	First Name	Job	Known Employment Dates
Barnes	Gertrude	Inspector	1943
Barnes	Hazel	Stenographer	1943
Bartells	Helen	String Department	1937
Bates	Ila J.	Inspector	1945
Bawkey	Virginia	Inspector	1945
Beason	Frances C.	Gluer of Inlays	1930
Beatty	Grace	Assembler	1943
Becker	Marion F.	Assembler	1945
Beekman	Adrian	Cost Clerk	1930
Beeman	Minnie	Machine Operator	1943
Beerstecher	Louis W.	Machinist	1943
Beilman	William	Finisher	1939
Belden	Bernitta E.	Stock Clerk	1945
Belden	Hilda	Inspector	1943
Bell	Mary O.	Assembler	1945
Bellisle	Maxine M.	Assembler	1943-1945
Bellson	Julius	Inspector, Personnel Director, Treasurer	1935-1970
Benner	Myrtle	Assembler	1943
Bennett	Elaine D.	Assembler	1945
Benson	Harmon C.	Finisher, Filler	1937 & 1945
Bergeon	Gerald J.	Finisher, Woodworker, General Foreman	1932-1970
Bergeon	Mildred A.	Assembler	1945
Bergeon	Ralph J.	Inspector, Foreman	1932-1939, 1943-1945
Berghuis	Sinnie	String Department	1937
Bertrand	Evelyn	Assembler, Machine Operator	1943-1945
Best	Charles Wallace	Cabinet Maker, Foreman	1910 - 1930
Betts	Wesley	Woodworker	1937
Betz	Beatrice	Assembler	1943
Bildon	Bernita	Stockroom	1945
Billman	Audrey M.	Machine Operator	1945
Bippes	Dorothy M.	Clerk, Secretary, Service Department Manager	1920-1945
Blackledge	James	Finisher	1937
Blackledge	Russell K. "Ralph"	Stringer	1937
Blaisdell	Jay	Finisher, Stainer	1930-1939
Blaisdell	Lily	Inlay	1930
Blaisdell	Lynn J.	Woodworker, Machinist	1930-1932 & 1937-1943
Blakely	N. Hale	Woodworker	1939
Blanchette	S. Jack	Industrial Engineer	1945
Blink	Marie	String Department	1937-1939
Blink	Thomas	Repair Bench	1937-1939
Bloom	Forrest C.	Inspector	1943
Bonnema	John J.	?	1939
Boguta	Martha T.	Inspector	1945
Bont	John	Spray Painter	1945
Boodt	Velura	Inspector	1943-1945

Last Name	First Name	Job	Known Employment Dates
Bos	Bertha	?	1939
Bos	Garrett "Gar"	Woodworker, Machinist, Patternmaker	1919-1965
Bos	Irene G.	Machine Operator	1943
Boven	Henry	Finisher	1937
Boven	Shirley A.	Assembler	1945
Bowersox	Hilda	Assembler	1943
Boyer	Harry A.	Woodworker	1930-1939
Bramble	Leroy C. "Curly"	Inspector, Repairman, Finisher, Woodworker	1920-1939
Brennan	Elizabeth A.	Coiler, Stringmaker	1937-1939
Brewer	Hollis P.	Setupman	1945
Britten	Barbara H.	Assembler	1945
Britton	Thelma J.	Assembler	1945
Brosseau	Rea	Stenographer	1930
Brown	Elsie	Assembler	1943
Brown	James R.	Radio Technician	1945
Brown	Jeanette	Assembler	1945
Brown	Mary	Inspector	1943
Brown	Neva L.	Burrer, Machine Operator	1944-1970
Brown	Rachel	Assembler	1943
Browne	Helena	Inspector	1943
Brownell	Barbara F.	Inspector	1945
Brumbaugh	Mabel	Clerk	1930
Brumfield	Mary A.	Assembler	1945
Buchanan	James Y.	Machinist	1943
Buck	Mary L.	Inspector	1945
Bullock	Bernice	Inspector	1945
Burch	Carolyn E.	Assembler	1945
Burchette	Doris R.	Assembler	1945
Burdette	Bernice	Assembler	1945
Burge	Floyd O.	Production Engineer	1945
Burns	Robert	Finisher	1930
Burpee	Mary E.	Inspector	1945
Bushell	Bertha M.	Assembler, Electronics Assembly	1944-1970
Bushouse	Eleanor J.	Assembler	1945
Bussard	Marion	Bookeeper	1930
Butler	Virginia M.	Assembler	1945
Buttelman	C.V.	Sales Manager	1918
Butus	Helen J.	Assembler	1945
Byers	Alice M.	Assembler	1945
Byholt	John	Woodworker	1937-1939
Caldwell	Wallace B. "Doc"	Salesman, Supervisor	1935-1945
Campbell	Frank Briggs	Advertising Manager	1925-1930
Campbell	Lucille	Clerk	1926
Canfield	Leona L.	Assembler	1945
Carey	Thomas W.	Factory Rep	1929

List of Gibson Employees: 1915-1945 (continued)

Last Name	First Name	Job	Known Employment Dates
Carver	Pauline	Inspector	1945
Cavanaugh	Eleanor	Inspector	1943
Cavanaugh	Eva	Assembler	1943
Cavanaugh	Russell J.	Woodworker	1915
Chambers	Philip A.	Woodworker	1926
Chandler	True A.	Assembler	1945
Channells	Glenn H.	Woodworker	1937-1939
Chapman	Ruth J.	Assembler	1945
Charkowski	Helen	Foreman	1943
Chenoweth	Gladys M.	Machine Operator	1945
Chevallier	Marion	Assembler	1943
Chittenden	Rodney E.	Accountant, Bookkeeper, Factory Foreman	1923-1930
Christian	Sue	Assembler	1945
Chriswell	June A.	Assembler	1945
Church	Elmer L.	Chief Accountant	1943-1945
Church	Lucille E.	Stenographer, Office Secretary	1943-1945
Clair	Harlan C.	Inspector, Foreman, Finish Specialist	1928-1970
Clark	Bertha A.	Typist	1930
Clark	Ernest J.	Woodworker	1937
Cleveland	Ruthelma	Solderer	1945
Cody	Constance H.	Assembler	1943
Coleman	Clarence U.	Cabinet Maker, Woodworker	1926-1939
Comee	George W.	Chief Accountant, Corp. Secretary & Controller	1935-1970
Comstock	Mary J.	Assembler	1945
Cone	Margaret M.	Assembler	1945
Connor	Revell D.	Buffer	1945
Cook	Glenn Owen	Bench Hand, Woodworker, Glue Mixer	1910-1951
Cook	Jack L.	Electronic Repairs	1939-1940
Cook	Theodore J.	Machinist, Engineer	1930-1939
Cornhill	Alfred H.	Benchman, Foreman	1926-1930
Cotterill	John R.	Brass Horn Bell Maker	1930
Courtney	Donna J.	Assembler	1945
Courtney	Earl L.	Buffer, Woodworker	1937-1939
Cox	Robert A.	String Department	1937
Crabtree	Dena E.	Assembler	1945
Craine	Minnie	String Wrapper	1930
Cramer	Florence	String Department	1937-1939
Cramer	Marion R.	Assembler	1945
Cramer	Wilma M.	Stenographer	1915
Crandall	John F.	Setupman	1945
Crandall	Joseph D.	Woodworker	1930
Cronk	Miriam F.	Assembler	1945
Crummel	Theda E.	String Maker	1939
Cummings	A.R.	?	1927
Currie	Virginia M.	Inspector	1945
Curtis	Joseph P.	Finisher, Stock Clerk, Woodworker, Watchman	1919-1960

Last Name	First Name	Job	Known Employment Dates
Dailey	Daniel L.	Machinist, Foreman	1937-1939
Dalla	Priscilla J.	Assembler	1945
Dalrymple	Edna E.	Machine Operator	1945
Davidson	Bobbie M.	Assembler, Instrument Adjuster	1943-1945
Davison	Coy	Stringer, Tester	1937-1939
Dean	Rosemary	Assembler	1943
De Bruin	Henrietta	Assembler	1943
Decker	Alberta	String Department	1937
Decker	Harry M.	Woodworker	1937
De Does	William	Stringer, Artist	1930-1937
De Haan	Harm G.	Machine Operator	1945
De John	Ila J.	Office Secretary	1945
Delach	Mary M.	Assembler	1943
De Nooyer	Henrietta	Bookeeper, Clerk	1930-1939
De Paepe	Ivan	Accountant	1930
De Roo	Theodore	Stainer	1930
De Rysle	Francis M.	Finisher	1930
De Smit	Peter A.	Finisher	1915
De Valk	Daniel "Dan"	Woodworker, Patternmaker	1920-1945
De Vries	Maxine	Inspector	1943
De Vries	Tillie	Assembler	1945
De Windt	Felista M.	Stenographer	1915
De Witte	Peter	Shipping Clerk	1937-1939
Dexter	Ralph	Demonstrator, Salesman	1925-1928
De Young	Cornelius C. "Neil"	Finisher, Foreman	1920-1939
De Zeeuw	Leota E.	Assembler	1945
Dickerson	Elizabeth J.	Inspector	1945
Doorenbos	Jacob C. "Jack"	Machinist & Setupman	1943-1964
Doornhaag	Johanna	Assembler	1943
Doornhaag	Kath	Assembler	1943
Doornhaag	Mary	Helper	1943
Dornak	Joe	Watchman	1930
Dostie	Louise E.	Solderer	1945
Dratt	Paul O.	Electrical Department	1937
Drolen	Sinnie	Stringmaker	1939
Drydyk	Clara B.	Inspector	1945
Dunklee	George D.	Contact Man, Employee Manager	1943-1945
Durien	Thelma	String Department	1937-1939
Dutton	Betty H.	Assembler	1945
Edgely	George M.	Demonstrator	1927-1929
Edwards	Charles	Salesman	1929-1930
Ellerton	Maurice Haynes "Max"	Clerk, Foreman, Shipping Clerk	1920-1945
Elliot	Nellie E.	Assembler	1945
Ellis	Fay	Employee	1939
Eshouse	Henry M.	Foreman	1937-1939
Estey	Marian	Assembler	1943

List of Gibson Employees: 1915-1945 (continued)

Last Name	First Name	Job	Known Employment Dates
Ettwein	Donald J.	Stringer	1937
Evans	Dorothy E.	?	1939
Everette	Wyant	Purchasing Agent	1939
Everts	Marybelle	Assembler	1944-1960
Ewing	Forest	Machinist	1945
Falvey	Elva I	Machine Operator	1943
Fenstermacher	Doris A.	Machine Operator	1945
Ferris	Harry L.	General Manager	1923-1924
Fetch	Helen	Assembler	1943
Fiant	Floyd	Finisher	1926
Filbrandt	John C.	Woodworker	1930
Fischer	Viola	Telephone Operator	1943
Fisher	Betty L.	Assembler	1945
Fisher	Marie B.	Clerk	1915
Flake	Ivan E.	Woodworker	1926
Flanders	Willard L.	Finisher, Woodworker	1937-1939
Fletcher	Bernard	Cost Clerk, Timekeeper	1937-1939
Flora	Ruth H.	Assembler	1945
Foster	Reuben	Packer	1937
Fox	Chester R. "Ray"	Janitor	1932-1945
Fox	Mabel E.	Stenographer	1915
Fraker	Doris R.	Clerk	1926
Frazee	Roy	Janitor	1926
Frederick	Elizabeth M.	Assembler	1943
Frederick	LaVon J.	Assembler	1945
Freeman	Lydia M.	Printer	1945
French	Lucile I.	Stenographer	1915
Frost	Margaret A.	Assembler	1943
Fry	Clinton	Inspector	1943
Fryling	Herman	Buffer, Finisher	1937-1939
Fuller	Clyde G.	Fireman, Watchman	1937-1943
Fuller	Lavern M.	Machine Operator	1945
Fuller	Walter W.	Experimental Work, Electrical Engineer	1933-1962?
Fuller	Warren B.	Salesman, Manager	1939-1945
Gallup	Charlotte	Assembler	1945
Gaut	William N.	Woodworker, Engineer	1937-1945
Geerligs	Folkert	Woodworker, Finisher	1930-1939
Gelow	Lavern E.	Salesman	1935-1937
Gerlofs	Jennie	Clerk	1939
Gernaat	Helen	Laborer, Sprayer	1930-1937
Gettys	Lydia M.	Assembler	1943
Gettys	Phyllis E.	Assembler	1945
Ghainer	Agnes M.	Stenographer	1915
Giddings	Claude	?	1945-1960?
Giddings	Orlo G.	Woodworker	1926
Gilkison	Thelma	Assembler	1945

Last Name	First Name	Job	Known Employment Dates
Gill	June L.	Assembler	1945
Glaspie	Belva E.	Assembler	1945
Glerum	Adrian	Woodworker, Finisher, Assembler, Cabinet Maker	1920-1932 & 1937-1945?
Goff	Howard W.	Woodworker	1929-1932
Goff	Myron F.	Woodworker	1926
Goff	Sharlott	Assembler	1943
Goldsmith	Dorothy J.	Inspector	1945
Goldsmith	Joyce P.	Machine Operator	1943
Gooch	Bertha	Stenographer	1930
Goodrich	Frank	Toolmaker	1945
Goodrich	Irene P.	Assembler	1945
Goodrich	Phillip C.	Finisher	1939
Gornick	Berniece H.	Assembler	1945
Gosney	Ruby E.	Clerk	1945
Grable	Judy	Inspector	1943
Graf	Minerva	Bookkeeper	1915
Graff	Moses J.	Woodworker	1915
Graham	Mildred L.	Assembler	1943
Grant	Helen A.	Clerk	1945
Green	Howard E.	Industrial Engineer	1945
Green	Maxine	Laborer, Sprayer	1930-1937
Green	Velma	Assembler	1943
Gregersen	Florence P.	Assembler	1943
Griffin	William L.	Woodworker	1943
Grigsby	Joyce E.	Machine Operator	1945
Grofvert	Frances I.	Stenographer, Clerk	1937-1939
Grover	Dorothy	Machine Operator	1943
Guess	Cath	Assembler	1943
Haan	Eleanor	Parcel Post	1937
Hadley	Thomas B.	Stringer / Finisher	1937-1939
Halbert	Dorothy	Assembler	1943-1945
Hale	Jewel M.	Machine Operator	1943
Hall	Dorothy M.	Assembler	1945
Hall	George E.	Musician, Inspector	1927-1933
Hall	Lucille	Assembler	1945
Hall	Myrl J.	Bench Hand	1930
Hall	Ruth E.	Machine Operator	1945
Hallam	Loretta A.	Assembler	1945
Hamden	Daniel C.	Stockroom, Clerk, Factory Manager	1937-1945
Hannah	Sylvester	Woodworker	1945
Harker	Myrtle	Assembler	1943
Harmelink	Donna	Clerk	1945
Harrington	Clifford W.	Woodworker	1926
Harris	Kathryn Lucille	Bookkeeper	1920-1971
Harris	Minnie	Inspector	1945
Harrison	Josephine E.	Assembler	1945

List of Gibson Employees: 1915-1945 (continued)

Last Name	First Name	Job	Known Employment Dates
Harrison	Martin Van Buren	Woodworker	1926
Hart	Bertha	Filing Clerk	1926-1930
Hart	Guy	Accountant, General Manager, President	1923-1948
Harvell	Monroe K.	Sander	1945
Haskins	Mary E.	Assembler	1945
Havenga	Clarence E.	Salesman, Sales Manager	1922-1962
Hawley	Herbert C.	Artist	1930
Hawley	John Barton "Jack"	Electroplater	1929-1930
Hawley	Koert De Boise	Woodworker, Maintenance Man	1926-1930
Heilman	Ruth	Assembler	1943
Hendrick	Walter G.	Machine Operator	1945
Hendricks	Louis L.	Woodworker	1943
Henratty	Ruth K.	Assembler	1945
Henry	Viola M.	Assembler	1945
Herbert	Estella G.	Assembler	1945
Herrema	Janet	Employee	1939
Hicks	Bertha	Assembler	1943
Hicks	Duane	Printer, Multi Operator	1937-1939
Hill	Elizabeth G.	Assembler	1943
Hill	Elizabeth H.	Solderer	1945
Hill	Hubert H.	Woodworker	1937-1939
Hill	Jeanne M.	Assembler	1945
Hinga	Anna M.	Clerk	1939
Hodapp	Pauline M.	Stock Clerk	1945
Holdeman	Shirley E.	Stock Clerk	1945
Holder	Sparlin M.	Machinist	1943-1945
Holder	William C.	Fireman	1937-1939
Holmes	Nema	Laborer, Sprayer	1930-1937
Holtzer	John A.	Watchman, Janitor	1937-1945
Hoogenboom	Gerrit	Woodworker	1939
Hoogstraten	Mathilda M.	Assembler	1945
Hoose	Audrey E.	Machine Operator	1945
Hope	Louis	Stringer, Salesman	1937-1939
Hornaday	Jean	Stenographer	1943
Hoskins	Melvin	Machinist	1943
Houghton	Charles	Woodworker	1939
Houvenar	Virginia	Assembler	1943
Howard	Charles A.	Finisher, Rip Sawyer	1926-1930
Howard	Edward F. "Pokey"	Machinist, Finisher, Woodworker, Lead Man	1915-1945?
Howard	Edwin J.	Scraper	1937
Howard	Manon	Woodworker	1937
Howard	Sylvia	Stenographer	1937
Howell	Walter A.	Assembler	1926
Huis	John	Bench Hand, Finisher, Inspector, Vice President	1926-1943 & 1947-1965
Huis	Raymond	Repair Bench / Woodworker	1937-1939
Humphrey	Dale W.	Guard	1943-1945

Last Name	First Name	Job	Known Employment Dates
Hurst	Donald E.	Bookkeeper / Accountant	1944-1970?
Huston	Harry Franklin	Assembler	1930
Hutchins	William W.	Machinist / Woodworker	1937-1939
Hutchinson	Flo R.	Assembler	1945
Ickes	Lillian	Assembler	1943
Irwin	D. William	Bender	1926
Irwin	Robert	Factory Superintendent	1943
Israel	James	Woodworker	1920-1926
Ivey	Violet J.	Assembler	1945
Jackson	Charles	Woodworker	1937
Jackson	Elmer	Machinist	1937
Jackson	Stanley J.	Factory Salesman	1930
Jager	Thomas	Woodworker, Finisher, Assembler	1920-1945?
Janiszewski	Leon B.	Woodworker	1937
Jarsma	John S.	Woodworker	1926
Jeffers	Gertrude V.	Assembler, Solderer	1943-1945
Johnson	Carrie	Credit Clerk	1926
Johnson	Charlene R.	Inspector	1945
Johnson	Dorene L.	Machine Operator	1945
Johnson	Jennie E	Binder	1945
Johnson	Vava	String Department, Woodworker	1937-1939
Johnston	Elmer	Stringer, Tester	1937-1939
Johnston	Harriett M.	Assembler	1945
Johnston	Joseph A.	Stringer	1915
Johnstone	James H.	Stringer, Clerk, Musician	1915-1939
Johus	Eleanor E.	Assembler	1945
Jones	Irene B.	Assembler	1945
Jones	John L.	Woodworker, Assembler	1926-1930
Joyce	Frances R.	Inspector	1945
Jury	Gwendolyn C.	Assembler	1945
Kassak	John F.	Woodworker	1937-1939
Kaufman	Zelda M.	Assembler	1943
Kautenberg	Marilyn L.	Inspector	1945
Kavanaugh	Joseph C.	Machinist, Tool Cribman	1943-1945
Keiper	Lucy	Case Liner	1930
Kelley	Raymond	String Department	1937
Kemp	Forrest	Lab	1943
Kemp	George M.	Lab	1943
Kennedy	Laura M.	Assembler	1943
Kievit	Cornelius	Finisher	1915
Kievit	Grace	Helper	1943
Kievit	Neil	Finisher, Artist	1926-1930
Kimball	Clara	Stenographer	1943
Kingsley	Henry R.L.	Woodworker, Bandsaw Operator, Patternmaker	1937-1939 & 1943-1970?
Kinney	Olin A.	Woodworker	1937-1939
Kite	Audrey	Clerk	1943

List of Gibson Employees: 1915-1945 (continued)

Last Name	First Name	Job	Known Employment Dates
Kivell	Clyde L.	Machinist, Foreman	1943-1945
Klapperich	Doris J.	Inspector	1945
Klein	John	Woodworker, Maintenance Man	1933-1960?
Klepper	Eleanor J.	Assembler	1945
Kloosterman	Ann	String Department	1937
Kloosterman	Prena	String Wrapper, Parcel Post Department	1930-1937
Klop	Cornelia	Finisher	1937
Kluge	Donna J.	Machine Operator	1945
Knapp	Helen V.	Assembler	1945
Knapp	Lavina J.	Inspector	1943
Kneper	Mary	Mechanic	1930
Kneper	Matt	Mechanic	1930
Knowlton	Eugene L.	Finisher, Woodworker	1937-1939
Koets	Virginia M.	Inspector	1943
Kopp	Carl J.	Sprayer, Finisher	1937-1939 & 1945-1960?
Kopp	Emma M.	Woodworker	1937
Korstange	Robert W.	Woodworker	1937-1939
Koster	Jane	Woodworker	1937
Kraft	John Frederick	Woodworker, Cabinet Maker	1920-1945?
Kraiger	Charles Roger	Wood Carver	1930
Kraiger	Leona N.	Case Maker	1930
Kramer	Margaret J.	String Department	1937-1939
Kraske	Victor	Foreman	1910-1926
Krueger	Frances	Telephone Operator	1937
Kuhn	Ernest F.	Machinist, Woodworker	1926-1971
Kuilema	Matt	Woodworker	1939
Kuney	Orvel Cyril "Red"	Woodworker, Cabinet Maker	1920-1945?
Kuras	Dorothy L.	Cost Clerk, Payroll Supervisor	1943-1970?
Kussy	Lillian J.	Woodworker	1939
Lacey	Clara L.	Woodworker	1937-1939
Ladd	Ethel	Clerk	1939
Lajiness	Harold	Woodworker	1939
Lakin	Andalene	Assembler	1943
Lambert	Virginia A.	Assembler	1945
Lampley	Vera M	Drill Press Operator	1945
Lampman	Phyllis A.	Assembler	1945
Land	Billie N.	Assembler	1945
Land	Katherine R.	Assembler	1945
Landes	David Wills	Woodworker	1915-1930?
Laurian	George D.	Superintendent	1909-1915
Larsen	Flans D.	Woodworker	1915
Leathers	Albert W.	Machine Operator	1943
Leedy	Jacqueline M.	Inspector	1945
Lehrman	Verda M.	Assembler	1945
Leland	Donald	Woodworker	1937
LeMieux	Doris L.	Assembler	1945

Last Name	First Name	Job	Known Employment Dates
Lemmers	Sarah E.	Assembler, Foreman	1943-1945
Lemon	Bessie	Stenographer	1930
Leonard	Ella	Assembler	1943
Leonard	Walter Nelson	Buffer, Finisher	1937-1939
LeRoy	Patricia	Assembler	1943
Levett	Carl	Lab	1943
Liedtke	Gust	Cabinet Maker	1930
Linderman	Theo G.	Instrument Adjuster	1945
Liles	Pearl L.	Machine Operator	1945
Lino	Gladys L.	Clerk	1915
Littlewood	Ruth	Machine Operator	1943
Livingston	Marguerite E.	Machine Operator	1945
Loar	Lloyd A.	Acoustical Engineer	1919-1924
Lockwood	Lillian E.	Inspector	1945
Long	Irving L.	Finisher, Woodworker	1925-1960?
Longman	Marion	Personnel Manager	1943
Lounsberry	Beverly E.	Assembler	1945
Lovens	Betty N.	Assembler	1943
Lover	Seth	Electrical Department	1941, 1945-47, 1952-67
Lowe	Morene	String Department	1937
Lozon	Martha	Assembler	1943
Lukins	John Paul	Machine Operator, Foreman String Division	1944-1970?
Lukins	Ruth	Assembler	1943
Luyendyk	Phyllis J.	Inspector	1945
McElroy	Kath L.	Assembler	1945
McFee	Ralph E.	Polisher	1915
McGowan	Marjorie F.	Assembler	1945
McHugh	Charles John	Machinist, Stock Clerk, Shipping Clerk	1915-1930
McHugh	Robert F.	Woodworker	1920
McHugh	Thaddeus J. "Ted"	Foreman, Machinist, Factory Superintendent	1907-1945
McIntyre	Lenn	Tester	1943
McKinney	Joyce I.	Assembler	1945
McLaughlin	Rosa	Assembler	1943
McNally	Jane	Assembler	1943
McNees	Eleanor	Assembler	1943
McNutt	Lynn M.	Fret Work	1930
MacDonald	Bette	Assembler	1943
Mafit	Delmont C.	Salesman, Production Manager	1916-1926
Mannion	Edna B.	Inspector	1945
Manski	Mildred	Stenographer	1937
Marble	Vesta Irene	Assembler, Foreman, Electronics Assembly	1942-1970?
Mark	Mildred L.	Assembler	1945
Marker	Wilbur C.	Marketing, Chief Inspector (Quality Control)	1938-1966
Marquardt	Jenerva	Assembler	1943
Marr	Barbara J.	Assembler	1943
Martin	James	Bench Hand	1926

List of Gibson Employees: 1915-1945 (continued)

Last Name	First Name	Job	Known Employment Dates
Martin	John S.	Salesman	1929
Massie	Austin	Woodworker	1937
Mastenbrook	Clara	Clerk	1937-1939
Mazer	Margaret J.	Assembler	1945
Mead	Charles E.	Shipping Clerk, Foreman	1930-1939
Meade	Lynn	Sander, Woodworker	1937-1939
Meacham	Nadine R.	Assembler	1945
Meech	Harry M.	Woodworker	1939
Mein	Barbara B.	String Department	1937
Mein	Jeanette	Machine Operator	1930
Meints	Barbara	Assembler	1943
Meints	Carly I.	Machine Operator	1943
Mentor	Edwin W.	Finisher	1937
Merica	George	Inspector	1940-1970?
Metcalf	Darlene F.	Assembler	1945
Meyle	Betty L.	Inspector	1945
Mielke	Frederick J.	Buffer	1945
Miller	Dorethea I	Assembler	1945
Miller	Frank	Salesman	1927
Miller	Fred M.	Instrument Maker, Machinist, Foreman	1909-1920
Miller	George Rush	Machinist, Superintendent	1930-1939
Miller	Robert D.	Woodworker	1937-1939
Mills	Allen M.	Toolmaker	1945
Mills	William J.	Machinist	1930-1939
Miner	R.Hazel	Machinist, Woodworker	1937-1939
Moelaart	Nellie K.	Assembler	1945
Moerman	Ivan H.	Draftsman	1945
Moffit	Geraldine D.	Stenographer, Clerk	1937-1939
Mohney	Marciel J.	Sander	1945
Mohney	Maxine F.	Assembler	1945
Molhoek	Annetta	Stenographer	1926
Monroe	Barbara J.	Assembler	1943
Monroe	Madalyn J.	Inspector	1943-1945
Moore	John J.	Mechanical Engineer	1943-1944
Morrison	Donna M.	Solderer	1945
Mottor	Maxine	Assembler	1943
Moyer	Eunice Q.	Foot Treadle Operator	1945
Muir	Anna	Group Leader	1945
Murphy	Edward F.	Assembler	1926
Murray	Alice V.	Assembler	1945
Myers	Glen	Helper	1937
Nanninga	Jacob	Sprayer	1937
Nap	Marguerite	Woodworker, Finisher	1937-1939
Nash	Raymond E.	Woodworker, Machinist	1930-1937
Neal	Iva R.	Assembler	1945
Neal	Lawrence B.	Salesman	1935-1939

Last Name	First Name	Job	Known Employment Dates
Nelson	Hazel	Assembler	1943
Nicholas	Gloria G.	Machine Operator	1945
Nichols	Lois	Assembler	1943
Nicol	Merle V.	?	1915
Nie	Winifred	Stringmaker	1939
Nieburger	Edward C.	Purchasing Director	1945
Niemi	Elizabeth	Machine Operator	1943
Noble	Clyde E.	Stringer, Woodworker	1937-1939
Nyman	Thelma I.	Assembler	1943-1945
O'Brien	Rita N.	Typist	1945
Oman	Florence E.	Assembler	1945
Orosz	Mary	String Department	1937
Orwig	Lenora	Helper	1943
Osborne	Christine	Inspector	1945
Ostrander	Dorothy	String Coiler	1937
Outman	Frank M.	Machine Operator	1945
Paauwe	Eleanore J.	String Maker	1939
Pape	Nellie	Janitor	1945
Patterson	John S.	Machinist, Wood Carver	1915-1920
Paul	Ray	Cleaner	1945
Peacock	Thomas	Salesman	1930-1939
Peapples	Ethel S.	Stenographer	1926
Pearl	Milton R.	Machinist	1915
Pearson	Theresa M.	Inspector	1945
Pease	Carleton G.	Time Studyman, Parcel Post & Service	1945-1970?
Pelton	Ray	Woodworker, Leadman	1929-1960?
Penhollow	Bernice A.	Machine Operator, Foreman	1943-1945
Penning	Henrietta	Stringmaker	1937-1939
Perigo	Laura M.	Stenographer	1945
Peterson	Carl W.	Machinist, Woodworker	1937-1939
Pfaff	George E.	Drill Press Operator	1945
Pfau	Frank C.	Woodworker	1926
Phelps	Harold	Time Clerk	1937
Phillippe	Mary	Case Liner	1930
Phillips	Arleta	String Maker	1939
Phillips	Ell F.	Woodworker	1926
Pickett	George W.	?	1920
Pickett	Robert	Woodworker	1939
Pickett	Wayne L.	Woodworker	1943
Pierce	Edward L.	Woodworker	1937-1939
Pifer	Isaiah Frank	Woodworker, Gluer	1926
Pillars	Marjorie J.	Machine Operator	1945
Piper	Vern A.	Stringer, Tester	1937-1939
Platt	James B.	Finisher	1915-1920
Post	George H.	Bookkeeper, Salesman, Sales Manager	1926-1941
Praeger	William E. (Jr.)	Bench Hand	1926

List of Gibson Employees: 1915-1945 (continued)

Last Name	First Name	Job	Known Employment Dates
Price	Judith L.	Assembler	1943
Prouty	Eugene F.	Machinist	1945
Pyle	Charles M.	Woodworker	1926
Quick	Clinton D.	Finisher	1926
Quigley	Phyllis L.	Switchboard Operator	1945
Raber	William Jefferson	Laborer, Sprayer	1930-1937
Randall	Edna	Secretary, Clerk	1937-1939
Randall	Mary	String Department, Woodworker	1937-1939
Rapp	Berneda	Machine Operator	1943
Rapp	Fred	Machinist, Woodworker	1937-1939
Rapp	Paul	Woodworker	1937-1939
Ray	Barbara J.	Inspector	1945
Raynes	Basil F.	Millwright, Maintenance Man	1933-1968
Reams	A. Jay Jr.	Associate Manager	1915
Reams	Sylvo	Company Secretary	1915
Reck	Gladys P.	String Department	1937-1939
Redmond	Patrick J.	Employee	1939
Reed	James F.	Superintendent	1930
Reeves	Henry T.	Chief Draftsman, Experimenter	1920-1926
Reinoehl	Berniece M.	Final Inspector	1945
Relaford	Mildred L.	Machine Operator	1943
Renauld	Margaret E.	Machine Operator	1945
Reynolds	Elaine	Assembler	1945
Rhyme	Bernice S.	Assembler	1945
Richardson	Jeanne M.	Inspector	1945
Rider	Rolle R.	Finisher	1926
Rife	Ona E.	Assembler	1943
Rinehart	Edwin E.	Maintenance Man	1945
Ringler	Ford	Woodworker	1937
Rix	Nathaniel L.	Woodworker, Assembler	1926-1930
Roberts	Earl	Machinist	1926
Roberts	La Donna R.	Machine Operator	1945
Robertson	Margaret N.	Assembler	1945
Robinson	Addie V.	Sander	1945
Rochester	Lillian	Assembler	1943
Rosenberger	Oliver Edward	Woodworker, Machinist, Foreman	1928-1945?
Rosenberger	Roger R.	Woodworker, Machinist, Tester, Leadman	1937-1945?
Rowland	Samuel	Woodworker	1937
Roy	Wanda V.	Machine Operator	1945
Russell	Hazel	Assembler	1945
Ruthrauff	Mary J.	Stenographer	1926
Ryskamp	Leona	Assembler	1943
Sager	Dorothy A.	Assembler	1945
Salo	Patricia L.	Assembler	1945
Sander	Gertrude M.	Assembler	1943
Sander	Neil	Clerk	1943

Last Name	First Name	Job	Known Employment Dates
Sands	Gertrude E.	Assembler	1945
Sawyer	Jean T.	Assembler	1945
Schauer	Donald F.	Scraper, Woodworker	1937-1939
Schauer	Florence H.	Stock Room	1937
Schipper	Gertrude	String Department	1937-1939
Schlough	Shirley J.	Instrument Stringer	1945
Schmidt	Neva J.	Assembler	1945
Schmuhl	Alford M.	Filler	1945
Schrier	Paul	Woodworker	1915-1939
Schwenck	Mildred C.	Inspector	1943
Scott	LaVern	Woodworker	1920-1930
Seburg	Orpha	Floor Lady	1930
Selegy	Matilda	?	1939
Seybert	Carl H.	Bandsaw Operator, Machinist, Woodworker	1920-1939
Shearer	Phyllis M.	Assembler	1943
Shedore	Leonard W.	Stringer, Tester, Assistant to Service	1928-1972
Shepard	Mae	Supervisor	1945
Shikoski	Fred W.	Inspector	1945
Short	Arthur D.	Woodworker	1926
Side	H.B.	Metalworker	1926
Siefert	George H.	Watchman	1943-1945
Siefert	John H.	Woodworker	1937-1939
Siefert	Margaret	Estimator, Industrial Engineer	1943-1945
Simonds	Alice	Assembler	1945
Simpson	Margaret K.	Assembler	1945
Skippers	Iris	Assembler	1945
Slager	Elizabeth	Laborer, Sprayer	1930-1937
Slater	Edith	Woodworker	1937
Slater	Gladys D.	Finisher, Woodworker	1937-1939
Slater	Mary	Assembler	1943
Sleeman	Almyra	Machine Operator	1943
Sliss	Henry A.	Errand Boy	1930-1934
Sliz	Rudolph	Assistant Purchasing Agent	1943
Sloyer	William J.	Woodworker	1926
Smith	Alonzo E.	Woodworker	1926
Smith	Ann L.	Assembler	1943
Smith	Beulah P.	Assembler	1945
Smith	Claude	Finisher	1939
Smith	Dick	Woodworker	1937-1939
Smith	George W.	Machinist	1937-1945?
Smith	Helen I.	Packer	1945
Smith	Mary Belle	Inspector	1945
Smith	Patricia M.	Assembler	1945
Smith	Paul	Finisher, Woodworker, Sander	1930-1945?
Smith	Trena	Solderer	1945
Smith	Virginia M.	Assembler	1943

List of Gibson Employees: 1915-1945 (continued)

Last Name	First Name	Job	Known Employment Dates
Smith	William H.	Machine Operator	1945
Snider	Hartford	Patternmaker	1943-1970?
Snyder	Leona	Bookkeeper	1926
Sootsman	William	Guard	1943-1945
Soule	Pauline W.	Bookkeeper	1926
Soule	William H.	Machinist, Woodworker, Fireman	1905-1939
Spalsbury	Wayne J.	Clerk	1926
Sparks	Constance E.	Assembler	1945
Spoor	Cornelia	Assembler	1945
Sportell	Winifred	String Department	1937
Stadler	Alf	Woodworker	1939
Stadler	Margaret G.	Assembler	1945
Staken	John P.	Woodworker	1945
Stanfield	Ruth	Case Liner	1930
Starbuck	Mary E.	Bookkeeper	1945
Stationery	Milford B.	Woodworker	1926
Stauffenberg	Luella	Assembler	1943
StClair	Erma C.	Assembler	1945
Steketee	Andrew J.	Finisher	1926
Stenger	Margaret	Machine Operator	1943-1945
Stenquist	Gottfried	Repairman	1930
Stephens	C. Carl	Tester	1943
Stevens	Leonard D.	Department Manager, Foreman	1930-1939
Stewart	Ernestine	Assembler	1943
Stewart	Lottye L.	Solderer	1945
Stewart	Phyllis A.	Assembler	1945
Stewart	Ralph E.	Woodworker	1937
Stine	Eleanor L.	Inspector	1943
Stirner	Milford B.	Laborer, Sprayer, Stainer	1930-1939
Storey	Margaret M.	Machine Operator	1945
Stout	Arthur C.	Sales Manager, Credit Manager	1915-1926
Stoutmeyer	Florence	Assembler	1945
Stowell	Harry	Packer	1945
Stratton	Bert W.	Woodworker, Department Manager, Finisher	1920-1939
Stratton	Ernest D.	Assembler, Stringer, Shipping Clerk	1920-1939
Strong	Thelma E.	Woodworker, Shipping Clerk	1937-1939
Sturgis	Margaret E.	Assembler	1943
Sullivan	Virgil	Superintendent	1930
Sutton	Corrine B.	Assembler	1943
Sutton	Donald E.	Woodworker	1939
Sweet	Ruth	Assembler	1943
Taylor	Bernice H.	Assembler	1945
Taylor	Frank E.	Errand Boy	1930
Taylor	Irene	Assembler	1943
Taylor	Mary E.	Assembler	1945
Teachout	Patricia A.	Assembler	1945

Last Name	First Name	Job	Known Employment Dates
Teal	Grace E.	Assembler	1943
Templin	Mildred L.	Inspector	1945
TenBrink	Geraldine R.	Typist	1945
Terpstra	Benjamin W.	Repair Bench	1937
Terrell	Anna	Stenographer	1937
Tetzlaff	Elwyn R.	Inspector	1945
Thomas	Alice M.	Solderer	1945
Thomas	Lyle	Repair Bench	1937
Thomas	Ruth L.	Inspector	1945
Thompson	Earl	Machinist, Woodworker	1937-1939
Thompson	Eleanor V.	Assembler	1945
Thompson	E.T.	Associate Sales Manager	1914-1918
Thompson	Eula W.	Inspector	1945
Timm	Lucille	Woodworker	1939
Tinklenberg	Alice M.	Assembler	1943
Tolmacs	Margaret	Liner, Silking Operator	1944-1970?
Tower	Leland G.	Laborer, Sprayer	1930-1937
Towne	Christine L.	Assembler	1945
Towne	Ruth E.	Assembler	1945
Tracy	Delores M.	String Department	1937
Triemstra	Henrietta	Stenographer	1937
Triemstra	Thomas	Buzzer, Woodworker	1937-1939
Triezenberg	Cornelius "Case"	Finisher, Woodworker, Foreman	1926-1976?
Try	Beverly C.	Woodworker	1937-1939
Turk	Jacob	?	1943-1960?
Tuttle	Phillip	Woodworker	1939
Tuzee	Josephine	String Department, Woodworker	1937-1939
Ufkes	Fred C.	Woodworker	1939
Ufkes	Helen G.	String Department, Machine Operator, Foreman	1937-1945?
Valentine	Arthur	Woodworker	1943
Valentine	Edna M.	Stenographer	1915
Van Denberg	Delores V.	Telephone Operator	1943
Van Dyke	Jacob	Inspector, Woodworker	1937-1939
Van Eck	Margaret	Stenographer, Clerk	1937-1939
Van Maaren	Freeda D.	Assembler	1945
Van Meter	Clara M.	Machine Operator	1945
Van Ooy	Darlene A.	Inspector	1945
Van Pelt	Alvin E.	Assembler	1945
Van Pelt	Dorothy E.	Assembler	1945
Van Stelle	Shirley J.	Inspector	1945
Van Weelden	Mary C.	Inspector	1945
Vander Velde	Henry W.	Finisher	1926
Verhage	John P.	Woodworker	1915
Vermeulen	Willard	Stringer, Woodworker	1937-1939
Virgin	W.J.	Case Maker	1930
Visker	Betty	String Maker	1939

List of Gibson Employees: 1915-1945 (continued)

Last Name	First Name	Job	Known Employment Dates
Voisine	John J.	Machinist, Woodworker	1915-1920
Voke	W. Lynn	Inspector	1943
Vovrick	Doris M.	Assembler	1945
Walls	Dorothy V.	Assembler	1945
Walsh	Dorothy M.	Assembler	1943
Ward	Louise M.	Burrer	1945
Ward	Russell	Salesman	1937
Warren	Donald	Finisher	1937-1939
Warren	Donna	Finisher	1937
Warren	Rose M.	Clerk	1945
Waters	Fern S.	Assembler	1945
Watkins	Harold C.	Inspector	1937
Watson	George	Guard	1943-1945
Weaver	James	Woodworker	1920
Webber	Marguerite L.	Inspector	1945
Weed	Frank Eugene "Gene"	Woodworker, Finisher, Cabinet Maker, Repairman	1920-1945?
Weessies	Anna	Office Girl, Clerk	1937-1939
Welch	Joyce F.	Assembler	1945
Weld	Frank E.	Woodworker	1926
Weld	George E.	Woodworker	1926
Werner	Rollo	Engineer, Director of Purchasing	1943-1970?
Westerberg	Joyce E.	Inspector	1945
Westman	William	Cabinet Maker, Acoustic Engineer	1944-1970?
Westman	William L.	Assembler	1945
Weston	Sylvia B.	Stenographer	1930
Wetherbee	Ella L.	Stenographer, Bookkeeper	1905-1915
Wheeler	Erma J.	Foot Treadle Operator	1945
Whelpley	Arthur E.	Metalworker	1926
Whipple	Evelyn A.	Assembler	1945
White	Mable	Assembler	1943
Whiteman	Peter	Laborer, Woodworker	1920-1926
Whitmore	Lucille G	Assembler	1945
Wiberg	Roy M.	Woodworker, Assembler, Fitter, Cabinet Maker	1919-1960
Wicke	Darrell	Employee	1943
Wiersma	Edith	Woodworker	1937
Wiersma	Merlie L.	Machine Operator	1945
Wilburs	Percy	Foreman	1930
Wilgenhof	Antone or Anthony	Cabinet Maker, Woodworker, Fretter	1920-1926 & 1937-1939
Wilkins	Clayton T.	Laborer	1930
Wilkins	Earl L.	Collector, Machinist, Sawyer, Cabinet Maker	1930-1945?
Wilkins	Helen	Assembler	1945
Wilkins	Leo H.	Woodworker, Machinist, Sander	1926-1939
Wilkins	Percy C.	Machinist, Foreman	1915-1920
Williams	Alma J.	Cabinet Maker	1930
Williams	Jean B.	Inspector	1945
Williams	Lewis A.	Sales Manager, General Manager	1902-1923

Last Name	First Name	Job	Known Employment Dates
Williamson	W. Ellwood	Industrial Engineer	1945
Wilson	Beverly V.	Assembler	1945
Wilson	Clarence	Machinist	1937
Wilson	Geraldine M.	Assembler	1943
Wilson	Raymond F.	Laborer, Foreman	1915-1926
Wise	Nelle M.	?	1945
Witt	Leta M.	Machine Operator	1945
Wolfe	John H.	Sander	1937
Wood	Thelma	Machine Operator	1943
Wood	William H.	Machine Operator	1945
Woodman	Mae E.	Assembler	1945
Woodworth	Gerald M.	Electrical Department, Tester, Foreman	1937-1945?
Woolston	Bernita D.	Assembler	1945
Workman	John	Finisher, Foreman	1939-1945?
Wright	Alice M.	Assembler	1945
Wright	Emma M.	Assembler	1945
Wright	William H.	Sander, Finisher, Inspector, Supervisor	1937-1945?
Wynn	Valma J.	Inspector	1945
Visker	Betty	String Department	1937
Yingling	Charles	Finisher	1926
Yoder	Mary	Stenographer	1943
Zidell	Mildred M.	Machine Operator	1945
Zimmer	Mary L.	Supervisor	1945
Ziolkowski	Hilda A.	Assembler	1945
Zuidema	Frances G.	Shipping & Receiving Clerk	1938-1945

Employees receiving service awards at Christmas 1944. Front row seated (left to right): Gene Reed, "Red" Kuney, Irving Long, Dan DeValk, Adrian Glerum, Ray Pelton, and Case Triezenberg. Standing (left to right): Earl Wilkins, Gar Bos, Frank Abnet, John Kraft, "Pokey" Howard, Roy Wiberg, Glenn Cook, Joe Curtis, Len Shedore, "Rusty" Adams, Tom Jaeger, and Ernie Kuhn.
Steve Huber Collection

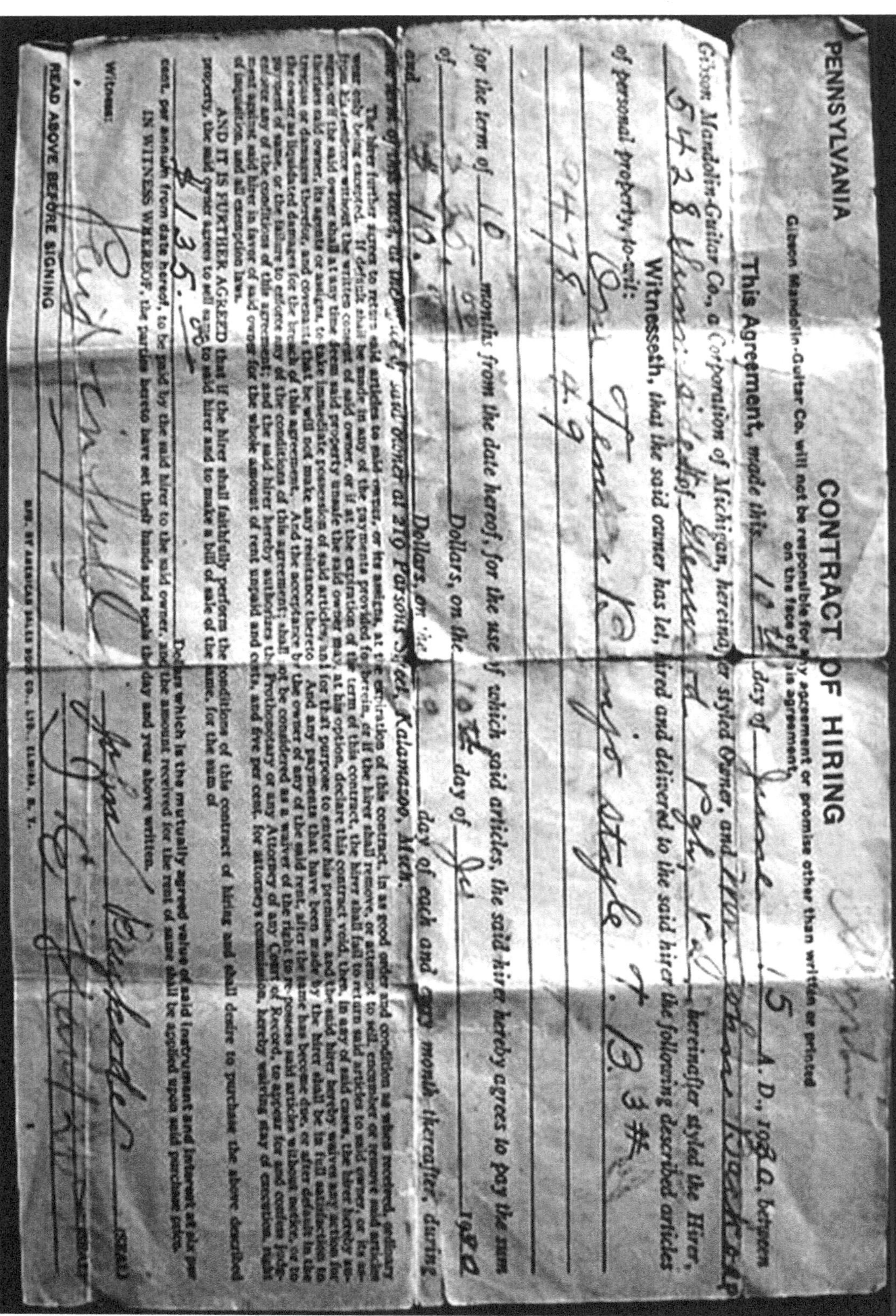

PENNSYLVANIA

CONTRACT OF HIRING

Gibson Mandolin-Guitar Co. will not be responsible for any agreement or promise other than written or printed on the face of this agreement.

This Agreement, made this 10th day of Jan A.D., 1930, between Gibson Mandolin-Guitar Co., a Corporation of Michigan, hereinafter styled Owner, and hereinafter styled the Hirer,

Witnesseth, that the said owner has let, hired and delivered to the said hirer the following described articles of personal property, to-wit:

for the term of 10 months from the date hereof, for the use of which said articles, the said hirer hereby agrees to pay the sum of Dollars, on the 10th day of 1930 and Dollars, on day of each and month thereafter, during the term of this lease at the office of said owner at 210 Parsons Street, Kalamazoo, Mich.

IN WITNESS WHEREOF, the parties hereto have set their hands and seals the day and year above written.

Witness:

READ ABOVE BEFORE SIGNING

This sales contract for a TB-3 (FON 9478-149) shows that the instrument was produced before January 10th 1930. Many similar documents were used to produce the revised factory order number charts in chapter 4.
Collection of Frank Schoepf

Chapter 3 – The Vendors: 1925-1931

Overview

During the pre-World War II period, Gibson dealt with a large number of vendors who provided a wide array of services, supplies, and parts to the company. Although most of Gibson's pre-war financial records have been lost, some records for the period 1925-1931 have survived. These are enough to allow us a detailed look at the vendors Gibson used before World War II.

Instrument Cases

For the most part, Gibson purchased their instrument cases pre-made. The exception to this rule was the brief period 1929-1931 when they employed several case makers and case liners at the factory in Kalamazoo. Gibson used all of the following companies between 1925 and 1931.

American Leather Handle Company, Newark, NJ
Maker of case handles.

Athol Manufacturing Company, Athol, MA
Makers of artificial leather.

Berlin Braid Manufacturing Company, New York City, NY
Makers of decorative braid work, possibly for case lining.

Cotex Corporation, Newark, NJ
Makers of a leather case covering material.

Geib & Schaefer Company, Chicago, IL
Gibson's main supplier of pre-made instrument cases through the end of World War II.

B.R. Hunt Manufacturing Company, Union City, IN
An alternate supplier of pre-made instrument cases used sporadically in 1927.

R.C. Jenkinson Company, Newark, NJ
Makers of case latches and locks.

Lifton Manufacturing Company, New York City, NY
An alternate supplier of pre-made instrument cases used sporadically in 1925.

Paragon Case Company, Oregon, IL
An alternate supplier of pre-made instrument cases used sporadically in 1925.

Specialty Handle Manufacturing, Newark, NJ
Maker of case handles.

A. Winpfheimer & Company, New York City, NY
Makers of velvet cloth, probably used for in-house built case lining 1929-1931.

Electroplating

Gibson subcontracted out their electroplating needs during most of the pre-war period. The exception was the brief period 1929-1931 when they employed John Barton "Jack" Hawley to do the job in-house. Hawley was an experienced electroplater from Grand Rapids, Michigan. His tenure at Gibson was destined to be brief; his job did not survive the January 1932 general purging of employees. When he died in 1976, his obituary did not mention his time at Gibson.

Gibson aficionados have vigorously debated the exact methodology of pre-war electroplating. Because Gibson itself used so many different electroplating vendors, this topic actually has very little to do with the company. In the 1932 catalog U on page 28, the Florentine banjo is described as being "quadruple gold plated" while page 20 of the same catalog describes the style 6 banjo as having "heavy gold plating." Likewise, the model specifications for the Granada banjo on page 31 call for "triple gold plating." Such terms have little or no significance in the real world of the electroplating industry and were no doubt originated in Gibson's advertising department.

The quality of the electroplating on pre-war Gibson instruments varied widely. In general, the plating was not very thick (regardless of the catalog copy) and wore off easily. The durability of the plating was directly linked to the characteristics of the part being plated. The die-cast pot-metal parts used on Gibson banjos after 1929 generally did not take plating very well and quickly began showing signs of deterioration. This situation improved somewhat in the late 1930's as the specifications of the pot metal were adjusted. Inspection of the actual instruments will show in particular that the gold plating was carried out in a number of ways; e.g., gold directly over copper, or gold over nickel over copper. Some parts were burnished before plating, resulting in a "satin" look. As the list given below suggests, the many differences were no doubt due to different methods used by each of the vendors at various times. Any quality control during the actual process was incumbent upon the vendor.

General Plate Company, Attleboro, MA
A supplier of gold-plating supplies used from 1929 to 1931. The company was founded in 1916 and eventually became part of Texas Instruments.

Grand Rapids Plating Company, Grand Rapids, MI
A company which Gibson used in 1927, probably for gold plating.

Hargie Plating Works, Kalamazoo, MI
Gibson's regular subcontractor for metal polishing, as well as nickel and chrome plating. Founded in 1925 by James S. Hargie and continued in business through 1964.

Matchless Metal Polish Company, Chicago, IL
A supplier of metal polish used 1929-1931.

J.C. Miller Company, Grand Rapids, MI
A supplier of metal polishing and electroplating supplies used in 1929.

Shephard Plating Company, Racine, WI
A subcontractor used in 1930.

Valley City Plating Company, Grand Rapids, MI
A subcontractor used in 1927.

Engraving

Like many other trade skills, Gibson subcontracted their engraving needs to a variety of individuals and companies before World War II. A 1927 publicity photo depicts Gibson employee O.C. "Red" Kuney standing at a workbench, in the process of engraving a banjo tone ring. However, the tool in Mr. Kuney's hand is not a graver, and Kuney himself was a woodworker, not an engraver. This type of misleading marketing was typical of Gibson catalogs in the pre-World War II period. Posed publicity photos to the contrary, financial records show that Gibson subcontracted out their engraving to the following vendors.

Henderson-Ames Company, Kalamazoo, MI
This company was primarily involved in the design and manufacture of uniform regalia. As part of this process, they also kept a number of jewelry engravers on staff for the purposes of decorating swords, medals, and other awards. Gibson used the company as its primary jobber for all types of metal engraving and etching. Henderson-Ames was founded in 1893 and was a successor to Ames Sword Company of Massachusetts.

Henderson-Ames Company, circa 1910
Collection of the author

Engraving (continued)

Ray W. Hoogenstyn, Grand Rapids, MI
A jewelry engraver of Grand Rapids used sporadically in 1927.

George Rickman, Kalamazoo, MI
A local jewelry engraver used sporadically in 1925.

William C. Schrier, Kalamazoo, MI
An employee of Henderson-Ames Company (see above) who did etching and engraving on the side for Gibson from 1928-1931. His workshop was located in the basement of his house in Kalamazoo. It is likely that he etched the famous Florentine, Bella Voce, and All-American banjo fingerboards.

Albert C. Wildermuth, Kalamazoo, MI
Another employee of Henderson-Ames Company (see above) who did engraving for Gibson. Wildermuth worked for Henderson-Ames from 1900 through 1926, then did independent job-lot work for Gibson in 1928 and 1929.

Finishing Supplies

Gibson did their own finish work in-house, using different materials and methods over the years. Prior to the invention of a sprayable, fast-drying nitrocellulose lacquer in 1923, Gibson used varnish finishes on their instruments. The quality of the finishes varied considerably. Some of the earliest nitrocellulose finishes (1925-1927) had a propensity to dry out, becoming brittle and flaking off. The finish work from the late 1930's was noticeably thicker and glossy, turning yellow with age. Page 57 of catalog X (1936) states that Gibson used custom-made lacquer and "oil sanded" between coats. It probably would be closer to the truth to say that Gibson mixed standard lacquer with additives (smoothers) prior to spraying. Various catalogs state that Gibson finish was hand-rubbed, yet factory photographs from the pre-war period clearly show machine-operated buffing wheels. As with other areas of the production process, it is likely that the catalog copy is not a reliable indicator of Gibson's actual methods.

Former Gibson employee Jim "Hutch" Hutchens recalled that by the time he came to work at Gibson in 1964, almost every surface inside the factory was covered in a fine coat of lacquer as a result of 40 years of overspray. This condition in combination with the railroad tracks on the east side of the building created a hazardous situation. "Hutch" related that sometimes a stray spark from a steam locomotive stack or one created by the grinding flange of a railroad car wheel would set the wooden fixtures inside the factory on fire. These small conflagrations were normally noticed quickly and extinguished rapidly by the employees. Contrary to popular legend, no evidence of a large, destructive fire at Gibson has ever been located.

The following companies all appear in Gibson's surviving financial records for 1925-1931.

H. Behlen & Brothers, New York City, NY
Makers of lacquer additives (smoothers) which Gibson used consistently throughout the period 1925-1931 and probably longer.

Herman Behr & Company, Chicago, IL
Makers of sandpaper products.

Behr Manning Corporation, Troy, NY
Maker of sandpaper products and other abrasives.

Brevolite Lacquer, North Chicago, IL
An alternate lacquer supplier which Gibson used after 1929. Brevolite had a 1933 patent for the dispersion of stains directly into nitrocellulose lacquer. The company may have been the source of the transparent lacquer used to create a blue, gray, or brown sunburst effect on Gibson's style 11 banjos. The appearance of this company in the financial records also coincides with the release of the style 11 banjos.

James B. Day & Company, Chicago, IL
Makers of lacquer thinner used at Gibson during 1930 and later.

DeVilbiss Company, Toledo, OH
The famous manufacturer of compressed-air paint brush equipment. Gibson used DeVilbiss equipment to spray their lacquer.

Devoe & Reynolds Company, Chicago, IL
Makers of finishing supplies.

Forbes Varnish Company, Cleveland, OH
This company was Gibson's main supplier of nitrocellulose lacquer from the early 1920's and onwards. They were still using Forbes products in the 1950's.

Gibson continued to use Forbes lacquer up into the 1950s. In this photograph Forbes sales representative Sherman W. Lees (on left) and long-time Gibson employee Case Triezenberg examine a small-body flattop guitar.
Steve Huber Collection

Grand Rapids Wood Finishing Company, Grand Rapids, MI
This company was evidently Gibson's main supplier of wood stain.

Paasche Airbrush Company, Chicago, IL
Makers of small "art" airbrushes and accessories. Probably used by Gibson to spray the stenciled logos and designs featured on certain models.

Zeller Lacquer Manufacturing Company, New York City, NY
An alternate lacquer supplier used sporadically by Gibson during this period.

Foundries

Kalamazoo was already a heavily industrialized city when Gibson was formed in 1902, and a number of local ferrous and non-ferrous foundries were in operation there from an early date. However, Gibson had no use for a foundry at all until they began producing banjos with cast tone rings in 1927. Surviving financial records show the company doing business with the following foundries after that time.

D.R.C. Foundry, Kalamazoo, MI
Very little is known about this company. Gibson made a payment of $10.24 to them in 1930.

Gerline Brass Company, Kalamazoo, MI
A very small, nonferrous foundry started by Otto Gerline in about 1913. This company was absorbed into Riverside Foundry & Galvanizing Company in 1935 and became their nonferrous division. Prior to that point, Riverside Foundry was exclusively a "grey iron" operation with no nonferrous capabilities. Gibson made small payments to Gerline Brass Company in 1930 and 1931.

Kalamazoo Foundry & Machine Company, Kalamazoo, MI
This company was exclusively a steel casting and fabricating jobber. Gibson made payments to them beginning in 1930. They were possibly the source of the steel coordinator rods used in Gibson banjo rims

Reed Foundry & Machine Company, Kalamazoo, MI
An iron and steel foundry. Gibson made a payment of $17.55 to them in 1930.

Riverside Foundry & Galvanizing Company, Kalamazoo, MI
A large operation which dealt exclusively in "gray iron" prior to 1935. They shared the same board of directors as the Kalamazoo Tank & Silo Company. Gibson made small payments to Riverside in 1930 and 1931. See Gerline Brass Company above for additional information.

Star Brass Works logo
Dean Hoffmeyer Collection

Star Brass Works, Kalamazoo, MI
A large foundry which began Kalamazoo operations in 1898. They specialized in fine brass, bronze, and aluminum casting. One of their *many* proprietary brass formulas used in the casting of electrical pickup wheels on trolley poles became world famous for its long wearing properties. Gibson used this company to cast brass banjo tone rings beginning in 1927. Company financial records show amounts payable to Star Brass varying from $677.50 in 1927 to as much as $3,688.51 in 1930. The foundry was located about 2.5 miles southeast of the Gibson factory and along the same railroad line. Star Brass Works ceased operations in 1961.

Much attention has been given in recent years to discovering the "secret formula" used by Gibson in their pre-World War II banjo tone rings. In my research I uncovered *absolutely no evidence* that any Gibson employee was skilled in the process of casting nonferrous metal. As with so many other production issues, it is clear that Gibson relied on the considerable expertise of their subcontractor, Star Brass Works, in the tone ring casting process. Gibson's tone ring specification probably simply called for "trolley brass" which Star Brass Works poured in many different alloys. Original information regarding the specific alloy used by Star Brass Works was lost when the company records were destroyed in 1961.

Pouring at Star Brass Works in 1948
Collection of the author

An intriguing look at the Star Brass Works operation is provided in a 1948 newspaper article which we quote as follows. "Back in the old days, the management used to have a little box of material in the safe. When the foundryman had his bronze melting pot to just about the right temperature he'd hurry to the office here. 'She's just about ready' he'd tell the company executive. That dignitary would pull on a pair of leather gloves, get a couple of pellets, or a pinch of the secret stuff from the box in the safe, hurry to the foundry and drop the mysterious mixture in the molten mass. That made it just right. That was the particular trade secret of the Star Brass Works."

Hardwood Lumber and Veneers

As described in their catalogs, Gibson purchased bulk hardwoods from all over the world. They accomplished this process by utilizing the services of long-established wholesale firms who sold mostly to the furniture and piano manufacturing trades. According to their 1936 catalog, Gibson allowed their hardwood to air-dry for five years before using it in production. During the period 1925-1931, Gibson did business with all of the following companies.

Julius Breckwoldt & Son, Dolgeville, NY
A maker of piano parts who likely sold Gibson spruce for use in soundboards.

Burnside Veneer Company, Chicago, IL
A "rotary cut" veneer company whose main factory was located in Pulaski, KY.

Walter Clark Veneer Company, Grand Rapids, MI
One of many smaller veneer companies that Gibson dealt with.

Evans & Retting Lumber Company, Grand Rapids, MI
Gibson made large purchases from this wholesale hardwood lumber supplier, probably northern Michigan maple.

Gill Lumber Company, Wausau, WI
A wholesale hardwood lumber supplier which Gibson dealt with on a smaller scale.

Grand Rapids Veneer Works, Grand Rapids, MI
One of many smaller veneer companies which Gibson dealt with.

Edward Hines Lumber Company, Chicago, IL
This company was one of the largest logging and wholesale lumber suppliers in the United States. Gibson would likely have purchased spruce from them.

Hoffman Brothers Company, Fort Wayne, IN
A medium-size wholesale lumber supplier.

Lane Lumber & Veneer Company, Grand Rapids, MI
One of two major wholesale veneer suppliers to Gibson.

J.H. Monteath Company, New York City, NY
One of two major importers and wholesalers of rare tropical lumber used by Gibson. They supplied rosewood and possibly mahogany as well. The Monteath Company was still in business as of 2011.

Nichols & Cox Lumber Company, Grand Rapids, MI
This company was Gibson's major supplier of northern Michigan curly maple.

C.H. Pearson & Son Hardwood Company, Brooklyn, NY
One of two major importers and wholesalers of rare tropical lumber used by Gibson. They supplied rosewood and possibly mahogany as well.

Pike Dial Lumber Company, Chicago, IL
A medium-sized supplier used sporadically by Gibson for wholesale hardwoods.

Posey Manufacturing Company, Hoquiam, WA
Gibson's major supplier of spruce for soundboards.

Rice Veneer & Lumber Company, Grand Rapids, MI
An alternate supplier of northern Michigan maple.

Manufactured Production Materials – Bulk

Gibson used large quantities of bulk manufactured materials in the production process. During the period 1925-1931, they did business with the following companies.

The Celluloid Company, Newark, NJ
Manufacturers of everything celluloid. They employed over 1,300 people in their Newark, New Jersey factory. Celluloid is a highly flammable, nitrocellulose-based plastic which was in use as far back as 1862. Gibson used the common form of celluloid for binding and other fancy forms for pickguards, decorative fingerboards, and trim on various models. Some varieties of celluloid plastic are known colloquially as "mother-of-toilet-seat."

DuPont Viscoloid Company, Chicago, IL
Viscoloid or Pyralin is a fancy form of pyroxylin plastic which resembles tortoise shell. DuPont used it to make hair brushes, combs, and other toiletry items. Gibson purchased large quantities of this material to use for pickguards.

Fiberloid Corporation, Indian Orchard, MA
Fiberloid is another variety of pyroxylin plastic and a member of the celluloid family. Gibson purchased large quantities of this material.

Joseph T. Ryerson & Son, Chicago, IL
Manufacturer of the 18% nickel-silver fret wire used by Gibson.

Steel Sales Corporation, Chicago, IL
Gibson did a continuing, substantial business with this company, which suggests that they provided the truss rod stock. Long-time Gibson employee Jim "Hutch" Hutchens indicated that the truss rod stock was a special alloy produced for Gibson by a subcontractor. The stock was cut to length at Gibson and then one end was threaded. Jim indicated this was usually a job done in odd moments when nothing else was happening.

Wigginton Company, Kalamazoo, MI
This company produced electric voltage testers. Gibson did a continuous business with them which once amounted to over $800 per month. Since Gibson did not produce any electrical instruments in the period 1925-1931, the purchases from Wigginton remain unexplained.

Pre-Manufactured Sub-Assemblies

Gibson purchased many pre-manufactured parts and sub-assemblies from vendors around the country including tuning machines, tailpieces, bridges, thumbscrews, banjo heads, and picks. The following list includes some of the more interesting companies with which they did business in the period 1925-1931.

Auburn Button Works, Auburn, NY
Makers of clothing buttons and other small plastic items. They may have made Gibson's line of picks and possibly the bridge pins used in guitars.

John S. Berger, Hamburg, PA
Maker and importer of wooden marquetry. Gibson used various types of marquetry on their instruments and on their banjos in particular. This man evidently filled most of Gibson's marquetry needs.

Doehler Die Casting, New York, NY
This company was founded in 1908 by Herman H. Doehler with a manufacturing plant in Brooklyn, New York and offices in Manhattan. Mr. Doehler is considered to be the inventor of modern die casting, a process in which molten pot metal is injected under high pressure into a steel die. In 1914 he opened a manufacturing facility in Toledo, Ohio and in 1921 another plant in Batavia, New York. The Doehler company is considered to be the major manufacturer of American hood ornaments before World War II. At the depth of the Great Depression in 1933, Doehler's administrative offices were also moved to Toledo. The company was merged with Jarvis Body in 1946 to become Doehler-Jarvis. Beginning in 1929 Gibson subcontracted the production of their banjo resonator bands (flanges) and stretcher bands (tension hoops) to Doehler. In 1937 Doehler also produced the "top-tension" parts for Gibson banjos. It has been previously assumed that the parts produced by Doehler for use on Gibson banjos were created using the "Zamak" alloy. However, recent metallurgical analysis by Jim Schroth has revealed that the earliest die-cast flanges were produced with a zinc alloy which predates the 1929 invention of "Zamak." This earlier alloy contains 90% zinc, 6% aluminum, 4% copper, and 0.1% magnesium. The percentage of aluminum and copper in these parts is higher than the amounts present in true Zamak, thereby reducing their impact strength and producing a more fragile part. Some of the earliest flanges and stretcher bands also tended to disintegrate over time, due to impurities in the alloy. In particular, the unwanted

presence of trace amounts of lead produced increased intergranular corrosion, more commonly known as "zinc pest."

Doehler Die Casting Stock Certificate – 1938
Frank Schoepf Collection

Grand Rapids Carved Moulding & Mfg. Co., Grand Rapids, MI
This company mass produced decorative wooden moulding. Gibson did business with them in 1927, which suggests that they may have produced the materials used on the resonator sides of the Florentine and Bella Voce banjos. Of course, in typical fashion, Gibson catalogs claimed that these items were "hand-carved."

Lincoln Manufacturing Company, Chicago, IL
A company catalog from this period shows that Lincoln Manufacturing Company produced thumbscrews, some of which appear to be identical to those used on Gibson banjos.

Albert D. Grover & Son, Long Island City, NY

Albert Deane Grover (1865 -1927) was a banjoist, composer, teacher, and inventor of banjo parts and accessories. His father Stephen Grover was a Boston piano maker. Albert was trained as a mechanical draftsman and had a successful early career manufacturing slot machines (for penny arcades, etc.). By 1920 he was widowed, living in Manhattan on 107th Street, and managing a "musical instrument accessory factory" with his son Walter. In 1929 the factory was located at 38 Payntar Avenue, Long Island City. A.D. held multiple patents, some of which were not granted until after his death. A.D. Grover & Son provided Gibson with tailpieces, tuners, bridges, and a myriad of other small accessory items.

However, the relationship between the two companies seems to have been a rocky one. In a letter dated April 17th, 1929, to C.F. Martin, Walter Grover seemingly takes great glee in revealing that Guy Hart (Gibson's general manager) has had a "nervous breakdown" and has left for Arizona. In return, the Gibson shipping ledgers reveal that on March 27th, 1935, Gibson sent the Grover Company "two bags of kindling," ostensibly as part of a practical joke (perhaps to light a fire and burn the place down). The ledgers also show many shipments of defective parts returned to Grover. In the early 1950's, Grover Musical Products of Cleveland, Ohio became the successors to A.D. Grover and Son.

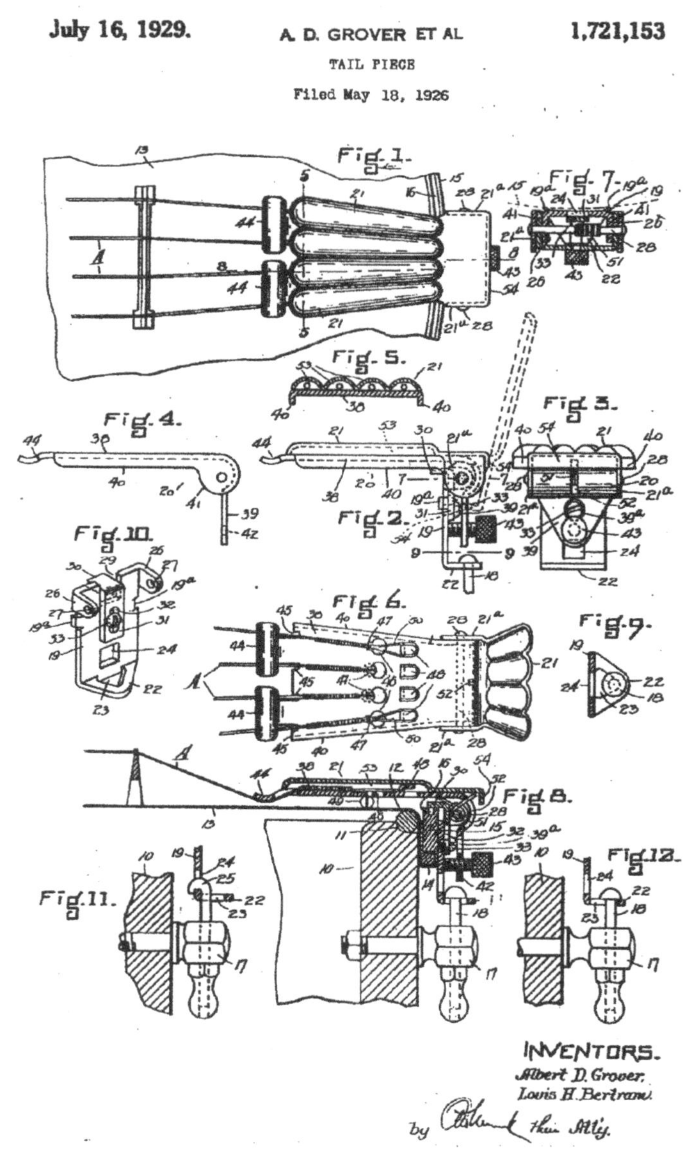

Grover's patent drawing for the "clamshell" banjo tailpiece

Collection of the author

Klise Manufacturing Company, Grand Rapids, MI
Founded in 1910 and still in business as of 2011, Klise Manufacturing is under the leadership of the same family's third generation. They produce decorative embossed wood products. In April of 1927 Gibson owed this company $1,810 for embossing sheets of veneer with the pattern used on the backs of the Florentine and Bella Voce banjo resonators. When shown the back of a pre-war Florentine resonator, current CEO Phil Veen said, "We could still do that today!" While Gibson catalogs and other promotional materials claimed that the Florentine and Bella Voce banjos were "hand-carved" examination of the banjos themselves and the financial records show that this was not true.

Ludwig & Ludwig, Chicago, IL
This famous drum manufacturer supplied Gibson with their proprietary "planetary" tuners for use on banjos.

Joseph D. Rogers Jr. & Son, Berlin, NY
The famous maker of high-quality calfskin banjo heads.

E.J. & J. Virzi, New York City, NY
The Virzi brothers are best known for their 1920 innovation the Virzi tone producer, which came as an option on Gibson F-5 mandolins, H-5 mandolas, K-5 mando-cellos, and L-5 guitars of the mid-1920's. In April of 1927 Gibson owed Virzi $1,486, probably not for tone producers but instead for a shipment of Virzi violins which Gibson marketed.

Waverly Musical Products Company, Long Island City, NY
This company was a manufacturer of stringed instrument accessories which Gibson used to supply many small sub-assemblies and parts. Waverly tuners and tailpieces were used on a wide variety of Gibson instruments. For Gibson banjos they also made the brass "E2" banjo stretcher bands (tension hoops), the head wire used inside the calfskin heads, banjo bracket wrenches, and the brass hooks and nuts used to tighten down the stretcher bands. Waverly was eventually purchased by the Stewart-McDonald Company of Athens, Ohio.

Pearl Inlay

Gibson instruments are well known for their beautiful mother-of-pearl inlays. Their pre-World War II patterns have been widely copied and reproduced in instruments by other makers. Gibson did not cut their own mother-of-pearl inlays at the factory. This function was outsourced to existing pearl houses. Except for simple shapes like dots, Gibson also did not inlay their own pearl, preferring again to allow the well-established pearl companies to do this work. The roughed-out fingerboard blanks were slotted at the factory and then shipped out to be inlaid. A similar procedure was followed for peghead overlays. After the inlays were installed, the pearl vendors shipped them back to Gibson. This system had been in place in the musical instrument industry as far back as the latter half of the 19th century.

We do not know who designed Gibson's pearl inlay patterns. Indeed, when Gibson wished to reproduce some of their *own* pre-war banjo patterns in the 1980's, they had to start from scratch because no official design drawings could be located in the files from Kalamazoo. Evidently there were no official names for the pre-war patterns. When banjo expert Davis Kennedy came to work at the Gibson factory in 1965, he specifically asked some of the remaining old-time employees about names for the mother-of-pearl patterns. In reply, he was told that the patterns had no official names. The names commonly used today like "flying eagle," "wreath," and "hearts & flowers" seem to date no further back than the late 1950's when demand for reproduction sets first arose. An unused pre-war "hearts & flowers" mandolin-banjo fingerboard in the possession of the author is simply inscribed "MB-4" on the back. It is likely that Gibson vendors and employees simply referred to the various patterns by their model or style number. Some of the elements in the earliest patterns seem to be "off-the-shelf" items that were arranged into pleasing patterns (e.g., dots, diamonds, squares, hearts, and spades). In the absence of any hard proof, it seems likely that the design work was done in-house and the original drawings were either lost or sent to the various pearl houses and not returned. Alternatively, the lack of trademark activity on Gibson's part may indicate that the designs were not theirs to begin with.

The pearl inlaying method used by pre-World War II pearl vendors was considerably different from the high-tech methods used currently. Employees in the pearl houses were paid "by the piece" and so speed was the most important criterion. After a pattern was marked out, a small pilot hole was drilled through the fingerboard or peghead overlay where each piece of pearl was to be inlaid. A jeweler's saw blade was threaded through the hole and then attached to a foot-powered sawing jig which was used to remove the remaining wood. The fingerboard or peghead overlay was then turned face down, and the pieces of pearl were placed in the holes from the rear, then the remaining space was packed with wood filler. The results were often sloppy, but this method had the advantage of being very fast.

Gibson primarily used the following pearl suppliers in the pre-World War II period.

Aumann Brothers Pearl, Detroit, MI
This company produced pearl work for Gibson throughout the pre-World War II period and was their major supplier from 1903 through 1930. In April of 1930 Gibson owed Aumann Brothers $760. The company cut mother-of-pearl and did the work of inlaying the patterns into fingerboards and peghead overlays. Adam Aumann (pronounced "OW-man") was born 1862 in Germany and became a naturalized American citizen in 1880. His two oldest sons were Frank Adam Aumann (1885 -1970) and Joseph A. Aumann (1887 - 1950). The family first lived in the Bronx and was doing inlay work there in the 1890's. They all moved to Detroit, Michigan in 1903 and founded a pearl shop at 46 Fordyce Avenue dedicated exclusively to cutting and inlaying pearl for furniture and musical instruments. After the death of their father in the 1920's, the business was carried on by Frank and Joseph and was known as Aumann Brothers Pearl.

An example of Aumann Brothers pearl
Collection of the Author

In a 2009 interview, a nephew of Frank and Joseph Aumann was able to give the author an eyewitness account of the Aumann Brothers Pearl shop in the 1930's. He remembered seeing Gibson orders at the shop and stated that his two uncles did all the work themselves at that time. He related that the original pearl shop stood in the back yard of the house at Fordyce Avenue. The shop had four jigsaw machines, probably because originally Adam Aumann and three of his sons were associated with the business. The operators stood up in front of the jigsaws and pumped a foot treadle at the bottom. The work platform was about chest high. He related that the mother-of-pearl used in the shop originated in Japan and arrived already cut into sheets. The sheets were glued together, sometimes as many as eight to ten layers thick with a piece of tracing paper on the top. The pattern to be cut was laid out with a sharp pencil, and then the sheets were all cut at the same time. The pearl was inlaid using the process already described above. The operation ceased to exist in the late 1940's when the brothers sold the house and moved away to Dearborn, Michigan.

An example of Union Pearl Works pearl
Jim Mills Collection

Union Pearl Works, Brooklyn, NY
This company supplied pearl to Gibson beginning in 1930 and probably became Gibson's major pearl vendor of the first half of the 1930's. The company was founded by Silas L. Lawles, and in operation by 1887 in New York City. Originally the offices and factory were located on the 6th and 7th floors of the Trenkmann Building at 241 Centre Street. On January 2, 1891, this building burned to the ground, due in part to a large supply of celluloid kept in the building by the Union Pearl Works. After the fire, the factory was relocated to 235 Berry Avenue in Brooklyn where it remained throughout the 20th century. The offices of the company remained at various locations in Manhattan. Joseph H. Lawles (1861-1936) and Thomas D. Lawles (1865 - lvg.1938), sons of Silas L. Lawles, assumed control of the operations in 1888. Like Aumann Brothers, this company both cut mother-of-pearl and did the inlay work. The quality of Union Pearl Works inlay is generally lower than that of Aumann Brothers and is easily distinguished visually by thicker lines and cruder cuts.

Howard W. Goff (1903-1970)
In a 2009 interview, one pre-war Gibson employee told the author that Kalamazoo resident Howard W. Goff also supplied pearl inlay work to Gibson in the late 1930's. Goff had

previously worked at Gibson during 1926-1932 along with his brother Myron F. Goff. Both men were woodworkers, and both were evidently laid off in the general purge of January 1932. Gibson found his pearl inlay product to be inferior and by 1937 he was working as a patternmaker at Clarage Fan Company of Kalamazoo. It has been speculated that the crudest pearl inlay work seen on Gibson peghead overlays of the late 1930's might have been the work of Howard W. Goff.

Strings

As a manufacturer of fretted instruments, Gibson obviously had a vested interest in strings. Originally Gibson purchased their strings pre-made from other manufacturers, just like many other parts. In his book *The Gibson Story*, historian Julius Bellson wrote that the company began making its own strings in the early 1920's. Surviving financial records seem to indicate that Gibson was still purchasing pre-made strings and re-packaging them in the late 1920's. That changed in 1929 when Gibson had a brief flirtation with bringing a few formerly outsourced functions into the factory. String-making was one of these and the only one to survive beyond 1931. Concurrently, about 1929 someone at Gibson had the idea of using Monel™ wire to produce strings. Monel™ is an alloy of nickel and copper which was patented by the Special Metals Corporation in 1906. This alloy has the disadvantage of "work hardening" very quickly but the advantage of being very resistant to corrosion. Because of the latter property, it was perfect for application as a long-lasting, musical instrument string. The idea was a tremendous success for Gibson. The String Department started with two employees in 1929 and by 1937 had increased to 24 workers, all women.

American Steel & Wire Company, Chicago, IL
This company was a division of U.S. Steel and began using the Monel alloy to make wire as early as 1910. From 1929 onward they were one of two major suppliers to Gibson of string-making wire.

Armour & Company, Kalamazoo, MI
This company supplied Gibson with gut strings throughout the pre-World War II period.

Driver Harris Company, Morristown, NJ
Founded in 1900 by brothers Frank & Wilbur Driver in partnership with Francis Harris. This company supplied Gibson with string-making wire.

Gibson Musical String Company, Belleville, NJ
This company had no connection to Gibson of Kalamazoo. The company was operated by brothers James and Frank Gibson, formerly employees of the National Musical String Company. Prior to the inception of Gibson's own string-making department in 1929, they were a major supplier of pre-made strings. This company evidently failed before 1932.

E. & O. Mari, New York City, NY
Manufacturers of LaBella brand strings. Gibson purchased pre-made strings from this company prior to 1929.

National Musical String Company, New Brunswick, NJ
Manufacturers of the famous "Bell Brand" and "Black Diamond" strings. The company was founded in 1897 by Thomas Nelson Jr., Alexander M. Paul, and George D. Emerson. In 1932 it came under the control of C. Bruno & Son who placed it under the day-to-day management

of ex-employees and former rivals James and Frank Gibson (see Gibson Musical String Company). The original records of this company are preserved at Rutgers University. Gibson purchased pre-made strings from this company prior to 1929.

V.C. Squier Company, Battle Creek, MI
Violin maker Victor Carroll Squier (b.1866) was a native of Battle Creek, Michigan. The company bearing his name made strings for all types of musical instruments but were perhaps best known for their violin-family strings. The V.C. Squier Company was acquired by Fender Musical Instruments in 1965. In that same year Fender was acquired by Columbia Broadcasting System, and they quickly shut the V.C. Squier Company down. Gibson made large purchases of pre-made strings from this company prior to 1929 and smaller purchases thereafter. The "Squier" name was used as of 2011 by Fender on a line of budget-brand guitars.

Standard Musical String & Manufacturing, Brooklyn, NY
This company was founded by Alexander M. Paul prior to 1917. Gibson purchased pre-made strings from this company prior to 1929.

Earl & Chappell – Patent Attorneys

No discussion of Gibson's pre-World War II vendors could be complete without a mention of their patent attorneys, the firm of Earl & Chappell. The name of this law firm can be found on most of Gibson's early patents. The firm was founded in 1895 by Fred L. Chappell Sr. He took in partner Otis A. Earl in 1905, and the practice flourished until 1955. In that year the surviving partner Otis A. Earl took in a new lawyer Austin A. Webb. The new firm of Earl & Webb lasted until 1964 when that firm dissolved. Mr. Earl became employed in another firm known as Woodham, Blanchard & Flynn and practiced law until his death at age 94 in 1967. As of this writing, the law firm of Flynn, Thiel, Boutell & Tanis, P.C. continues the long tradition of Earl & Chappell in Kalamazoo. In a 2010 interview with partner David G. Boutell, Esq., he indicated that Gibson's patent files made the long journey all the way from Earl & Chappell to the law firm of Woodham, Blanchard & Flynn. They were eventually destroyed due to expiration of the patents.

Factory interior view, circa 1936
Kalamazoo Public Library Local History Collection

The smokestack at Parsons Street was built by the M.W. Kellog Company in 1917
Steve Huber Collection

Chapter 4 - Factory Order Numbers

Overview

From the beginning of the company in 1902, Gibson used a factory order number (FON) system to track production costs and control inventory. Gibson's first production manager Sylvo Reams was probably responsible for introducing this process to the company. These factory order numbers are often confused with serial numbers, even by vintage instrument experts. While both types of numbers may be found on Gibson instruments, factory order numbers are related to the accounting process while serial numbers are linked to shipping and warranty issues. In the next chapter we will cover the serial number system.

All pre-World War II Gibson instruments were produced under a factory order number, even if it was not stamped or inked onto the instrument. Some instruments were also given a serial number. On the instruments themselves, some have only a FON, some have only a serial number, some have *both*, and thousands have *neither.* Gibson factory order numbers (if present or available on an instrument) are the best indicators of when the instrument was *manufactured*, while serial numbers (if present or available on an instrument) are the best indicators of when the instrument was *shipped*.

Factory Order Number Assignment

Under the factory order number system each prospective batch of instruments was assigned a unique number (FON) before production began. Therefore, *every* Gibson instrument produced in the pre-World War II period had a FON at the time it was manufactured, even if it does not appear on the instrument. Then, as the instruments moved along the production line the employees tracked the quantities of raw materials used, the number of pre-assembled parts pulled from the stockroom and the hours of labor used in the process. These were duly reported to the accounting staff who then charged their costs back to the FON.

Observed evidence indicates that the instruments contained in any one particular FON batch were all of the same type (i.e. banjos, guitars or mandolins) but not necessarily of the same model. Banjos and guitars in particular might have different neck types (i.e. tenor, plectrum or regular) within the same FON batch. The size of a batch might vary from only one (a custom order) or up into the hundreds.

Factory Order Number Placement on the Instruments

At an early stage of the production process each instrument within a given batch was marked with the FON (either die-stamped or ink-stamped) and given an additional sequential number indicating its position within the batch. The apparent exceptions to this rule are the lowest priced instruments which inexplicably did not receive any markings which are detectable today. The sequential positional number was separated by a hyphen from the batch number (e.g. 554-2.)

For instruments marked with a FON, the location varied. On mandolins with a round soundhole the FON was usually ink stamped on one of the interior side walls, and it is visible through the

soundhole. Instruments with f-holes had their FON ink-stamped on the interior back, visible through the lower f-hole. One exception to this rule is the FON for Master Model mandolin family instruments built during Lloyd Loar's tenure with the company (1922-1924). The FON on these instruments was handwritten on the interior of the back before it was glued up and then later covered with a paper label bearing Loar's signature. For banjos Gibson used a set of metal dies to stamp the FON inside the banjo rim wall. It was also often written in pencil on the banjo neck heel and in chalk across the inside surface of the banjo resonator. About 1927 Gibson also began using red paint to recopy the FON on the resonator's inside surface just to the right side of the neck notch. This was probably done so the shipping clerks could read the number without taking off the banjo resonator. During the period 1941-45 banjos had a FON stamped on the back of the peghead. Some types and models of pre-World War II Gibsons do not have a FON that is visible on the instrument.

Production Meetings

In the pre-World War II period, Gibson held a weekly production meeting in which management decided what the factory would produce in the coming weeks. There is clear evidence that Gibson built some instruments for inventory as well as producing others to meet orders from their retail dealers. We believe that custom orders also entered the production process at the weekly meetings.

Throughout the pre-World War II period, all orders were initiated using a preprinted form. In a 1970 interview, long-time Gibson employee Wilbur Marker stated that Gibson purchased padded receipt books from a local stationery store for that purpose. External evidence suggests that these books had four or five identical, sequentially numbered forms on each page and that each book contained about 150 pages. The preprinted number on the form became the factory order number (FON). Wilbur Marker also related that the pads were kept on a shelf at Gibson and the secretaries would simply grab one on the way into the weekly production meeting. This may have introduced an element of randomness to the sequence of factory order numbers because a book used in a previous meeting may not have always been the same one used at the next meeting.

Rollovers

Gibson reused the same factory order numbers many times for different instrument batches. This is true from the beginning of the company right up into the 1950's. Because the FON's were a function of the accounting department and never actually intended to uniquely identify an instrument (in the way that a serial number does) this practice did not create a problem at the factory. However, it is problematic for us today when we attempt to identify a production date for an instrument using only the FON. Such investigations are best performed when using a combination of constructional features, provenance and any identifying numbers.

After a batch of instruments was produced and sold, there was no reason not to use a specific FON again. Study has shown that after reaching a certain point in FON's, Gibson would start all over again at batch #1. In common usage these have come to be called "rollovers." The highest FON used *before* the occurrence of a "rollover" seems to have been random and was probably a direct result of whatever the highest pre-printed number was in the receipt books used to originate the FON. Obviously, whenever a pile of receipt books was entirely used up, a new batch was obtained from the local stationery store to replace them. Beginning in 1934 Gibson seems to have started over again with batch #1 at some point every year.

Summary of Gibson Factory Order Number Series (1902 – 1945)

Years	FON's used
1902-1916	1 through 3650
1917-1923	11000 through 12000
1924-1925	11000 through 11250 (with "A" suffix)
1925	1000 through 1250 (with "A" suffix – banjos only)
1925-1931	8000 through 9999
1927-1928	0110 through 0442 (banjos only)
1931-1933	1 through 890 (with some isolated higher numbers)
1934	1 through 1500 (with some isolated higher numbers)
1935	1 through 1520 (with some isolated higher numbers, some with "A" suffix)
1936	1 through 1100 (with some isolated higher numbers, some with "B" suffix)
1937	1 through 1400 (with some isolated higher numbers, some with "C" suffix)
1938	1 through 1000 (with some isolated higher numbers, some with "D" suffix"
1939	1 through 980 (with some isolated higher numbers, some with "E" suffix)
1940-1945	1 through 7900 (some with letter suffix, some with letter prefix, some without)

Example of a die-stamped FON in a Gibson banjo rim
Collection of the author

Example of a chalked FON in a Gibson banjo resonator
Collection of the author

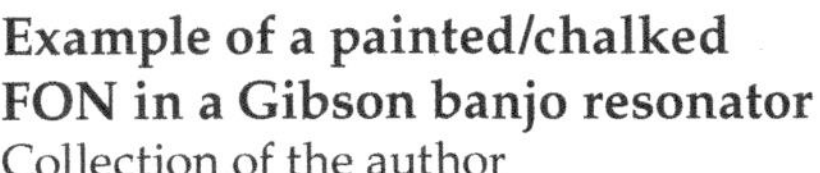

Example of a painted/chalked FON in a Gibson banjo resonator
Collection of the author

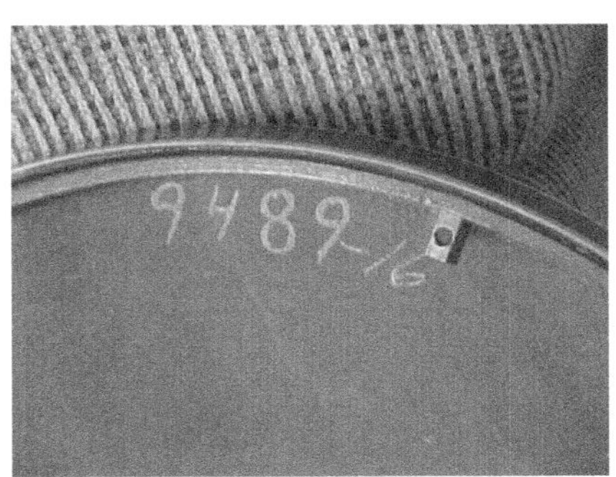

1902-1916 FON Series

FON's used during this earliest period of Gibson production have been obtained by observation of extant instruments by myself and others. No shipping ledgers for the period have survived. Collected numbers suggest that Gibson started with the numeral 1 and had reached FON's as high as 3650 by 1916. Many FON's from this series are missing because they are from batches whose instruments have yet to be discovered and examined. The following table is not meant to be all-inclusive.

FON	Model	Production Year
133	L-1	1904
171	A-4	1905
190	F-2	1905
200	F-2	1905
220	A	1905
230	A-1	1905
232	F-4	1905
243	A-2	1905
249	F-4	1905
258	A	1905
259	A	1905
264	F-2	1905
268	A-4	1905
283	F-4	1906
284	F-4	1906
285	A	1906
286	A-1	1906
304	A	1906
309	A-4	1906
324	F-2	1906
409	A-4	1906
411	A-3	1906
421	O-2	1906
424	L-1	1906
433	L-1	1906
434	A-1	1906
484	A-2	1907
486	A	1907
507	F-2	1907
540	A-2	1908
545	A	1908
546	A	1908
547	A-3	1908
548	A-4	1908
683	H-1	1909
726	K-1	1909
911	A-4	1909
927	F-2	1909
1015	A-1	1910
1027	F-4	1910

FON	Model	Production Year
1037	F-2	1910
1041	H-2	1910
1046	F-4	1910
1057	A	1910
1114	L-1	1910
1186	A-4	1910
1191	F-4	1910
1199	F-4	1910
1204	A	1910
1219	A	1910
1242	A	1910
1260	A-4	1910
1295	F-4	1910
1302	A-1	1910
1317	F-4	1910
1333	A-4	1910
1339	F-4	1910
1356	A-1	1910
1357	A	1910
1408	F-4	1910
1420	L-1	1910
1445	A-1	1910
1450	A-4	1911
1462	F-4	1911
1473	K-1	1911
1517	F-4	1911
1528	K-1	1911
1537	H-1	1911
1538	H-2	1911
1546	F-4	1911
1582	A-1	1911
1584	A-3	1911
1593	F-4	1911
1600	K-2	1911
1604	L-1	1911
1661	K-4	1911
1663	F-4	1911
1678	F-2	1911
1691	A-1	1911
1733	F-4	1911

FON	Model	Production Year
1753	F-4	1911
1765	A	1911
1779	F-4	1911
1789	F-4	1911
1811	A	1911
1812	F-2	1912
1837	A-1	1912
1845	O	1912
1900	F-4	1912
1902	A	1912
1929	F-4	1912
1936	A-4	1912
1937	A-3	1912
1938	A-1	1912
1939	A	1912
1985	F-4	1912
1998	A	1912
2010	L-1	1912
2017	J	1912
2038	K-1	1912
2040	H-1	1912
2044	A-4	1912
2053	A	1912
2069	F-2	1912
2109	A-1	1912
2129	L-3	1912
2132	F-4	1912
2143	A-4	1912
2145	A-3	1912
2152	L-1	1912
2153	A	1912
2160	F-4	1912
2181	H-1	1912
2206	A-1	1913
2207	F-2	1913
2209	A	1913
2215	O	1913
2216	A-4	1913
2229	F-4	1913
2230	K-2	1913
2282	F-4	1913
2290	A-4	1913
2291	A-1	1913
2307	F-2	1913
2313	H-2	1913

FON	Model	Production Year
2329	A-1	1913
2337	L-3	1913
2364	A	1913
2375	A-4	1913
2384	A	1913
2409	A-3	1913
2415	U	1913
2416	O	1913
2421	H-2	1913
2430	A	1913
2438	F-4	1913
2489	A-4	1913
2491	F-2	1913
2496	A-1	1913
2497	F-4	1913
2505	A	1913
2513	F-4	1913
2535	A-3	1913
2542	A	1913
2543	A-1	1913
2548	A-1	1913
2562	A-4	1913
2572	L-4	1914
2591	A	1914
2606	A-4	1914
2616	A-1	1914
2622	F-4	1914
2626	A	1914
2627	K-1	1914
2634	U	1914
2652	A-4	1914
2659	A-1	1914
2666	F-4	1914
2667	A-3	1914
2672	H-2	1914
2673	O	1914
2741	A-4	1914
2742	F-2	1914
2743	F-4	1914
2754	K-1	1914
2767	A	1914
2806	A-4	1914
2825	A	1914
2867	L-4	1914
2868	A-1	1914

1902-1916 FON Series (continued)

FON	Model	Production Year
2871	H-2	1914
2882	F-4	1914
2899	H-4	1914
2908	F-2	1914
2909	A-3	1914
2950	A	1915
2959	A-4	1915
2980	A-1	1915
2983	U	1915
2985	F-4	1915
3006	A	1915
3023	F-4	1915
3032	A	1915
3033	A-1	1915
3072	A-1	1915
3073	A	1915
3083	L-1	1915
3116	A	1915
3118	F-4	1915
3122	A-1	1915
3125	U	1915
3153	A-3	1915
3159	K-4	1915
3160	L-1	1915
3171	A-4	1915
3200	A	1915
3201	O	1915
3236	A-3	1915
3246	F-2	1915
3247	F-4	1915
3256	A-4	1915
3262	A	1915
3268	A-3	1915
3269	A-4	1915
3285	A-4	1915
3288	A-4	1915
3289	L-3	1915
3322	A-1	1916
3324	A-4	1916
3325	F-2	1916
3326	F-4	1916
3366	A-1	1916
3381	A	1916
3382	A-1	1916
3383	A-4	1916

FON	Model	Production Year
3385	F-4	1916
3400	F-4	1916
3417	A	1916
3418	A-1	1916
3428	H-4	1916
3458	H-1	1916
3459	H-2	1916
3493	H-2	1916
3503	A-4	1916
3505	H-2	1916
3555	A-1	1916
3580	L-4	1916
3586	O	1916
3635	A	1916
3636	A-1	1916
3638	F-2	1916
3639	F-4	1916

1917-1923 FON Series

FON's used during this second period of Gibson production have been obtained by observation of extant instruments by myself and others. In addition, some shipping information from this period survives. Collected data shows that Gibson initiated a new sequence of FON's beginning with the numeral 11000 in 1917 and continued with this series reaching FON's near 12000 by the end of 1923. Many FON's from this series are missing because they are from batches whose instruments have yet to be discovered and examined. The following table is not meant to be all-inclusive.

FON	Model	Production Year
11000	A	1917
11001	L-3	1917
11007	A	1917
11008	A-1	1917
11009	A-3	1917
11010	A-4	1917
11012	A	1917
11014	A	1917
11017	A-3	1917
11018	A-4	1917
11020	F-4	1917
11027	A	1917
11028	A	1917
11030	A-4	1917
11031	F-2	1917
11032	F-4	1917
11033	H-1	1917
11042	O	1917
11045	H-1	1917
11048	H-1	1917
11049	A-1	1917
11050	A-1	1917
11051	A-1	1917
11056	A	1917
11058	A	1917
11059	A-1	1917
11062	A-4	1917
11066	A-4	1917
11067	F-4	1917
11069	H-2	1917
11070	H-2	1917
11077	U	1917
11079	A	1917
11080	A	1917
11082	A	1917
11085	A-3	1917
11086	A-3	1917
11088	A-4	1917
11090	F-2	1917

FON	Model	Production Year
11095	O	1917
11096	L-1	1917
11102	A-1	1918
11103	A	1918
11104	A-1	1918
11112	A	1918
11113	A	1918
11114	A	1918
11121	A-4	1918
11122	A-4	1918
11128	L-3	1918
11131	F-4	1918
11132	H-1	1918
11133	H-4	1918
11144	A	1918
11145	A	1918
11146	A	1918
11147	A	1918
11163	A-3	1918
11164	A-3	1918
11166	A-2	1918
11186	F-4	1918
11193	A-3	1918
11200	O	1918
11205	F-4	1918
11288	F-4	1919
11310	A-4	1920
11311	A-2	1920
11318	A-2	1920
11320	K-1	1920
11321	GB-3	1920
11323	DY	1920
11324	A	1920
11325	A-1	1920
11326	A-3	1920
11329	A	1920
11330	A-2	1920
11338	A-4	1920
11343	A-2	1920

1917-1923 FON Series (continued)

FON	Model	Production Year
11345	K-2	1920
11347	A-2	1920
11348	F-2	1920
11349	F-2	1920
11356	O	1920
11358	L-4	1920
11364	H-1	1920
11365	F-4	1920
11367	F-4	1920
11374	A-2	1921
11375	A-4	1921
11384	A-4	1921
11385	A-4	1921
11392	A-2	1921
11409	A	1921
11413	GB	1921
11414	GB	1921
11415	MB	1921
11418	A-2	1921
11419	F-4	1921
11420	A-Jr	1921
11422	A-4	1921
11424	A	1921
11425	A-Jr	1921
11426	A-4	1921
11427	MB	1921
11434	A	1921
11435	A-4	1921
11436	L-1	1921
11437	L-3	1921
11438	TB-4	1921
11439	MB	1921
11442	A	1921
11444	A-2	1921
11446	H-4	1921
11449	F-4	1921
11453	A-2	1921
11460	TB-4	1921
11461	MB-4	1921
11464	H-4	1921
11468	A-4	1921
11473	MB	1921
11480	H-1	1921
11483	F-4	1921
11486	F-4	1921
11487	O	1921
11488	CB	1921
11489	GB	1921
11491	MB	1921
11495	F-4	1921
11496	A	1921
11499	MB	1921
11501	TB-0	1921
11505	L-1	1921
11506	TB-4	1921
11507	A-2	1921
11508	MB	1921
11509	MB	1921
11510	GB	1921
11511	CB	1922
11513	TB-0	1922
11525	A-4	1922
11527	F-4	1922
11531	TB-4	1922
11534	MB	1922
11536	MB	1922
11537	TB-4	1922
11542	TB-Jr	1922
11543	MB-0	1922
11544	F-4	1922
11548	F-4	1922
11550	MB-4	1922
11553	MB-0	1922
11554	GB-3	1922
11557	MB-4	1922
11558	F-4	1922
11562	TB-0	1922
11564	A	1922
11567	TB	1922
11568	MB	1922
11569	TB-4	1922
11571	MB-1	1922
11575	F-4	1922
11576	A-3	1922
11577	GB	1922
11578	A-3	1922
11579	MB-2	1922
11580	TB	1922
11581	MB	1922
11583	MB	1922

FON	Model	Production Year
11588	MB	1922
11590	F-4	1922
11597	A-4	1922
11599	TB-4	1922
11603	A	1922
11605	H-4	1922
11609	F-5	1922
11612	A-3	1922
11617	GB-4	1922
11618	F-2	1922
11619	A	1922
11620	TB-3	1922
11621	TB-0	1922
11623	A	1922
11626	A-2	1922
11627	A	1922
11628	MB-1	1922
11633	O	1922
11634	A-Jr	1922
11638	MB-1 & MB-2	1922
11642	A-3	1922
11645	MB-Jr	1922
11648	A	1922
11650	A-4	1922
11655	F-4	1922
11656	A	1922
11658	A-2	1922
11659	F-4	1922
11660	TB	1922
11667	F-2	1922
11668	L-1	1922
11669	L-3	1922
11674	TB-1	1922
11661	MB	1922
11671	TB	1922
11676	TB	1922
11677	MB-4	1922
11678	GB-3 & GB-4	1922
11680	O	1922
11686	MB	1922
11691	TB-4	1922
11692	A	1922
11693	A-2	1922
11696	F-4	1922
11698	L-Jr	1922

FON	Model	Production Year
11699	A-2	1922
11700	MB	1922
11703	F-4	1922
11704	A-Jr	1922
11707	H-4	1922
11709	MB-4	1922
11711	A-4	1922
11713	TB	1922
11715	TB	1922
11716	MB	1922
11719	TB	1922
11720	A	1922
11721	F-4	1922
11724	TB	1922
11729	Mando-viola	1922
11733	MB	1922
11737	GB-4	1922
11739	F-5	1922
11741	TB	1922
11742	TB-1	1922
11746	H-4	1922
11747	GB	1922
11749	TB-4	1922
11750	A-2	1922
11754	MB-4	1922
11755	A	1922
11756	F-2	1922
11758	TB	1922
11760	A-2	1922
11761	A-Jr	1922
11763	F-4	1922
11765	MB-2	1922
11766	TB	1922
11769	A	1922
11772	MB	1922
11776	A	1922
11777	A-2	1922
11778	TB	1922
11780	MB	1923
11782	A	1923
11783	A-2	1923
11784	A-3	1923
11785	A-4	1923
11786	TB	1923
11796	A-2	1923

1917-1923 FON Series (continued)

FON	Model	Production Year
11799	TB	1923
11800	TB-4	1923
11801	TB	1923
11810	F-4	1923
11811	F-2	1923
11812	H-4	1923
11815	A-Jr	1923
11816	TB	1923
11818	TB-Jr	1923
11821	GB	1923
11827	F-4	1923
11834	MB-2	1923
11835	A	1923
11836	A-2	1923
11837	A-4	1923
11842	MB	1923
11844	TB-4	1923
11845	TB-1	1923
11846	MB	1923
11847	TB	1923
11850	A	1923
11851	A-2	1923
11852	F-4	1923
11854	MB-1	1923
11858	TB	1923
11862	MB-1	1923
11863	MB-4	1923
11864	A	1923
11865	A-2	1923
11867	F-4	1923
11879	A	1923
11882	L-3	1923
11883	A	1923
11884	L-2	1923
11889	MB-Jr	1923
11897	A-4	1923
11900	TB-Jr	1923
11902	A-2z	1923
11908	MB-Jr	1923
11909	MB-3 9"	1923
11918	A-1	1923
11919	A-2z	1923
11920	A-4	1923
11921	A-1	1923
11922	F-4	1923

FON	Model	Production Year
11932	A-1	1923
11934	A-2z	1923
11943	MB-Jr	1923
11947	GB-4	1923
11948	A-4	1923
11949	A-2z	1923
11951	A-2z	1923
11953	H-1	1923
11954	MB-4	1923
11955	MB-4	1923
11962	A-Jr	1923
11963	A-2z	1923
11971	A-2z	1923
11982	F-4	1923
11984	TB-5	1923
11985	F-5	1923
11986	A-1	1923
11990	F-4	1923
11991	A-2z	1923
11995	A-2z	1923
11999	A-2z	1923

1924-1925 FON Series

FON's used during this third period of Gibson production have been obtained by observation of extant instruments by myself and others. During this period the letter suffix "A" was added to FON's. The rationale for this addition is not clear. Collected data shows that Gibson initiated a new sequence of FON's beginning with 11000A in 1924 and continued through the first quarter of 1925. Many FON's from this series remain to be discovered, and the following table is not meant to be all-inclusive.

FON	Model	Production Year
11002A	A-2z	1924
11006A	A-Jr	1924
11008A	TB-4	1924
11009A	TB-1	1924
11011A	TB-4	1924
11012A	TB	1924
11015A	MB-4	1924
11019A	TB-Jr	1924
11021A	TB	1924
11022A	TB-4	1924
11021A	A-1	1924
11024A	TB-5	1924
11026A	MB	1924
11029A	TB-1	1924
11033A	GB-4	1924
11034A	L-4	1924
11039A	TB-3	1924
11041A	MB-4 & TB-4	1924
11043A	A-Jr	1924
11044A	A-Jr	1924
11048A	TB	1924
11049A	TB	1924
11051A	RB-Jr	1924
11052A	RB-3	1924
11053A	RB-4	1924
11054A	PB-Jr	1924
11056A	MB-4	1924
11057A	TB-4	1924
11058A	H-5	1924
11062A	J	1924
11063A	MB-3	1924
11064A	MB-4	1924
11065A	MB-4	1924
11066A	A-4	1924
11067A	F-4	1924
11068A	TB-4 & PB-4	1924
11070A	TB-Jr	1924
11075A	TB-3	1924
11077A	TB-4	1924
11078A	TB-4	1924

FON	Model	Production Year
11086A	TB-5	1924
11089A	TB	1924
11091A	TB	1924
11093A	H-4	1924
11097A	TB-5	1924
11101A	RB-4	1924
11105A	K-1	1924
11106	K-4	1924
11110A	MB-4	1924
11112A	MB	1924
11113A	MB-3	1924
11114A	TB	1924
11117A	TB	1924
11123A	MB-Jr	1924
11124A	TB-1	1924
11127A	UB	1924
11130A	MB-Jr	1924
11132A	RB-Jr	1924
11133A	PB-Jr	1924
11134A	RB-3	1924
11135A	TB	1924
11141A	TB-5	1924
11142A	O	1924
11144A	TB	1924
11147A	A-4	1924
11148A	F-2	1924
11149A	H-1	1924
11156A	MB-Jr	1924
11157A	MB-3	1924
11159A	UB	1924
11161A	TB-3	1924
11172A	Tenor Lute	1924
11177A	Tenor Lute	1924
11180A	Tenor Lute	1924
11185A	A-Jr	1924
11186A	L-Jr	1924
11188A	TB-1	1924
11190A	Tenor Lute-4	1924
11191A	A-Jr	1924
11192A	UB	1924

1924-1925 FON Series (continued)

FON	Model	Production Year
11196A	TB-4	1924
11197A	A	1924
11198A	MB-Jr	1924
11199A	TB-Jr	1924
11201A	TB-Jr	1925
11204A	A	1925
11206A	MB-1	1925
11209A	A-Jr	1925
11211A	MB	1925
11212A	TB-Jr	1925
11214A	TB	1925
11218A	MB-Jr	1925
11221A	TB-3	1925
11231A	A-Jr	1925
11232A	A	1925
11241A	TB	1925

A typical example of a guitar FON with a blurred ink-stamp on the headblock. This is 11698.

Collection of the author

1925 Banjo FON Series

In the first quarter of 1925 and concurrent with the third FON series, Gibson used a totally separate group of batch numbers for *some* of their banjo production. The rationale for this action remains unclear. FON's used in this series have been obtained by observation of extant instruments by myself and others. This series ran from 1000 to 1250 and uses the letter "A" suffix. Many FON's from this series remain to be discovered, and the following table is not meant to be all-inclusive.

FON	Model	Production Year
1003A	TB-4	1925
1007A	TB-4	1925
1008A	TB-4	1925
1010A	TB-1	1925
1011A	TB-4	1925
1014A	MB-3	1925
1017A	MB	1925
1018A	MB-4	1925
1020A	TB	1925
1021A	TB	1925
1022A	TB-4	1925
1024A	TB-5	1925
1026A	MB	1925
1030A	TB-3	1925
1031A	TB-4	1925
1035A	CB-4	1925
1038A	TB-Jr	1925
1041A	TB-4	1925
1051A	RB-Jr	1925
1052A	TB-3	1925
1053A	RB-4	1925
1055A	PB-3	1925
1063A	MB-3	1925
1064A	MB-4	1925
1068A	TB-4 & PB-4	1925
1072A	TB-Jr	1925
1075A	TB	1925
1077A	TB-4	1925
1083A	TB-3	1925
1084A	RB-1	1925
1085A	RB-3	1925
1088A	TB-Jr	1925
1090A	TB-Jr	1925
1096A	MB-Jr	1925
1099A	GB-4	1925
1101A	RB-4	1925
1109A	TB & MB	1925
1111A	TB-3	1925
1112A	MB-Jr	1925
1113A	MB-3	1925

FON	Model	Production Year
1114A	TB-4	1925
1123A	MB-Jr	1925
1125A	TB-Jr	1925
1131A	TB-1	1925
1135A	TB-4	1925
1139A	MB-Jr	1925
1144A	TB	1925
1145A	TB-3	1925
1146A	CB-4	1925
1156A	MB-Jr	1925
1160A	TB-1	1925
1161A	TB-3	1925
1164A	TB-3	1925
1169A	TB-3	1925
1176A	UB-1	1925
1178A	TB	1925
1187A	TB-Jr	1925
1188A	TB	1925
1190A	TB-Jr	1925
1193A	UB	1925
1194A	TB-Jr	1925
1195A	TB-1	1925
1197A	PB-4	1925
1198A	TB-Jr	1925
1199A	TB-Jr	1925
1213A	TB-1	1925
1214A	TB-3	1925
1226A	UB	1925
1241A	TB	1925

1925-1931 FON Series

FON's used during this fourth period of Gibson production have been obtained from shipping ledgers and by direct observation of instruments by myself and others. In the second quarter of 1925, Gibson initiated a new sequence of FON's beginning with the numeral 8000 and reaching 9999 early in 1931. No FON's with a letter suffix have been seen. Many FON's from this series remain to be discovered, and the following table is not meant to be all-inclusive.

FON	Model	Production Year
8004	TB-0	1925
8012	TB-3	1925
8013	TB-2	1925
8014	TB-0	1925
8015	TB-0	1925
8016	TB-3	1925
8018	TB-2	1925
8021	A	1925
8024	A	1925
8031	TB-3	1925
8033	TB-4	1925
8034	TB-Granada	1925
8035	TB-5	1925
8039	TB-5	1925
8040	TB-0	1925
8041	TB-3	1925
8042	TB-2	1925
8043	TB-2	1925
8044	TB-3	1925
8045	TB-4	1925
8046	TB-Granada	1925
8047	TB-5	1925
8049	TB-3	1925
8052	TB-3	1925
8053	TB-0	1925
8054	TB-2	1925
8057	PB-3	1925
8058	PB-4	1925
8059	TB-5	1925
8060	TB-Granada	1925
8061	TB-3	1925
8064	TB-3	1925
8065	TB-2	1925
8066	TB-2	1925
8067	TB-0	1925
8068	TB-5	1925
8069	TB-3, RB-3 & GB-3	1925
8073	TB-2	1925
8075	TB-Jr	1925

FON	Model	Production Year
8076	TB-2	1925
8077	TB-0	1925
8078	F-4	1925
8079	UB	1925
8082	TB-4	1925
8083	TB-Granada	1925
8086	TB-3	1925
8087	TB-Jr	1925
8089	A	1925
8090	TB-3	1925
8091	TB-5	1925
8092	A-Jr	1925
8094	A	1925
8095	A	1925
8097	F-4	1925
8103	TB-3	1925
8104	TB-Granada	1925
8105	TB-5	1925
8106	MB-Jr	1925
8109	TB-5 & PB-5	1925
8111	MB	1925
8112	MB-2	1925
8113	MB-3	1925
8116	TB-3	1925
8117	TB-4	1925
8118	TB-Granada	1925
8120	TB-3 & PB-3	1925
8122	A & A-1	1925
8123	A-4	1925
8124	TB-3	1925
8125	TB-3	1925
8126	TB-3	1925
8127	TB-3 & RB-3	1925
8130	TB-1	1925
8131	TB-3	1925
8132	TB-4 & PB-4	1925
8133	TB-Granada & PB-Granada	1925
8134	RB-4	1925
8135	TB-3	1925
8138	TB-3	1925
8139	TB-Granada	1925
8141	MB-Jr	1925
8142	TB-2	1925
8143	TB-0 & TB-1	1925
8146	TB-4	1925

FON	Model	Production Year
8153	A-Jr	1925
8156	TB-5	1925
8157	TB-Granada	1925
8158	TB-5	1925
8159	TB-5	1925
8161	TB-3 & RB-3	1925
8162	TB-3	1925
8163	TB-3	1925
8164	TB-4	1925
8165	TB-3	1925
8166	TB-3	1925
8168	PB-1	1925
8169	TB-4 & RB-4	1925
8170	TB-3	1925
8171	TB-4 & RB-4	1925
8172	PB-3	1925
8176	TB-0	1925
8179	TB-3	1925
8182	PB-4	1925
8187	TB-0 & TB-1	1925
8188	TB-0	1925
8190	A-Jr	1925
8193	L-Jr	1925
8200	TB-2	1925
8201	TB-3	1926
8204	TB-3	1926
8205	TB-3	1926
8206	TB-3	1926
8207	TB-3	1926
8208	TB-Granada	1926
8209	TB-Granada	1926
8210	TB-2	1926
8211	TB-2	1926
8214	PB-Granada	1926
8215	TB-4 & PB-4	1926
8216	GB-1	1926
8217	GB-3	1926
8218	MB-0 & MB-1	1926
8219	TB-3	1926
8223	TB-3	1926
8225	TB-3 & GB-3	1926
8226	TB-3	1926
8227	TB-5	1926
8228	MB-3	1926
8229	A	1926

FON	Model	Production Year
8230	F-4	1926
8231	F-5	1926
8232	PB-3	1926
8233	L-1	1926
8234	L-1	1926
8235	L-1	1926
8244	TB-2	1926
8245	TB-2	1926
8246	TB-3 & PB-3	1926
8248	TB-4	1926
8249	TB-4	1926
8250	TB-Granada	1926
8251	TB-5	1926
8252	TB-5	1926
8254	TB-1	1926
8255	TB-0	1926
8256	TB-1	1926
8257	TB-0	1926
8258	TB-1	1926
8259	TB-1 & PB-1	1926
8260	TB-1	1926
8262	PB-3	1926
8265	TB-2	1926
8266	TB-2	1926
8267	RB-Custom	1926
8270	MB-3 & RB-3	1926
8278	TB-3	1926
8279	TB-3	1926
8280	TB-3	1926
8281	TB-3	1926
8284	A	1926
8285	L-0	1926
8288	L-1	1926
8296	A-Jr	1926
8297	MB-0 & MB-1	1926
8298	MB-2	1926
8299	TB-0	1926
8300	PB-3	1926
8313	TB-1	1926
8314	TB-1 & RB-1	1926
8316	TB-2	1926
8317	TB-2	1926
8318	TB-3 & PB-3	1926
8319	TB-3	1926
8322	MB-1 & MB-2	1926

1925-1931 FON Series (continued)

FON	Model	Production Year
8323	TB-3	1926
8324	GB-3	1926
8325	TB-1	1926
8326	TB-1 & MB-1	1926
8333	L-0	1926
8334	L-1	1926
8335	MB	1926
8336	MB-3	1926
8337	TB-1	1926
8338	TB-2	1926
8339	TB-2	1926
8340	TB-2	1926
8341	TB-4	1926
8350	L-5	1926
8351	GB-1	1926
8352	TB-1	1926
8353	TB-2	1926
8355	F-2	1926
8356	H-1	1926
8357	TB-5	1926
8359	TB-1	1926
8360	RB-1	1926
8361	TB-Granada	1926
8376	TB-4	1926
8377	TB-5	1926
8379	TB-1	1926
8383	TB-1	1926
8385	TB-2	1926
8386	L-0	1926
8401	L-0	1926
8405	A-Jr	1926
8406	L-1	1926
8407	L-0 & L-1	1926
8408	L-0	1926
8411	TB-0 & TB-1	1926
8412	TB-1	1926
8413	TB-1	1926
8414	TB-3	1926
8415	TB-3	1926
8416	PB-4	1926
8423	TB-1	1926
8425	TB-3	1926
8426	TB-1	1926
8428	TB-4	1926
8429	TB-3	1926

FON	Model	Production Year
8430	A	1926
8432	L-1	1926
8433	L-1	1926
8437	TB-0	1926
8438	TB-1	1926
8439	TB-2	1926
8443	TB-Granada	1926
8444	TB-5	1926
8445	PB-1	1926
8446	TB-3 & PB-3	1926
8447	RB-3	1926
8448	GB-3	1926
8457	UB-3, UB-4 & UB-5	1926
8465	TB-Granada	1926
8475	L-0	1926
8476	L-1	1926
8478	TB-0	1926
8479	TB-1	1926
8482	TB-3	1926
8483	TB-4	1926
8485	TB-3 & PB-3	1926
8486	PB-4	1926
8487	PB-Granada	1926
8488	PB-5	1926
8489	MB-0	1926
8490	MB-1	1926
8491	MB-3	1926
8498	UB-4 & UB-5	1926
8506	F-4	1926
8508	A-Jr	1926
8510	A	1926
8512	F-4	1926
8514	L-0	1926
8516	L-1	1926
8521	TB-1	1926
8522	TB-0	1926
8523	TB-1	1926
8524	TB-1	1926
8527	TB-3	1926
8528	TB-3	1926
8532	TB-Granada	1926
8535	TB-1 & PB-1	1926
8540	GB-1	1926
8541	GB-3	1926
8542	MB-0	1926

1925-1931 FON Series (continued)

FON	Model	Production Year
8543	MB-1	1926
8544	MB-3	1926
8552	TB-Florentine & TB-Bella Voce	1927
8553	TB-Florentine & TB-Bella Voce	1927
8559	A-Jr	1927
8562	MB-0	1927
8563	F-2	1927
8567	L-0	1927
8568	L-1	1927
8574	TB-1	1927
8575	TB-1 & PB-1	1927
8580	TB-Bella Voce	1927
8584	PB-1	1927
8592	MB-1	1927
8593	MB-2	1927
8594	MB-1 & MB-2	1927
8596	MB	1927
8597	UB-4 & UB-5	1927
8598	TB-2	1927
8601	RB-3	1927
8602	TB-Florentine, PB-Florentine & TB-Bella Voce	1927
8603	TB-Florentine	1927
8604	MB-Bella Voce	1927
8605	UB-Bella Voce	1927
8606	GB-Bella Voce	1927
8614	A	1927
8615	TB-Florentine & TB-Bella Voce	1927
8617	TB-Bella Voce	1927
8623	TB-3	1927
8624	A-Jr	1927
8626	A	1927
8627	TB-1	1927
8632	H-4	1927
8649	TB-1	1927
8650	TB-2	1927
8651	TB-1	1927
8652	RB-1	1927
8653	TB-Florentine	1927
8657	L-5	1927
8660	PB-Florentine	1927
8661	TB-Granada	1927
8662	TB-3 & PB-3	1927
8663	PB-Granada	1927
8665	L-0	1927
8666	L-0	1927

FON	Model	Production Year
8667	L-1	1927
8670	MB-0	1927
8671	TB-1	1927
8672	TB-2	1927
8673	TB-3	1927
8674	TB-3	1927
8675	TB-4	1927
8676	TB-5	1927
8677	TB-0 & PB-1	1927
8678	PB-4	1927
8680	TB-Florentine & TB-Bella Voce	1927
8682	TB-Florentine	1927
8684	GB-1	1927
8685	TB-Bella Voce	1927
8686	TB-Florentine & TB-Bella Voce	1927
8687	TB-Bella Voce	1927
8689	TB-Bella Voce	1927
8692	PB-Florentine	1927
8694	PT-3	1927
8695	TB-Bella Voce	1927
8698	MB-2	1927
8699	MB-2	1927
8700	TB-3	1927
8701	TB-4	1927
8702	TB-Granada	1927
8703	TB-3	1927
8704	PB-Granada	1927
8705	RB-3	1927
8706	TB-Bella Voce	1927
8708	TB-Florentine	1927
8711	Nick Lucas Special	1927
8712	A-Jr	1927
8716	TB-0 & MB-0	1927
8717	MB-0	1927
8718	TB-1	1927
8719	TB-3	1927
8720	GB-1	1927
8721	TG-1	1927
8724	PB	1927
8725	TB-Bella Voce	1927
8726	A-Jr	1927
8727	TB-3	1927
8739	TB-3	1927
8742	RB-Florentine	1927
8750	TB-3	1927

1925-1931 FON Series (continued)

FON	Model	Production Year
8751	TB-4	1927
8752	TB-3 & PB-3	1927
8755	TB-Florentine	1927
8756	TB-Florentine & TB-Bella Voce	1927
8757	TB-Bella Voce	1927
8759	TB-Florentine	1927
8760	TB-Florentine & PB-Florentine	1927
8761	TB-Florentine	1927
8762	TB-3 & RB-3	1927
8763	TB-1	1927
8766	A-Jr	1927
8767	L-0	1927
8768	PB	1927
8769	TB-Granada	1927
8773	TB-3	1927
8776	RB-1	1927
8779	TB-3	1927
8782	TB-Granada	1927
8785	TB-Florentine	1927
8789	TB-3	1927
8793	TG-0	1927
8794	TG-0	1927
8795	TG-0	1927
8797	TG-1	1927
8798	TG-1	1927
8799	A	1927
8804	TB-3	1927
8808	A	1927
8809	F-4	1927
8810	L-0	1927
8811	L-0	1927
8812	L-1	1927
8814	TB-3 & RB-3	1927
8815	Nick Lucas Special	1927
8818	UB-4 & UB-5	1927
8819	MB-0	1927
8820	MB-1	1927
8822	TB-1	1927
8823	TB-3	1927
8824	TB-3 & PB-3	1927
8825	TB-Custom	1927
8826	TB-3 & PB-3	1927
8828	TB-3	1927
8829	PB-Florentine	1927
8830	TB-3	1927

FON	Model	Production Year
8831	TB-Granada & PB-Granada	1927
8832	TB-Granada & PB-Granada	1927
8834	TB-3 & PB-3	1927
8835	TB-Granada	1927
8836	TB-4	1927
8837	TB-1	1927
8838	TB-1 & TB-2	1927
8845	TB-4	1927
8847	PB-Oriole	1927
8848	GB-1	1927
8849	PG-1	1927
8850	MB-2	1927
8851	TB-2	1927
8852	GB-3	1927
8853	PB-Bella Voce	1927
8855	GB-Granada	1927
8856	TB-Florentine	1927
8859	TB-3	1927
8862	RB-4	1927
8863	MB-1	1927
8864	TB-3	1927
8867	MB-3	1927
8873	TB-5 & PB-5	1927
8874	TB-5	1927
8875	TB-5 & PB-5	1927
8876	TB-5	1927
8877	RB-Granada	1927
8878	TB-5	1927
8880	PB-4	1927
8882	TB-Granada	1927
8883	PB-3	1927
8885	TB-Granada	1927
8886	TB-Granada & PB-Granada	1927
8889	TB-1	1927
8890	TB-1	1927
8894	TB-Bella Voce	1927
8897	RB-Granada	1927
8900	TB-2	1927
8901	TB-3	1928
8907	TB-3	1928
8910	RB-3	1928
8911	TB-4	1928
8914	RB-4	1928
8917	PB-Granada	1928

1925-1931 FON Series (continued)

FON	Model	Production Year
8919	TB-5	1928
8920	TB-5	1928
8921	TB-Granada	1928
8922	TB-4	1928
8930	TB-0	1928
8932	A-4	1928
8933	A	1928
8935	TB-2	1928
8936	PB-Florentine	1928
8943	L-1	1928
8945	UB-4 & UB-5	1928
8947	TB-2	1928
8948	TB-3	1928
8949	TB-4	1928
8950	TB-5	1928
8952	RB-1	1928
8953	RB-3	1928
8954	GB-1	1928
8955	L-0	1928
8957	PB-3	1928
8959	PB-Florentine	1928
8960	TB-Florentine & PB-Florentine	1928
8961	TB-Florentine	1928
8962	TB-0 & TB-1	1928
8964	TB-3	1928
8965	PB-Bella Voce	1928
8966	PB-Florentine	1928
8968	TB-Bella Voce	1928
8970	TB-Granada	1928
8971	TB-Granada	1928
8972	TB-5	1928
8974	TB-3	1928
8975	TB-1 & TB-2	1928
8976	TB-3	1928
8977	TB-3	1928
8978	TB-4	1928
8979	TB-4	1928
8988	L-0	1928
8989	Nick Lucas Special	1928
8998	A-4	1928
8999	F-4	1928
9001	L-1	1928
9002	L-1	1928
9003	L-0	1928

FON	Model	Production Year
9004	L-1	1928
9005	L-3	1928
9006	L-5	1928
9007	L-5	1928
9009	Nick Lucas Special	1928
9010	Nick Lucas Special	1928
9013	PB-3	1928
9014	TG-1	1928
9018	MB-0	1928
9021	TB-1 & TB-2	1928
9022	TB-2	1928
9023	TB-2	1928
9024	TB-3	1928
9025	TB-3	1928
9026	TB-4	1928
9027	TB-4	1928
9028	TB-Granada	1928
9029	TB-5	1928
9030	TB-2	1928
9031	TB-3 & PB-3	1928
9032	TB-3 & RB-3	1928
9033	L-0	1928
9034	GB-3	1928
9035	TG-1 "8 string"	1928
9042	Trujo "style C"	1928
9043	TB-Bella Voce & RB-Bella Voce	1928
9044	TB-3	1928
9046	Trujo "style B"	1928
9049	Trujo "style C"	1928
9050	F-5	1928
9051	L-1	1928
9052	L-1	1928
9055	MB-3	1928
9056	MB-3	1928
9057	TB-3	1928
9058	TB-Granada	1928
9063	TB-0	1928
9068	TB-Bella Voce	1928
9073	GB	1928
9074	L-0	1928
9075	L-0	1928
9076	L-0	1928
9077	L-1	1928
9078	TB-1 & TB-2	1928
9079	TB-1	1928

1925-1931 FON Series (continued)

FON	Model	Production Year
9080	TB-3	1928
9081	PB-4	1928
9087	TB-0, TB-1 & TB-2	1928
9088	GB-Granada	1928
9090	TB-Florentine	1928
9094	TB-3	1928
9096	TB-1	1928
9097	TB-3	1928
9098	TB-3	1928
9099	TB-3 & PB-3	1928
9100	GB-3	1928
9101	PB-6	1928
9102	TB-0 & TB-1	1928
9106	TB-6	1928
9107	Nick Lucas Special	1928
9109	TB-5	1928
9111	TB-2	1928
9112	TB-3	1928
9113	TB-3	1928
9114	TB-4	1928
9115	TB-Granada	1928
9116	TB-6 & PB-6	1928
9120	PB-3	1928
9123	MB-4	1928
9127	L-0	1928
9128	L-0	1928
9130	RB-3	1928
9131	GB-1	1928
9132	TB-Granada	1928
9135	TB-Florentine & PB-Florentine	1928
9136	TB-Florentine	1928
9137	TB-Florentine & PB-Florentine	1928
9138	PB-Florentine	1928
9139	TB-Florentine & PB-Florentine	1928
9140	F-5	1928
9142	L-0	1928
9144	L-0 & TG-0	1928
9145	L-0	1928
9146	L-1	1928
9150	TB-3	1928
9151	TB-3	1928
9152	TB-Granada & MB-Granada	1928
9153	TB-6	1928
9154	TB-6 & PB-6	1928
9156	PB-6	1928

FON	Model	Production Year
9157	TB-3	1928
9159	MB-5	1928
9160	TB-5	1928
9162	PB-4	1928
9166	RB-Granada	1928
9167	TB-3	1928
9169	TB-6 & PB-6	1928
9172	A	1928
9174	L-0	1928
9175	L-0	1928
9176	L-0	1928
9181	L-0	1928
9188	TB-1	1928
9189	TB-1	1928
9190	TB-1	1928
9191	TB-1	1928
9192	TB-1 & PB-1	1928
9193	TB-Granada & PB-Granada	1928
9196	PB-3	1928
9197	TB-6	1928
9200	L-0	1928
9201	L-0	1928
9202	L-1	1928
9203	L-1	1928
9204	TB-3 & MB-3	1928
9210	A-Jr	1928
9212	L-1	1928
9213	L-3	1928
9214	TB-Granada	1928
9215	TG-1	1928
9219	TB-1 & MB-1	1928
9220	TB-3	1928
9221	TB-3	1928
9222	TB-4	1928
9223	RB-3	1928
9224	GB-3	1928
9226	TB-6 & PB-6	1928
9227	TB-Florentine & PB-Florentine	1928
9230	TB-3	1929
9231	A-Jr	1929
9232	TB-6	1929
9234	PB-3	1929
9236	RB	1929
9237	L-1	1929
9238	L-1	1929

1925-1931 FON Series (continued)

FON	Model	Production Year
9240	A-Jr	1929
9242	Royal PT	1929
9245	F-4	1929
9246	L-0	1929
9247	L-0	1929
9248	TB-1	1929
9250	TB-3	1929
9251	L-5	1929
9252	TG-0	1929
9253	TB-6 & PB-6	1929
9259	TB-3	1929
9260	TB-3	1929
9261	TB-Granada	1929
9262	TB-6	1929
9263	Royal PT & TB-6	1929
9264	PB-3	1929
9265	PB-4	1929
9266	TB-6 & PB-6	1929
9267	RB-3	1929
9268	RB-Granada	1929
9269	MB-1	1929
9270	MB-3	1929
9271	TB-4	1929
9274	PB-Florentine	1929
9275	PB-Bella Voce & TB-Florentine	1929
9279	Trujo "style A"	1929
9280	TB-3	1929
9281	Trujo "style A"	1929
9284	Royal PT	1929
9288	F-5	1929
9289	L-1	1929
9291	L-0	1929
9292	TB-4	1929
9294	TB-1 & RB-1	1929
9295	GB-1	1929
9301	Royal PT, TB-6 & PB-6	1929
9304	L-1	1929
9307	TB-1	1929
9308	TB-3, PB-3 & MB-3	1929
9309	MB-1	1929
9310	TB-3	1929
9311	RB-1	1929
9312	GB-1	1929
9313	TB-3	1929
9317	L-1	1929

FON	Model	Production Year
9323	Nick Lucas Special	1929
9324	PB-3	1929
9328	H-1	1929
9330	TB-1	1929
9331	TB-2	1929
9332	TB-4	1929
9334	F-5	1929
9336	TB-Custom & GB Custom	1929
9337	TB-Custom	1929
9344	TB-Granada	1929
9349	L-1	1929
9351	TB-6	1929
9354	MB-1	1929
9355	TB-3 & PB-3	1929
9356	TB-Granada	1929
9359	RB-1	1929
9360	TB-6 & Royal PT	1929
9361	TB-Custom	1929
9363	TB-Studio King	1929
9365	Bass banjo	1929
9366	TB-3	1929
9368	TB-6	1929
9369	TB-3	1929
9372	PB-Truett	1929
9373	PB-Truett	1929
9374	Experimental banjo	1929
9375	L-0	1929
9376	L-1	1929
9379	L-0	1929
9380	L-1	1929
9381	L-2	1929
9383	TB-1	1929
9384	TB-1	1929
9385	TB-3	1929
9387	TB-6	1929
9388	TB-1	1929
9392	TB-Granada	1929
9393	TB-3	1929
9394	TB-4	1929
9398	RB-Custom	1929
9400	TB-2	1929
9405	Nick Lucas Special Custom	1929
9406	L-1	1929
9408	TB-6	1929
9409	L-0	1929

1925-1931 FON Series (continued)

FON	Model	Production Year
9411	F-5	1929
9415	PB-4	1929
9417	Nick Lucas Special	1929
9418	L-5	1929
9419	TB-1	1929
9420	GB-1	1929
9422	RB-3	1929
9425	TB-4	1929
9426	TB-Recording King #506	1929
9427	TB, PB & RB-Studio King #641 & #645	1929
9428	TB-1	1929
9434	RB-6	1929
9435	L-1	1929
9437	L-0	1929
9438	TB-1	1929
9439	TB-1	1929
9440	TB-3 & PB-3	1929
9441	GB-3	1929
9442	TB-4	1929
9446	L-0	1929
9447	L-1	1929
9453	TB-6	1929
9454	TG-1	1929
9456	L-0	1929
9457	L-1	1929
9461	Nick Lucas Special	1929
9462	RB-4	1929
9463	MB-1	1929
9464	TB-1	1929
9465	TB-3	1929
9466	TB-4	1929
9467	PB-3	1929
9468	RB-1	1929
9469	TB-2	1929
9470	TB-Granada	1929
9471	PB-4	1929
9472	PB-Granada	1929
9473	RB-3	1929
9474	RB-4	1929
9475	RB-Granada	1929
9476	L-2	1929
9477	TB-1 & PB-1	1929
9478	TB-3	1929
9480	Kel Kroydon KK-2	1929
9482	TB-4	1929

FON	Model	Production Year
9486	TB-1	1929
9487	TB-2 & RB-2	1929
9488	TB-3	1929
9489	TB-3	1929
9490	L-1	1929
9491	H-4	1929
9495	TB	1929
9496	Kel Kroydon KK guitars	1929
9497	L-0	1929
9499	L-1	1929
9500	Kel Kroydon KK-2	1929
9501	TB-Custom	1930
9505	L-2	1930
9506	L-0	1930
9507	L-0	1930
9508	L-1	1930
9511	L-1	1930
9513	TB-1 & PB-1	1930
9515	Kel Kroydon KK guitars	1930
9518	TB-1	1930
9519	TB-1 & RB-1	1930
9520	TB-2	1930
9521	TB-4	1930
9522	TB-Granada & PB-Granada	1930
9523	TB-1, PB-1 & RB-1	1930
9524	TB-3 & PB-3	1930
9525	PB-4	1930
9526	PB-Granada & RB-Granada	1930
9527	RB-1	1930
9528	RB-3	1930
9529	RB-4	1930
9530	PB-Granada & RB-Granada	1930
9531	GB-1	1930
9532	TB-3 & GB-3	1930
9536	TB-4	1930
9538	TB-2	1930
9539	TB-1	1930
9540	TB-1	1930
9541	TB-1	1930
9542	TB-1	1930
9543	TB-1	1930
9544	TB-1	1930
9545	TB-1	1930
9546	TB-2	1930
9547	TB-2	1930

1925-1931 FON Series (continued)

FON	Model	Production Year
9548	TB-2	1930
9549	TB-3	1930
9550	TB-3	1930
9551	TB-3	1930
9552	TB-3	1930
9553	TB-4	1930
9554	TB-4	1930
9556	TB-Granada & RB-Granada	1930
9557	TB-Granada & RB-Granada	1930
9559	PB-1	1930
9560	TB-1, PB-1 & RB-1	1930
9562	TB-Granada & PB-Granada	1930
9563	RB-1	1930
9564	L-0	1930
9565	L-0	1930
9566	L-0	1930
9567	L-0	1930
9568	L-1	1930
9569	L-1	1930
9570	L-1	1930
9571	L-1	1930
9572	L-2	1930
9573	L-2	1930
9574	L-2 "Hawaiian"	1930
9575	A	1930
9577	Nick Lucas Special	1930
9579	L-2	1930
9580	TB-3 & PB-3	1930
9581	PB-4	1930
9582	PB-Granada	1930
9583	RB-4	1930
9584	RB-Granada	1930
9585	L-0	1930
9587	TB-3	1930
9588	TB-3	1930
9589	PB-3	1930
9591	TB-2	1930
9592	TB-Recording King	1930
9594	TB-2	1930
9595	L-1	1930
9597	TB-1	1930
9598	TB-2 & RB-2	1930
9599	PB-2	1930
9601	TB-1 & RB-1	1930
9602	RB-3	1930

FON	Model	Production Year
9604	L-1	1930
9611	PB-6	1930
9613	TB-3 & PB-3	1930
9614	TG-3	1930
9615	TB-Studio King #645	1930
9616	TB-Studio King #645	1930
9617	TB-Recording King #506 & #507	1930
9618	A-Jr	1930
9619	F-5	1930
9621	K-1	1930
9622	Kel Kroydon KK-1	1930
9623	TG-1	1930
9625	PG-1	1930
9626	A	1930
9629	L-0	1930
9630	L-2	1930
9633	TB-All American	1930
9636	MB-1	1930
9637	MB-1	1930
9638	TB-1 & PB-1	1930
9639	TB-4, PB-4 & RB-4	1930
9640	TB-6 & PB-6	1930
9642	Kel Kroydon KK-1	1930
9645	Kel Kroydon KK-1 & KK-2	1930
9646	Kel Kroydon KK-3	1930
9649	Marshall Special	1930
9652	Kel Kroydon KK-11 banjo	1930
9653	TB-Florentine	1930
9654	TB-Florentine	1930
9661	TG-1	1930
9662	Nick Lucas Special	1930
9663	MB-1	1930
9666	PB-Trujo	1930
9667	Nick Lucas Special	1930
9671	TB-4	1930
9673	TB-3	1930
9681	F-5	1930
9683	TG-0 3/4	1930
9685	L-2	1930
9686	L-3	1930
9688	Nick Lucas Special	1930
9689	Nick Lucas Special	1930
9690	TB-1	1930
9691	TB-2	1930
9702	GB-3	1930

1925-1931 FON Series (continued)

FON	Model	Production Year
9703	RB-4	1930
9704	S.S. Stewart guitars	1930
9705	TG-5	1930
9711	TB-1	1930
9715	PB-Trujo	1930
9717	TB-Studio King	1930
9719	TB-1	1930
9724	TG-1	1930
9726	Kel Kroydon KK-2	1930
9728	Nick Lucas Special	1930
9729	TB-2	1930
9731	Trujo guitars	1930
9732	Kel Kroydon KK banjos	1930
9735	L-0	1930
9736	L-1	1930
9737	Kel Kroydon KK banjos	1930
9738	TB-3	1930
9740	L-2 & TG-2	1930
9741	TG-2	1930
9742	TB-All American	1930
9744	TB-S.S. Stewart	1930
9747	TB-All American	1930
9748	TB-All American	1930
9752	TG-0	1930
9753	L-0	1930
9755	L-0	1930
9756	L-1	1930
9757	TB-Custom	1930
9759	L-1	1930
9760	L-2	1930
9763	H-5	1930
9767	L-0	1930
9768	L-1	1930
9769	L-2	1930
9771	L-5	1930
9772	Nick Lucas Special	1930
9773	MB-1	1930
9774	TB-1	1930
9775	RB-1	1930
9776	TB-3 & GB-3	1930
9777	GB-1	1930
9778	RK guitars	1930
9779	TB-Recording King	1930
9781	Kel Kroydon KK-11	1930
9782	Kel Kroydon KK-11	1930

FON	Model	Production Year
9783	MB-1	1930
9785	L-0	1930
9786	L-1	1930
9788	Kel Kroydon KK banjos	1930
9789	Kel Kroydon KK banjos	1930
9792	Kel Kroydon KK banjos	1930
9793	L-2	1930
9794	Kel Kroydon KK banjos	1930
9797	Kel Kroydon KK banjos	1930
9801	PB-Custom	1931
9804	Trujo guitars	1931
9807	L-2	1931
9808	L-0	1931
9809	L-1	1931
9812	TB-1	1931
9819	Kel Kroydon KK guitars	1931
9820	A	1931
9820	L-1	1931
9822	Kel Kroydon KK banjos	1931
9824	Kel Kroyden KK-11	1931
9828	TG-1	1931
9829	PB-11	1931
9842	L-5	1931
9845	TB-1	1931
9846	RB-1	1931
9847	TB-1 & GB-1	1931
9848	MB-1	1931
9849	MB-2	1931
9851	Kel Kroydon KK banjos	1931
9854	Kel Kroydon KK guitars	1931
9857	MB-1	1931
9865	RB-Granada	1931
9873	L-0	1931
9875	L-0 "3/4 size"	1931
9877	TB-1	1931
9878	TB-2	1931
9881	F-4	1931
9887	TG-1	1931
9889	F-5	1931
9890	Kel Kroydon KK-1	1931
9893	Kel Kroydon KK banjos	1931
9896	TB-1	1931
9897	L-1	1931
9902	TB-1	1931
9903	TB-3	1931

1925-1931 FON Series (continued)

FON	Model	Production Year
9904	MB-3	1931
9907	TB-3	1931
9908	TB-3	1931
9919	L-0	1931
9920	L-1	1931
9921	Nick Lucas Special	1931
9923	Kel Kroydon KK-1	1931
9925	TB-1	1931
9926	TB-3	1931
9927	TB-1 & RB-1	1931
9928	PG-00	1931
9929	PG-0	1931
9938	RB-11	1931
9941	TB-3	1931
9942	Kel Kroydon KK banjos	1931
9943	Kel Kroydon KK-20	1931
9944	Kel Kroydon KK-1 "tenor guitars"	1931
9947	TB-All American	1931
9948	TB-All American	1931
9951	TG-0 3/4	1931
9952	L-5	1931
9954	L-0	1931
9956	Kel Kroydon KK-1	1931
9959	TB-2	1931
9960	TB-3	1931
9961	Nick Lucas Special	1931
9964	PB-3	1931
9965	L-5	1931
9969	TG-0	1931
9970	GB-1	1931
9971	PB-Truett	1931
9975	RB-2	1931
9976	TB-3	1931
9983	TB-3	1931
9984	TB-3	1931
9985	L-1	1931
9987	L-0	1931
9988	L-1	1931

1927-1928 Custom Banjo FON Series

Early in 1927 Gibson launched a line of custom-made banjos and concurrently began using a sequence of FON's which had a leading zero. No instruments other than banjos have been observed which utilized these FON's. These "leading zero" FON's range from 0110 through 0442 and their use ended in 1928. Many FON's from this period remain to be discovered, and the following table is not meant to be all-inclusive.

FON	Model	Production Year
0110	TB-Bella Voce	1927-1928
0114	TB-Bella Voce	1927-1928
0121	TB-Bella Voce & TB-Florentine	1927-1928
0136	TB-4	1927-1928
0146	TB-3	1927-1928
0170	TB-3	1927-1928
0171	PB-3 & TB-3	1927-1928
0181	TB-Bella Voce & PB-Florentine	1927-1928
0196	TB-Granada	1927-1928
0206	PB-Bella Voce & TB-Bella Voce	1927-1928
0218	TB-Bella Voce	1927-1928
0223	TB-Bella Voce	1927-1928
0228	TB-Custom	1927-1928
0253	TB-Florentine	1927-1928
0259	TB-Bella Voce	1927-1928
0263	PB-Florentine & TB-Florentine	1927-1928
0283	PB-Bella Voce & TB-Bella Voce	1927-1928
0292	TB-Bella Voce & TB-Florentine	1927-1928
0313	TB-Bella Voce	1927-1928
0325	PB-Bella Voce	1927-1928
0329	TB-4	1927-1928
0344	TB-4	1927-1928
0359	TB-Granada	1927-1928
0369	PB-Granada & TB-Granada	1927-1928
0394	TB-5	1927-1928
0404	TB-5	1927-1928
0419	TB-3	1927-1928
0425	TB-3	1927-1928
0429	TB-4	1927-1928
0434	PB-Granada	1927-1928
0439	PB-5 & TB-5	1927-1928
0442	TB-Bella Voce	1927-1928

1931-1933 FON Series

FON's used during this fifth period of Gibson production have been obtained from shipping ledgers and by direct observation of instruments by myself and others. External and internal sources indicate that musical instrument production virtually ceased in 1932 and 1933 due to the effects of the economic depression. However, Gibson also produced a line of wooden toys during this time that also would have required FON's. In the second quarter of 1931, Gibson initiated a new sequence of FON's which began all over again with the numeral 1, eventually reaching 890 late in 1933, with isolated numbers higher. Many FON's from this period remain to be discovered, and the table is not meant to be all-inclusive.

FON	Model	Production Year
1	RB-1	1931
2	L-1	1931
3	TB-1	1931
13	Kel Kroydon KK-1	1931
19	TB-3 & MB-3	1931
20	TB-2	1931
21	L-00	1931
25	TB-3	1931
28	L-0	1931
30	L-1	1931
33	L-0	1931
34	RB-1	1931
35	L-00	1931
36	L-0	1931
37	L-1	1931
39	PG-1	1931
40	L-1	1931
42	TB-3	1931
44	MB-3	1931
48	L-0	1931
49	L-1	1931
54	TG-00	1931
59	L-2	1931
66	L-00	1931
67	L-00	1931
68	TG-00	1931
70	L-00	1931
78	TG-1	1931
79	L-0	1931
80	L-1	1931
83	L-00	1931
87	RB-1	1931
88	L-00	1931
89	TB-1	1931
99	L-0	1931
100	L-1	1931
101	L-4	1931
105	MB-1	1931

FON	Model	Production Year
107	RB-2 & TB-2	1931
108	L-00	1931
113	L-2	1931
114	Nick Lucas Special	1931
115	TB-3	1931
116	PB-3 & RB-3	1931
117	RB-1	1931
120	TB-2	1931
121	RB-1	1931
122	TB-1	1931
123	TB-1	1931
124	TB-1	1931
125	F-4	1931
126	L-1	1931
127	L-0	1931
128	TB-1	1931
130	TB-2	1931
132	L-00	1931
135	A	1931
139	L-00	1931
141	TB-11	1931
142	C-1	1931
149	L-0	1931
151	MB-3	1931
153	TB-3	1931
155	L-0	1931
156	L-00	1931
157	TB-1	1931
158	TB-3	1931
160	HG-24	1932
163	L-0	1932
167	L-1	1932
168	L-00	1932
169	Nick Lucas	1932
170	RB-1 & TB-1	1932
176	RB-2	1932
177	RB-3 & TB-3	1932
178	L-0	1932
181	L-0	1932
186	TG-0	1932
188	L-0	1932
189	L-10 & L-12	1932
190	L-00	1932
191	TG-00 (black finish)	1932
196	RB-2	1932

FON	Model	Production Year
197	HG-22	1932
200	L-4	1932
203	L-00	1932
205	HG-20	1932
206	HG-22	1932
207	L-1	1932
208	L-0	1932
209	HG-24	1932
211	L-00	1932
212	TB-3, PB-3 & RB-3	1932
213	RB-1	1932
214	L-0	1932
216	TB-3	1932
217	L-0	1932
218	TB-1	1932
219	L-00	1932
228	L-0	1932
229	L-00 “12 fret”	1932
234	TB-1	1932
235	TB-3	1932
238	MB-1	1932
239	MB-2	1932
240	TB-3 & MB-3	1932
242	L-00	1932
246	TG-0	1932
250	L-00	1932
251	L-1 “12 fret”	1932
252	TB-1	1932
254	L-0	1932
256	L-00	1932
263	L-00	1932
268	MB-1	1932
269	L-00 “13 fret”	1932
270	MB-3	1932
271	TB-3	1932
272	L-1	1932
276	TB-4 & RB-4	1932
281	L-00	1932
282	HG-20	1932
283	HG-22	1932
284	HG-24	1932
293	TB-1	1932
296	TG-0	1932
298	L-1 “14 fret”	1932

FON	Model	Production Year
301	A	1932
302	HG-20	1932
306	MB-3	1932
308	HG-22 (tenor)	1932
309	L-00	1932
310	L-10	1932
314	F-5	1932
315	L-00	1932
316	L-00	1932
317	L-00	1932
318	HG-20	1932
321	L-00	1932
322	L-00	1932
323	L-1	1932
325	L-00	1932
328	L-00	1932
335	L-0	1932
336	L-0	1932
337	L-0	1932
338	L-0	1932
340	HG-20	1932
351	L-00	1932
353	L-2	1932
358	HG-20	1932
361	L-1	1933
363	L-7	1933
364	L-0	1933
365	L-0	1933
369	L-0	1933
370	L-0	1933
371	L-0	1933
372	TG-1 & KTG-14	1933
373	L-Century	1933
374	KJ "mando-bass"	1933
378	L-50	1933
380	UB	1933
382	L-Century	1933
386	L-1	1933
388	L-1	1933
392	L-0	1933
393	L-00 & L-1	1933
395	L-00	1933
396	F-4	1933
397	PG-1	1933
398	L-0	1933

1931-1933 FON Series (continued)

FON	Model	Production Year
403	L-1	1933
405	L-00	1933
407	L-0	1933
409	L-0	1933
415	L-00	1933
417	L-0	1933
418	L-00	1933
420	KJ "mando-bass"	1933
422	L-75	1933
427	L-1	1933
429	TG-00	1933
430	L-0	1933
432	L-75	1933
433	L-00	1933
436	L-75	1933
437	L-1	1933
438	KG-11	1933
442	L-00	1933
443	L-50	1933
444	KG-31	1933
445	L-00	1933
447	L-4	1933
450	L-1	1933
453	L-2	1933
456	L-00	1933
461	C-1	1933
462	TG-00	1933
466	L-0	1933
467	L-00	1933
477	TG-1	1933
478	L-00	1933
479	L-00 & TG-00	1933
481	L-0	1933
484	Martell Special	1933
488	L-00	1933
489	MB-1	1933
499	L-00	1933
500	KM-11	1933
504	L-12	1933
509	TG-1	1933
510	L-00	1933
511	KG-11	1933
512	L-2	1933
514	L-2	1933
516	TB-"12" (not top-tension)	1933

FON	Model	Production Year
517	PB-"12" (not top-tension)	1933
526	KG	1933
528	A-0	1933
530	KG-11	1933
531	L-00	1933
532	L-1	1933
539	L-Century	1933
545	L-00	1933
550	TG-00	1933
551	L-00	1933
555	L-Century	1933
556	L-Century	1933
559	TU	1933
560	KG-11	1933
567	L-1	1933
571	A-00	1933
572	A-50	1933
573	L-Century	1933
575	L-00	1933
577	L-00	1933
593	KG	1933
594	L-00	1933
595	L-2 & TG-2	1933
597	KG-11	1933
598	KG-11	1933
599	KG	1933
605	L-50	1933
606	TB-"12"	1933
607	A-50	1933
608	L-Century	1933
609	L-1	1933
612	L-1	1933
617	RB-"12" (not top-tension)	1933
618	KG-11 & RK #926 "Carson Robison"	1933
623	L-Century	1933
632	L-1	1933
633	L-00	1933
643	L-00	1933
650	L-00	1933
651	L-1	1933
652	KG	1933
653	KG	1933
654	L-00	1933
655	L-Century	1933
658	KM-11	1933

1931-1933 FON Series (continued)

FON	Model	Production Year
659	A-00	1933
661	KG-Sr.	1933
665	L-00	1933
668	L-Century	1933
672	L-00	1933
673	KG-11	1933
674	L-1	1933
675	L-00	1933
676	KG-11	1933
682	L-Century	1933
691	KG-11	1933
692	L-0	1933
694	KG-Sr. "Haw."	1933
695	L-Century	1933
698	L-Century	1933
699	L-Century	1933
700	L-75	1933
701	L-00 & L-1	1933
702	L-00	1933
704	TG-00	1933
706	KG-11	1933
707	KG-11	1933
708	L-00	1933
710	L-00	1933
712	A-50	1933
714	A-1	1933
715	L-1	1933
719	KM-11	1933
725	TG-00	1933
728	L-Century	1933
730	L-1	1933
732	KG-Sr.	1933
733	L-00	1933
734	KG	1933
735	KG-11 & RK #926 "Carson Robison"	1933
741	L-Century	1933
742	L-00 & Martell Special	1933
745	L-1	1933
748	A-00	1933
750	A-1	1933
751	TB-11	1933
752	L-1	1933
755	KG-Sr.	1933
757	TB-Truett	1933
759	A-50	1933

FON	Model	Production Year
762	L-00	1933
768	L-00	1933
776	KG-Sr.	1933
777	L-00	1933
778	L-Century	1933
779	L-1	1933
785	A-50	1933
786	L-Century	1933
787	KG-11	1933
788	L-Century	1933
795	KHG-11	1933
805	L-Century	1933
806	KG-11	1933
808	KTG-11	1933
809	F-5	1933
812	L-1	1933
814	A-00	1933
815	L-00 & L-1	1933
821	L-0	1933
823	L-Century	1933
827	A-Century	1933
833	L-00	1933
835	L-00	1933
836	A	1933
838	L-Century	1933
845	L-00	1933
846	A-00	1933
848	KM-11	1933
849	A-00	1933
850	A-1	1933
851	A-1	1933
852	A-50	1933
853	L-00	1933
855	L-Century	1933
856	L-1	1933
862	L-10	1933
865	L-00	1933
866	A	1933
871	KG-11 & RK #1201	1933
872	KG-11	1933
873	KM & RK #1610	1933
874	KTG	1933
875	TG-00	1933
876	L-00	1933
877	L-00	1933

1931-1933 FON Series (continued)

FON	Model	Production Year
883	HG-24	1933
884	L-1	1933
887	L-0	1933
1304	RK #807	1931
2365	L-4	1933
2544	Deluxe Flattop	1933
2784	A-00	1933
3391	L-00	1933

Students of Gibson teacher-agent Betty Reichenbach, circa 1939

Joy Musselman Collection

1934 FON Series

During 1934 Gibson used FON's between 1 and 1500, with a few isolated numbers being higher. The following data was compiled from shipping ledgers and direct observation of instruments by myself and others. Many FON's from this period remain to be discovered, and the table is not meant to be all-inclusive.

FON	Model	Production Year
51	L-50	1934
64	S-1	1934
65	S-2	1934
133	RK #926 "Carson Robison"	1934
138	PG-50	1934
161	Jumbo	1934
201	L-Century	1934
272	RK #1201	1934
278	A-1	1934
280	A-50	1934
297	A-00	1934
331	TB-1	1934
334	A-50	1934
344	TB-1	1934
345	TB-3	1934
346	TB-3	1934
347	TB-3	1934
348	CB-3	1934
357	TB-3	1934
381	PB-1	1934
387	F-2	1934
406	L-50	1934
413	TB-1	1934
416	L-50	1934
431	RK #1201	1934
441	TB-4	1934
485	TB-Recording King	1934
524	KHG-11	1934
554	TB-3	1934
568	L-50	1934
584	Roy Smeck Special	1934
588	L-50	1934
667	L-50	1934
670	TG-50	1934
683	L-50	1934
720	TB-1	1934
726	TG-50	1934
729	L-50	1934
737	L-50	1934
753	L-50	1934
789	TG-50	1934

1934 FON Series (continued)

FON	Model	Production Year
797	L-50	1934
798	TG-50	1934
800	TB-Granada	1934
803	TB-Recording King	1934
809	L-75	1934
817	S-1	1934
818	S-2	1934
822	L-50	1934
824	TB-2	1934
831	S-1	1934
832	L-50	1934
839	Jumbo	1934
854	KG	1934
859	L-50	1934
860	L-50	1934
864	RK #1201	1934
867	TB-1	1934
878	L-50	1934
879	S-1	1934
881	S-1	1934
882	Jumbo	1934
888	S-2	1934
889	Jumbo	1934
890	MB-1	1934
891	MB-1	1934
894	L-50	1934
895	TG-00	1934
896	PG-1	1934
897	L-Century	1934
898	L-Century	1934
902	L-00	1934
903	L-Century	1934
908	L-1	1934
910	KG & RK #1201	1934
911	KG-11	1934
912	KG-11 & RK #926 "Carson Robison"	1934
913	KG	1934
914	KG-11 & RK #1283 "Carson Robison"	1934
915	L-00	1934
916	L-00	1934
917	L-00	1934
918	L-00	1934
919	L-00	1934
920	L-00	1934
921	L-00	1934

FON	Model	Production Year
922	Jumbo	1934
923	L-50	1934
924	L-50	1934
925	L-50	1934
926	L-50	1934
928	L-00 & L-1	1934
929	L-1	1934
930	L-75	1934
931	L-75	1934
932	L-75	1934
933	L-75	1934
934	L-75	1934
935	L-Century	1934
936	L-Century	1934
937	L-Century	1934
938	L-Century	1934
939	L-Century	1934
940	L-Century	1934
944	Roy Smeck guitars	1934
946	L-Century	1934
950	A-00	1934
952	A-00	1934
953	A-00	1934
955	A-1	1934
956	S-2	1934
958	A-00	1934
959	A-50	1934
960	A-50	1934
961	KM-11	1934
965	S-2	1934
966	S-1	1934
967	L-4	1934
971	L-00	1934
973	L-Century	1934
976	KG-Sr	1934
978	L-00	1934
983	L-00 & TG-00	1934
988	GB-1	1934
990	S-1	1934
991	S-2	1934
992	Jumbo	1934
999	L-5	1934
1001	L-7	1934
1002	L-1	1934
1003	PB-Trujo	1934

1934 FON Series (continued)

FON	Model	Production Year
1004	KTG-11	1934
1006	L-7	1934
1010	S-1	1934
1012	S-1	1934
1013	RB-1	1934
1016	TB-3	1934
1017	L-50	1934
1019	TB-1	1934
1022	L-1	1934
1025	KG-11 & RK #926 "Carson Robison"	1934
1026	KG-11	1934
1027	KG-11	1934
1028	KG-11	1934
1031	TG-00	1934
1032	KM-11	1934
1034	TB-3	1934
1043	Jumbo	1934
1044	L-50	1934
1045	Jumbo	1934
1046	Jumbo	1934
1048	TB-1	1934
1051	TB-3	1934
1058	L-00 & L-1	1934
1060	KM-11	1934
1061	L-50	1934
1066	TB-1	1934
1071	F-5	1934
1073	GB-1 "Roy Smeck"	1934
1075	Jumbo	1934
1080	L-50	1934
1082	KG-11	1934
1084	PG-1 & RK #1206	1934
1085	L-00 & RK	1934
1088	L-00	1934
1091	KG-11	1934
1092	S-1	1934
1093	KG-11	1934
1094	KG	1934
1100	S-1	1934
1101	Jumbo	1934
1114	KM	1934
1123	KG	1934
1129	L-4	1934
1135	A-00	1934
1136	A-0	1934

FON	Model	Production Year
1137	A-1	1934
1138	A-50	1934
1139	A-Century	1934
1144	F-5	1934
1145	L-75	1934
1146	KG-11	1934
1147	KG-11	1934
1155	L-75	1934
1166	KG	1934
1167	L-4	1934
1173	KG-31	1934
1174	KG-11	1934
1178	KG	1934
1183	L-00	1934
1185	L-4	1934
1189	A-Century	1934
1195	L-75	1934
1197	Cromwell G-4	1934
1199	A-Century	1934
1204	L-1	1934
1207	KHG-11	1934
1212	L-00	1934
1216	KG-31 & Cromwell G-4	1934
1220	A-50	1934
1227	PB-6	1934
1229	Cromwell G-6	1934
1235	KG-21	1934
1236	KG-31 & Cromwell G-4	1934
1237	A-00	1934
1239	KG-11	1934
1254	L-00 "14 fret"	1934
1256	A-00	1934
1257	A-1	1934
1259	L-5	1934
1267	A-50	1934
1281	A-00	1934
1303	L-1	1934
1308	L-1	1934
1313	KG-31	1934
1316	A-50	1934
1317	A-00	1934
1320	A-00	1934
1321	A-1	1934
1322	A-1	1934
1323	A-00	1934

1934 FON Series (continued)

FON	Model	Production Year
1325	L-00	1934
1334	KG	1934
1344	KG-31 & Cromwell G-4	1934
1346	Cromwell G-4	1934
1369	A-1	1934
1370	A-00	1934
1388	Black Special	1934
1389	L-Century	1934
1397	L-Century	1934
1399	L-5	1934
1411	L-7	1934
1412	L-Century	1934
1433	A-00	1934
1441	Cromwell G-4	1934
1442	KG-31 & Cromwell G-4	1934
1450	L-1	1934
1454	KG-21	1934
1455	KG-11	1934
1472	A-00	1934
1473	A-50	1934
1496	Jumbo	1934
1499	KG-21	1934
1515	Capital J-2	1934
1645	Jumbo	1934

Early mandolin orchestra
Centerstream Archives

1935 FON Series

During 1935 Gibson used FON's between 1 and 1520, with a few isolated numbers being higher. The addition of a letter suffix "A" occurred at the start of 1935, but only some models were singled out for that distinction. The rationale for the "A" is not clear. No duplication of numbers is seen between FON's with a letter suffix "A" and those without. This suggests that the letter suffix was added later on the production floor and was not part of the original pre-printed form used in the weekly production meetings. It may be that the accounting staff wanted to differentiate certain batches for inventory or cost purposes. The following data was compiled mainly from shipping ledgers. Some FON's from this period remain to be discovered, and the following table is not meant to be all-inclusive.

FON		Model	Production Year
1	A	L-1	1935
2		KG-31	1935
3		KG-31	1935
4		KG-31 & KTG-31	1935
7	A	KG-31	1935
8	A	KG-31	1935
9	A	KG-31	1935
12	A	A-00	1935
14	A	L-30 & Black Special	1935
15	A	L-37 & L-50	1935
17	A	Black Special	1935
19	A	RK #1205	1935
20	A	L-00	1935
21	A	KG-31, RK #1201 & Capital J-2	1935
22	A	TG-50	1935
23	A	L-37 & L-50	1935
24	A	RK #1201	1935
25	A	L-30 & Black Special	1935
26	A	L-30	1935
27	A	KG-31, Cromwell G-4 & Capital J-2	1935
28	A	A-50	1935
29	A	A-50	1935
30	A	L-37 & L-50	1935
31	A	L-30 & Black Special	1935
32	A	Cromwell G-6 & Capital J-3	1935
33	A	L-37	1935
34	A	KTG-21 & RK #1203	1935
35	A	KG-21 & RK #1205	1935
36	A	KG-31	1935
37	A	Cromwell G-4	1935
38	A	KG-31	1935
39	A	KG-31 & RK #1241	1935
40	A	RK #1242	1935
41		Cromwell GM-2	1935
42	A	RK #1607	1935
43	A	KM-11	1935
44	A	KM-11 & RK #1610	1935

1935 FON Series (continued)

FON		Model	Production Year
45	A	Cromwell GM-4	1935
47	A	RK #1242	1935
48	A	KG-31 & RK #1206	1935
49	A	RK #1201	1935
50	A	RK #1204	1935
51	A	KG-21, RK #1205 & Fascinator #4970	1935
52	A	RK #1203	1935
53	A	RK #1206	1935
54	A	RK #1241 & Cromwell G-6	1935
55	A	RK #1242	1935
56	A	Cromwell GM-2 & Capital J-10 (or JM-1)	1935
57	A	RK #1607	1935
61	A	KG-31 "Special", Cromwell G-4, Capital J-2, Fascinator #4970	1935
64	A	KG-31	1935
65	A	Cromwell G-4	1935
66		PB-3	1935
69		TB-1	1935
71	A	RK #1205	1935
72	A	KG-21 & RK #1205	1935
73	A	RK #1241 & Cromwell G-6	1935
74	A	RK #1242	1935
75	A	RK #1607	1935
79	A	RK #1241	1935
81	A	KG-31, KTG-31 & RK #1206	1935
84	A	S-1	1935
85	A	S-2	1935
88	A	KG-31 & RK #1206	1935
90	A	KG-21	1935
91	A	KG-21 & RK #1205	1935
92	A	RK #1206	1935
93	A	KG-21 & RK #1205	1935
94	A	RK #1204 (TG)	1935
95	A	KTG-21 & RK #1203	1935
96	A	L-37	1935
97	A	L-30	1935
98	A	KG-21 & RK #1203	1935
99	A	KG-31 & RK #1206	1935
101	A	KG-31	1935
103	A	RK #1201	1935
104	A	KG-21 & RK #1201	1935
105	A	KTG-21 & RK #1203	1935
106	A	KG-31 & RK #1206	1935
107	A	KG-21 & RK #1205	1935
108	A	KG-31, RK #1206, Cromwell G-4 & Fascinator #4970	1935
109	A	Fascinator #4960	1935

FON		Model	Production Year
110	A	KG-31 & Fascinator #4970	1935
111	A	Fascinator #4980	1935
112	A	KM-21	1935
113	A	RK #1241 & Cromwell G-6	1935
114	A	RK #1242	1935
115	A	RK #1607	1935
116	A	A-1	1935
117	A	A-1	1935
118	A	Cromwell G-4 & GTG-4	1935
120	A	L-30 & Black Special	1935
121	A	L-37	1935
122	A	L-37 & L-50	1935
123	A	L-75	1935
124		L-50	1935
125	A	RK #1203	1935
127	A	L-37	1935
129	A	L-30 & L-37	1935
130	A	L-50	1935
131		Cromwell G-4	1935
132	A	KM-21 & RK #1607	1935
133	A	KTG-21	1935
134	A	KG-31, RK #1206, Cromwell G-4 & Capital J-2	1935
136	A	L-1	1935
137	A	KTG-11	1935
138	A	L-30	1935
141		L-30 & Black Special	1935
142	A	Cromwell G-4	1935
143	A	L-50	1935
144	A	L-75	1935
145	A	RK #1201	1935
149	A	KG-21	1935
150	A	RK #1242, Cromwell G-4 & Ambassador	1935
151	A	L-30 & Black Special	1935
154		TB-1	1935
158	A	L-30 & Black Special #2	1935
159		MB-3 & TB-3	1935
160		TB-2	1935
162		KG-21	1935
163	A	A-50	1935
166	A	KG-31, Cromwell G-4, GTG-4 & Coast CWTG-4	1935
167	A	KG-21	1935
168	A	TG-50	1935
169	A	KG-21	1935
170	A	KM-11 & RK #1610	1935
172	A	L-1	1935

1935 FON Series (continued)

FON		Model	Production Year
178	A	L-30 & Black Special	1935
180	A	KG-21	1935
181	A	L-50	1935
182	A	KG-21	1935
184	A	TG-50	1935
187	A	RK #1201	1935
191	A	L-00	1935
193	A	KTG-21	1935
194	A	KG-31	1935
195		TB-3	1935
198	A	KG-31	1935
199	A	L-75	1935
200	A	L-30 & Black Special	1935
201	A	L-00	1935
202	A	Cromwell G-4 & Capital J-2	1935
203	A	KG-11	1935
204	A	A-00	1935
205	A	F-7	1935
207	A	L-00	1935
208	A	TG-00	1935
210		MB-1	1935
211		TB-1	1935
212	A	L-75 & TG-75	1935
213	A	L-Century	1935
214	A	Cromwell G-4 & Ambassador	1935
216	A	L-30 & Black Special	1935
217	A	L-37	1935
218	A	TG-37	1935
219	A	L-Century	1935
220	A	TG-30	1935
222	A	KM-21	1935
223		KTG-11	1935
224	A	KTG-21	1935
225	A	KTG-31 & Cromwell GTG-4	1935
228	A	TG-50	1935
229	A	Cromwell G-4	1935
231	A	KG-11	1935
232	A	KH-21 "mandola"	1935
233	A	L-37	1935
234	A	H-0	1935
235	A	KJ "mando-bass'	1935
237	A	Cromwell G-4	1935
238	A	L-00	1935
239	A	RK #1201	1935

FON		Model	Production Year
241	A	L-37 & Black Special	1935
242	A	KG-21	1935
243	A	L-50	1935
244	A	L-30 & Black Special	1935
245	A	L-30 & Black Special	1935
246	A	L-37	1935
247	A	L-30	1935
248	A	Black Special	1935
249	A	S-1	1935
250	A	Jumbo	1935
251	A	Black Special	1935
252	A	L-50 & TG-50	1935
253	A	L-50	1935
254	A	Cromwell G-4	1935
255	A	KG-21	1935
258		TB-1	1935
260	A	KG-31 & Cromwell G-4	1935
261	A	L-1 & Cromwell G-4	1935
262	A	TG-1	1935
266	A	Cromwell G-4	1935
268	A	Cromwell G-4 & Ambassador	1935
269	A	L-75 & TG-75	1935
270	A	L-50	1935
271	A	L-37 & L-50	1935
272	A	Black Special	1935
273	A	L-50 & Black Special	1935
276	A	KG-21	1935
278	A	TU	1935
279	A	A-00	1935
280	A	L-50 & Black Special	1935
281	A	L-50	1935
282	A	KG-11	1935
283	A	L-00	1935
284	A	KG-31	1935
285	A	KG-11	1935
287	A	Cromwell G-4	1935
288	A	L-50 & Black Special	1935
289	A	L-30	1935
290	A	KG-31 Capital J-2 & Cromwell G-4	1935
291	A	KG-31 & KTG-31	1935
292	A	L-50	1935
293	A	L-Century	1935
295	A	KG-21	1935
300	A	KG-21	1935

1935 FON Series (continued)

FON		Model	Production Year
303	A	A-50	1935
305	A	Black Special	1935
306	A	Black Special	1935
307	A	S-1	1935
309	A	Cromwell G-4	1935
311		TB-1	1935
312		TB-3	1935
313	A	Cromwell G-4	1935
315	A	L-50	1935
316	A	L-30	1935
320	A	TG-30	1935
323	A	L-37	1935
325	A	Black Special	1935
327	A	L-75	1935
328	A	L-37	1935
330	A	KG-21	1935
332	A	KG-21	1935
335	A	L-37	1935
336	A	L-30 & Black Special	1935
337	A	Cromwell G-4	1935
338	A	KG-21	1935
339	A	Black Special	1935
340	A	L-37 & L-50	1935
341	A	L-75 & TG-75	1935
342	A	RK #1242	1935
343	A	L-30	1935
344	A	Black Special & L-37	1935
345	A	L-30 & L-75	1935
346	A	S-2	1935
348		L-00 "14 fret"	1935
350	A	A-75	1935
351	A	KK-31 "mando-cello"	1935
352	A	S-1	1935
353	A	L-50	1935
354	A	Cromwell G-4 & Coast CW-4	1935
355	A	KTG-21	1935
359	A	Cromwell G-4	1935
360	A	Cromwell G-4	1935
361	A	L-30	1935
362	A	Cromwell G-4	1935
363	A	KG-31, Cromwell G-4, Coast CW-4, Capital J-2, & Kraftsman 4	1935
364	A	L-00	1935
366	A	S-1	1935
367	A	L-37	1935

FON		Model	Production Year
368	A	A-00	1935
370	A	L-30	1935
371	A	A-1	1935
372	A	Cromwell G-4	1935
373	A	KG-31, Cromwell G-4, Coast CW-4, Capital J-2 & Kraftsman 4	1935
375	A	L-50 & Black Special	1935
376	A	L-30	1935
377	A	Cromwell G-4	1935
378	A	KG-31	1935
379		TB-2	1935
380	A	L-50	1935
382	A	KG-11	1935
384	A	KG-11	1935
386	A	L-00 & TG-00	1935
389	A	L-00	1935
390	A	KG-21, Cromwell G-4 & Capital J-2	1935
391	A	KHG-11	1935
392	A	L-50	1935
393	A	L-30	1935
394	A	Black Special	1935
395	A	KG-21	1935
398	A	KG-21	1935
399	A	Black Special	1935
402	A	KG-31	1935
404	A	L-30	1935
405	A	TB-3	1935
407	A	KG-31	1935
409	A	S-1	1935
414	A	L-37 & L-50	1935
415	A	L-30 (?)	1935
431	A	KG-31	1935
440	A	KG-31	1935
480	A	KG-21	1935
511	A	L-12	1935
515	A	L-00	1935
518	A	TG-50	1935
629	A	KG-31	1935
636	A	Cromwell G-4	1935
748	A	L-75	1935
768		MB-3	1935
777	A	Cromwell G-4	1935
794	A	TB-1	1935
827	A	TB-3	1935
863		Black Special	1935

1935 FON Series (continued)

FON		Model	Production Year
899	A	L-7	1935
905	A	Black Special	1935
907	A	S-1	1935
923	A	L-37	1935
954	A	Cromwell G-4	1935
990	A	KG-21	1935
1010	A	A-50	1935
1012		RK #682	1935
1013		KG-31	1935
1044		RK #1201	1935
1059		MB-3	1935
1088	A	CB-3	1935
1092		RK #682	1935
1104		L-50	1935
1125		L-50	1935
1126		L-50	1935
1127		L-37 & L-50	1935
1128		L-50	1935
1129		L-75	1935
1130		Jumbo	1935
1133		PB-1	1935
1140		A-75	1935
1144		RK #1242	1935
1158		Jumbo	1935
1159		S-1	1935
1161	A	TB-3	1935
1162		RK #926 & RK #1201	1935
1165		RK #926 "Carson Robison"	1935
1175		RK #1242	1935
1176		L-30 & Black Special	1935
1180		RK #1610	1935
1191		KG & RK #1201	1935
1194		TB-X "Reser model"	1935
1196		RK #1242	1935
1198		L-50	1935
1200		L-50	1935
1201		L-50	1935
1203		L-30	1935
1206		Jumbo	1935
1208		RK #926 & RK #1201	1935
1210		L-30 & Black Special	1935
1213		KG-21 & RK #1007	1935
1219		RK #1242	1935
1228		KG-21 & RK #807	1935
1242		L-50	1935

FON		Model	Production Year
1243		Black Special	1935
1245		MB-3	1935
1247		PB-1	1935
1252		RK #926	1935
1255		L-50	1935
1259		TB-1	1935
1262		L-50	1935
1263		L-50	1935
1264		L-50	1935
1265		L-50	1935
1266		RK #926 "Carson Robison"	1935
1268		TG-50	1935
1270		L-30 & Black Special	1935
1272		RK #1007	1935
1273		TB-3	1935
1274		TG-75	1935
1275		TU	1935
1279		KG-21 & RK #1007	1935
1280		KG & RK #926 "Carson Robison"	1935
1283		L-30 & Black Special	1935
1290		KG-21, RK #926 & RK #1201	1935
1291		L-50	1935
1292		MB-1	1935
1293		MB-3	1935
1294		L-1	1935
1295		L-50	1935
1296		L-30 & Black Special	1935
1297		KG-21	1935
1299		KG-21	1935
1300		Black Special	1935
1301		KG-21	1935
1302		L-75	1935
1303		L-37	1935
1304		KG-21 & RK #1007	1935
1305		L-75	1935
1307		L-50	1935
1308		Black Special	1935
1309		KG-31 & Cromwell G-4	1935
1310		KG-31 & Cromwell G-6	1935
1311		KG-31 & Cromwell G-4	1935
1312		KG-31 & Cromwell G-4	1935
1313	A	Cromwell G-6	1935
1314		Black Special	1935
1315		Black Special & Cromwell G-6	1935
1317		MB-2	1935

1935 FON Series (continued)

FON		Model	Production Year
1318		TG-50	1935
1319		RK #1242	1935
1321		L-50	1935
1324		A-75	1935
1326		MB-1	1935
1330		KM-21	1935
1331		RK #926 & RK #1201	1935
1332		Black Special	1935
1333		KM-11 & RK #807	1935
1334	A	Cromwell G-6 & Coast CW-6	1935
1335		A-75	1935
1337		Cromwell G-4	1935
1340		KG-31 & Cromwell G-4	1935
1341		KG-31 & Cromwell G-4	1935
1342		Black Special	1935
1343		Cromwell G-4	1935
1344		L-00	1935
1345		Cromwell G-4	1935
1346		RB-1	1935
1348		KG-31 & Cromwell G-4	1935
1349		Black Special	1935
1350		MB-1	1935
1351		L-50	1935
1352		L-50	1935
1354		Black Special	1935
1357		L-75	1935
1359		L-30 & Black Special	1935
1360		TB-3	1935
1361		KG-21, KTG-21 & Capital J-2	1935
1362		KG-21 & KTG-21	1935
1363		KG-21 & KTG-21	1935
1364		L-50	1935
1365		L-37 & L-50	1935
1367		RK #1201	1935
1372		KG-31 & Cromwell G-4	1935
1373		KG-31 & Cromwell G-4	1935
1374		TG-50	1935
1375		KG-21	1935
1376		Jumbo	1935
1377		Cromwell G-2	1935
1382		KM-11 & RK #1610 mandolins	1935
1383		Cromwell G-4	1935
1384	A	KG-11	1935
1385		L-30 & Black Special	1935

FON		Model	Production Year
1386		L-50	1935
1387		L-50	1935
1391		RK #1610	1935
1393		Cromwell G-4	1935
1395		L-00	1935
1396		KG-11	1935
1399		KG-21	1935
1400		KG-21	1935
1401		TG-30 & Black Special tenor gtr.	1935
1402		KG-21	1935
1403		KG-21	1935
1404		Cromwell G-4	1935
1405		KTG-21	1935
1407		TG-50	1935
1408		TB-3	1935
1409		TB-4 & PB-4	1935
1410		Cromwell G-2	1935
1411		Coast CW-6	1935
1414		TG-1	1935
1415		Cromwell G-2	1935
1416		Black Special	1935
1418		L-37, TG-37, L-50 & TG-50	1935
1419		KG-21	1935
1420		KG-31 Capital J-2 & Cromwell G-4	1935
1421		Cromwell G-4	1935
1422		KG-31	1935
1423		L-00	1935
1424		KG-21	1935
1425		KTG-31	1935
1427		TG-30	1935
1430		KM-21	1935
1431	A	KG-31, Cromwell G-6 & Capital J-3	1935
1432		Black Special	1935
1437		Black Special	1935
1438		Cromwell G-2	1935
1439		KG-11	1935
1440		Cromwell G-2	1935
1441		L-37	1935
1442		L-50	1935
1443		KG-31 & Cromwell G-4	1935
1444		KG-31 Capital J-2 & Cromwell G-4	1935
1445		L-30 & Black Special	1935
1446		L-30 & Black Special	1935
1447		KM-21	1935

1935 FON Series (continued)

FON		Model	Production Year
1449		TG-50	1935
1451		S-1	1935
1452		L-75	1935
1453		Jumbo	1935
1455		L-4	1935
1457		KM-21	1935
1458		KG-31	1935
1459		Cromwell G-6	1935
1461		KG-31, Cromwell G-4 & Capital J-2	1935
1462		Cromwell G-6 & Capital J-3	1935
1463		TG-50	1935
1464		Black Special	1935
1465		Black Special	1935
1466		Capital J-2	1935
1467		KM-21	1935
1468		Cromwell G-4	1935
1469	A	TG-50 or KG-11	1935
1470		KHG-21 & KTG-21	1935
1471		L-00	1935
1473		KG-31 & Cromwell G-4	1935
1474	A	RK #1242	1935
1477	A	L-00	1935
1478		KG-31, Cromwell G-4 & Capital J-2	1935
1480		KG-31, Cromwell G-4 & Capital J-2	1935
1481	A	MB-3	1935
1483		KG-31	1935
1484		TG-50	1935
1485		TB-Granada	1935
1487		Cromwell G-4 "new model"	1935
1488		KG-21 & RK#1205	1935
1489		KM-21	1935
1490		KG-21	1935
1491		L-37 & L-50	1935
1492		L-37 & L-50	1935
1495	A	KG-11	1935
1496		KG-21	1935
1504		KG-31, Cromwell G-4 & Capital J-2	1935
1505		L-37 & L-75	1935
1506	A	TG-0	1935
1507		L-30 & Black Special	1935
1508		L-30 & Black Special	1935
1509		KG-31, Cromwell G-4 & Capital J-2	1935
1510		Cromwell G-4 & Capital J-2	1935
1511		KTG-21	1935

FON		Model	Production Year
1512		KG-31 & Cromwell G-4	1935
1513	A	KG-31, Capital J-3, Cromwell G-6 & Coast CW-6	1935
1515	A	L-00	1935
1517		KG-31	1935
1628		TG-37	1935
1737		L-50	1935
2538		L-50	1935
2544	A	RK #1242, Cromwell G-6 & Fascinator #4970	1935
4758		TB-X "Reser model"	1935

Gibson teacher-agent William McMichael and his students in 1935

Ruth Glover Collection

1936 FON Series

During 1936 Gibson used FON's between 1 and 1100, with a few isolated numbers being higher. The addition of a letter suffix "B" occurred at the start of 1936, but only some models were singled out for that distinction. The rationale for the "B" suffix is not clear. No duplication of numbers is seen between FON with a letter suffix "B" and those without. This suggests that the letter suffix was added later on the production floor and was not part of the original pre-printed form used in the weekly production meetings. Some 1935 FON's with a letter "A" suffix (like 199-A) were carried over into 1936 and then received a "B" suffix (becoming 199-B.) This seems to be the case where production of a batch occurred at the end of 1935 and was prolonged into 1936. Some FON's from this period remain to be discovered, and the following table is not meant to be all-inclusive. Data in this table was taken mainly from shipping ledgers.

FON		Model	Production Year
11	B	KG-21	1936
19		KM-11	1936
25	B	MB-1	1936
35		TB-3	1936
40	B	KG-31	1936
69	B	KG-11	1936
77	B	KG-31	1936
82	B	KG-31	1936
87	B	KHG-21	1936
94	B	L-5	1936
98	B	KG-21	1936
100	B	KG-14	1936
105	B	L-30	1936
107	B	Advanced Jumbo	1936
113	B	KG-21	1936
115	B	L-30	1936
118	B	KG-21	1936
124	B	L-30	1936
135	B	Bass Violin	1936
137	B	ES-150	1936
164	B	TG-50	1936
171	B	MB-2	1936
175	B	E-150	1936
183	B	RB-1	1936
186		PB-3 & RB-3	1936
199	B	L-75	1936
203	B	L-00	1936
209	B	L-30	1936
212	B	KG-14	1936
219	B	TG-37	1936
222	B	KG-31	1936
233	B	KK-31 "mando-cello"	1936
251	B	L-50	1936
257		TB-4	1936
259	B	MB-1	1936

FON		Model	Production Year
262	B	Cromwell G-4	1936
280	B	Black Special	1936
281		PB-1	1936
292	B	KG-21	1936
294	B	Black Special	1936
295	B	MB-1	1936
298	B	KG-21	1936
299	B	KG-31	1936
304	B	L-30	1936
307	B	S-1	1936
316	B	KG-21	1936
319	B	KG-21	1936
327	B	L-37 & L-75	1936
337	B	L-00	1936
340	B	KG-21	1936
348	B	KG-31	1936
350	B	L-30	1936
354	B	L-0	1936
359	B	L-50	1936
360	B	KG-21	1936
366		KTG-21	1936
368	B	KG-21	1936
376	B	KG-21	1936
378		MB-3	1936
386	B	Cromwell TG-4	1936
400	B	Super 400	1936
406	B	A-Century	1936
407	B	A-1	1936
408	B	RK #1242	1936
410	B	L-37	1936
414	B	L-37 & L-50	1936
415	B	L-30	1936
416	B	L-30 & L-37	1936
417	B	KG-11	1936
418	B	KG-21	1936
419	B	TU	1936
421	B	Black Special	1936
422	B	KG-31	1936
430	B	TG-1	1936
431	B	Black Special	1936
432		EH-150	1936
433		EH-150	1936
434	B	Cromwell G-4, Capital J-2, Coast CW-4 & Kraftsman 4	1936
435	B	L-1	1936

1936 FON Series (continued)

FON		Model	Production Year
436	B	L-00	1936
437	B	L-50	1936
439	B	L-50	1936
440	B	L-37	1936
443	B	L-30, Black Special, L-37 & PG-37	1936
445		EH-100	1936
447	B	L-5	1936
449	B	KM-11	1936
450	B	A-1	1936
451		TB-X "Reser model"	1936
452		EH-150	1936
453	B	TG-50	1936
454		EH-150	1936
456	B	KG-21	1936
458	B	L-Century	1936
459	B	A-1	1936
460	B	Super 400	1936
462		EH-150	1936
463	B	KG-11 & RK #1201	1936
464	B	KG-11	1936
465	B	L-30	1936
466	B	A-1	1936
467	B	A-1	1936
468	B	KG-21 & RK #1242	1936
469	B	KM-11	1936
470	B	KG-31	1936
472	B	KTG-14	1936
473	B	TG-30	1936
475	B	L-50	1936
476	B	TG-4, Cromwell GTG-4, Capital TG-2, Coast TGCW-4	1936
477		EH-150	1936
478		EH-150	1936
479		EH-150	1936
480		EH	1936
482	B	KG-31 "Special," Ambassador M-5 & Coast CW-4	1936
483	B	Ambassador M-7	1936
484	B	Ambassador M-9	1936
485	B	Ambassador M-11	1936
489	B	A-1	1936
491	B	Jumbo	1936
492	B	L-Century	1936
494	B	L-30	1936
495	B	L-50 & Black Special	1936
496	B	L-75	1936

FON		Model	Production Year
498	B	NL	1936
500	B	KG-21 & RK #1201	1936
501	B	KG-21	1936
503	B	KG-21	1936
504		EH-150	1936
505		EH-150	1936
506	B	A-00	1936
507		EH-100	1936
508	B	HG-00	1936
509	B	KG-21 & L-30	1936
510	B	L-37	1936
514	B	KJ "mando-bass"	1936
515	B	L-30	1936
516	B	KG-21	1936
517		TB-X "Reser model"	1936
519	B	KG-21	1936
520	B	Cromwell GM-4	1936
521	B	L-50	1936
522	B	TG-30	1936
523	B	TG-50	1936
524	B	KHG-11	1936
525		EH-100	1936
526		EH-100	1936
527		EH-100	1936
529	B	L-00	1936
530	B	KG-21	1936
531	B	L-50	1936
532	B	HG-00	1936
533	B	L-00	1936
534	B	L-30 & Cromwell G-5	1936
535	B	Cromwell GM-4	1936
536	B	Cromwell GM-6	1936
537	B	Cromwell G-4, Capital J-2	1936
538	B	KG-31	1936
539	B	KM-21	1936
540	B	KG-21	1936
545		EH-100	1936
546		EH-100	1936
549	B	L-50	1936
550	B	L-30	1936
551	B	Jumbo	1936
552	B	L-30 & L-37	1936
553	B	L-75	1936
558		PB-Granada	1936

1936 FON Series (continued)

FON		Model	Production Year
559	B	KG-31	1936
560	B	KG-11	1936
561	B	KG-31	1936
562	B	L-30	1936
563	B	A-1	1936
566		EH-150	1936
567	B	KG-31 "Special" & Cromwell G-5	1936
568	B	KG-31 "Special"	1936
569	B	KG-31 "Special", Cromwell G-5 & Coast Wholesale CW-5	1936
570	B	KG-21 & Cromwell G-5	1936
571	B	KG-21	1936
573	B	L-75	1936
574	B	Cromwell GM-5	1936
576	B	KG-21 & Cromwell G-5	1936
577	B	KG-21	1936
578		EH-100	1936
579		EH-100	1936
580		EH-100	1936
581		EH-100	1936
584	B	L-30	1936
585	B	L-00	1936
587	B	L-30 & L-37	1936
588	B	L-50 & Black Special	1936
590	B	Black Special	1936
592	B	KG-11	1936
593	B	KJ "mando-bass"	1936
594	B	Cromwell G-4 & G-6	1936
595	B	Cromwell GTG-4, Capital J-16 & Coast TG-CW-4	1936
596	B	KG-21 & Cromwell G-5	1936
598	B	L-00	1936
600	B	A-00	1936
603	B	L-30	1936
604	B	L-37	1936
605		EH-100	1936
606		EH-100	1936
607		EH-100	1936
608		EH-100	1936
610	B	KG-21	1936
611	B	KG-31	1936
612	B	HG-00	1936
613	B	KG-11	1936
614	B	RK #1281	1936
618	B	L-1	1936
619	B	L-00	1936

FON		Model	Production Year
620		EH-150	1936
621		EH-150	1936
622		EH-150	1936
623		EH-150	1936
627	B	A-75	1936
632	B	S-2	1936
634	B	L-00	1936
637	B	L-50 & Black Special	1936
639	B	L-30	1936
640	B	Black Special	1936
642	B	KG-11? or KG-21?	1936
644	B	L-30 & Black Special	1936
645		MB-3	1936
646	B	L-Century	1936
647	B	RK #1281	1936
648	B	KG-31	1936
649	B	KG-31, RK #1283 & Kraftsman 10	1936
650	B	KG-31 & RK #1284	1936
651	B	RK #1285	1936
653	B	L-75	1936
655	B	Coast Wholesale CW-4	1936
657		EH-150 “special”	1936
659	B	KG-31, Cromwell G-4 & Kraftsman 4	1936
660	B	KG-21	1936
661	B	L-50	1936
663	B	TG-50	1936
664	B	KG-31	1936
666	B	A-00	1936
668		TB-X “Reser model”	1936
669	B	L-30 & Black Special	1936
670	B	Cromwell G-4	1936
672	B	L-00	1936
673	B	Black Special	1936
675	B	L-50	1936
678	B	KG-21	1936
679	B	KG-31	1936
683	B	Coast Wholesale CW-6	1936
685		TB-1 & RB-1	1936
688	B	Jumbo	1936
689	B	L-30	1936
693	B	L-75	1936
694	B	L-37	1936
695	B	Coast TG-CW-4	1936
697	B	L-37	1936

FON		Model	Production Year
698	B	L-37	1936
699	B	L-30	1936
700	B	KG-21	1936
701	B	KG-21	1936
702	B	L-30	1936
703	B	L-00	1936
704	B	KG-31, Cromwell G-5 & Coast Wholesale CW-5	1936
707	B	KG-31 "Special"	1936
708	B	KG-21	1936
711	B	RK #1283 "Carson Robison"	1936
713	B	KG-31	1936
714	B	KG-31, RK #1283 & Kraftsman 4	1936
716	B	KG-31 & Kraftsman 4	1936
717	B	L-0	1936
718	B	RK #1283 & Kraftsman 10	1936
719	B	RK #1283 "Carson Robison"	1936
720	B	RK #1284 & KG-31	1936
721	B	RK #1285	1936
722	B	KG-21	1936
723	B	L-Century	1936
724	B	L-30, Black Special, RK #1283 & Kraftsman 10	1936
725	B	L-50	1936
726	B	L-30	1936
727	B	Kraftsman 10	1936
729		TB-3	1936
730	B	L-00	1936
731	B	A-00	1936
732	B	A-1	1936
735	B	Kraftsman 10 & Kraftsman 38-S	1936
737	B	L-37	1936
738	B	L-30	1936
739	B	A-50	1936
740	B	L-50	1936
744	B	L-30	1936
745	B	H-4	1936
746	B	KG-11	1936
747	B	L-00	1936
748	B	L-75	1936
749		TB-1 & RB-1	1936
755	B	Coast Wholesale CW-4	1936
756	B	L-00	1936
758	B	KG-21	1936
759	B	RK #1283 "Carson Robison"	1936
760	B	Coast Wholesale CW-4 & KG-21	1936

FON		Model	Production Year
762	B	L-30 & KG-21	1936
764	B	KG-21	1936
765	B	L-50	1936
767	B	Coast Wholesale CW-4	1936
768	B	KG-21	1936
769	B	KG-21	1936
770	B	KG-31 & Cromwell G-4	1936
771	B	HG-00	1936
772	B	L-00	1936
773	B	L-00	1936
774	B	L-30	1936
775	B	L-50	1936
778	B	KG-21	1936
779	B	KG-31 & RK #1281	1936
780	B	Cromwell TG-4	1936
782	B	L-37 "Special"	1936
783	B	KG-14	1936
786	B	KTG-11	1936
787	B	KTG-31	1936
788	B	KG-21	1936
790	B	KG-21 & TG-50	1936
791	B	KG-21 & TG-50	1936
792	B	KG-21 & KHG-21	1936
793	B	Kraftsman 10	1936
794	B	KG-21	1936
796	B	PG-50	1936
797	B	KG-31 & RK #1284	1936
798	B	KG-21	1936
799	B	KG-31, Cromwell G-4 & Coast Wholesale CW-4	1936
800	B	KG-21	1936
801	B	S-1	1936
802	B	L-30	1936
803	B	L-30, L-37 & Black Special	1936
804	B	L-37 & Black Special	1936
805	B	L-50 & Black Special	1936
806	B	L-37 & Black Special	1936
807		RB-3	1936
809		RB-1	1936
810	B	KG-21	1936
811	B	KG-11	1936
812	B	KG-14	1936
813	B	KG-14	1936
816	B	KG-31, Cromwell G-4 & Capital J-2	1936
820	B	KG-31 & RK #1284	1936

1936 FON Series (continued)

FON		Model	Production Year
821	B	KG-31	1936
822	B	KG-31	1936
823	B	KG-31	1936
824	B	KG-31, RK #1283 & Kraftsman 10	1936
825	B	L-Century	1936
827	B	KG-14	1936
828	B	KG-31, Cromwell G-4 & Capital J-2	1936
829	B	KG-31 & Coast Wholesale CW-6	1936
831	B	KG-14 & KHG-14	1936
832	B	KG-31	1936
834	B	KG-31	1936
837	B	L-00	1936
838	B	L-00	1936
839	B	L-37	1936
840	B	Black Special	1936
841		TB-1 & RB-1	1936
842	B	KG-21	1936
843		EH-150	1936
844		EH-150	1936
845		EH-150	1936
846		EH-150	1936
847	B	L-50	1936
848	B	KG-31	1936
849	B	RK #1285	1936
851	B	L-00	1936
854	B	L-0	1936
855	B	TB	1936
856	B	L-50	1936
860	B	KG-21 & L-30	1936
861	B	KG-14	1936
862	B	KG-21 & “Special Guitar”	1936
864	B	KG-21	1936
865	B	Bristow Radio Spc. & KG-21	1936
866	B	L-30 & Black Special	1936
867	B	L-37	1936
869	B	Cromwell G-4	1936
870	B	KH-21 “mandola”	1936
871	B	KJ “mando-bass”	1936
872	B	KG-14, RK #1115 & RK #1281	1936
875	B	KG-31, Cromwell G-4, Capital J-2 & Coast Wholesale CW-4	1936
876	B	A-00	1936
877	B	L-30	1936
878	B	L-37 & TG-37	1936
879	B	S-1	1936

FON		Model	Production Year
880	B	KG-21	1936
881	B	RK #1283 "Carson Robison"	1936
883	B	TG-50	1936
887	B	L-00	1936
888	B	RK #1283 "Carson Robison"	1936
889	B	L-Century	1936
890	B	L-50, TG-50 & PG-50	1936
892	B	KG-31 "Special," Cromwell G-5 & Coast Wholesale CW-5	1936
893	B	RK #1285	1936
895	B	L-00	1936
898	B	KG-21 & L-37	1936
899	B	KG-31 & Cromwell G-4	1936
900	B	KG-21	1936
901	B	KTG-21	1936
903	B	L-30	1936
904	B	RK #1283 "Carson Robison"	1936
907		TB-1	1936
908	B	RK #1228	1936
909	B	KG-31 "Special"	1936
911	B	Advanced Jumbo	1936
912	B	L-50	1936
913	B	L-00	1936
914	B	L-30 & Black Special	1936
915	B	L-37	1936
916	B	L-00	1936
917		TB-1	1936
918		TB-3	1936
919		RB-1	1936
920	B	KG-31 & RK #1284	1936
921	B	KG-31	1936
922	B	KG-21 & KHG-21	1936
923	B	KG-31 & Cromwell G-4	1936
924	B	RK #1281 & RK #1283	1936
925	B	A-00	1936
926	B	KG-31	1936
927	B	RK #1228, RK #1283 & KG-21	1936
928		EH-150	1936
929		EH-150	1936
930		EH-150	1936
931		EH-150	1936
932	B	L-50	1936
933	B	KG-31	1936
934		TB-3	1936
935	B	Black Special	1936

1936 FON Series (continued)

FON		Model	Production Year
936	B	L-75	1936
939	B	F-7	1936
940	B	RK #1283 "Carson Robison"	1936
941	B	RK #1285	1936
942	B	KG-21	1936
946	B	KG-21	1936
947	B	L-00	1936
948	B	L-00	1936
949	B	L-00	1936
950	B	L-30	1936
951	B	L-50 & Black Special	1936
955	B	KG-21	1936
956	B	KG-21 & KHG-21	1936
958	B	RK #1228 & RK #1283	1936
959	B	TG-50	1936
960	B	J-35	1936
961	B	J-35	1936
962	B	KG-14 & RK #1281	1936
963	B	L-30	1936
964	B	L-30	1936
965	B	A-00	1936
966	B	L-00	1936
967	B	L-75	1936
968	B	L-30	1936
969	B	KM-11	1936
970	B	KG-31	1936
972	B	L-50	1936
973	B	KG-31, KHG-31 & Cromwell G-4	1936
974	B	KG-31	1936
975	B	KG-11	1936
977		MB-3	1936
979	B	KG-31 & RK #1284	1936
982	B	L-37	1936
983	B	L-30 & Black Special	1936
984	B	L-50	1936
985	B	Black Special	1936
986	B	KG-21	1936
987	B	KG-14	1936
988	B	KG-14	1936
989	B	KH-21 "mandola"	1936
990	B	KG-31 & Cromwell G-4	1936
992		EH-150	1936
993		EH-150	1936
994	B	EH-150	1936

FON		Model	Production Year
995		EH-150	1936
997	B	RK #1228	1936
998	B	RK #1228 & RK #1283	1936
999	B	RK #1285 & Cromwell G-4	1936
1000	B	RK #1127 & RK #1270	1936
1002	B	KTG-31	1936
1004	B	L-30 & L-37	1936
1005	B	KG-31	1936
1006	B	A-1	1936
1008	B	A-75	1936
1009	B	L-50	1936
1010	B	L-5	1936
1011	B	KG-31	1936
1012		TB-3	1936
1014	B	KG-14	1936
1015	B	KG-31	1936
1018	B	Advanced Jumbo	1936
1019	B	L-5	1936
1020	B	RK #1281	1936
1021	B	KG-14	1936
1022	B	TB-Trujo	1936
1023	B	J-35	1936
1024	B	S-1	1936
1025	B	L-75	1936
1028	B	J-35	1936
1029	B	KM-21 & RK #1228	1936
1030	B	KG-31	1936
1031	B	Kraftsman 225-S & KG-31	1936
1032	B	J-35	1936
1034	B	RK #1285	1936
1038	B	Black Special	1936
1039	B	L-50 & Black Special	1936
1040	B	KG-21 & RK #1115	1936
1042	B	J-35	1936
1043	B	KG-14	1936
1044	B	KG-21	1936
1046	B	Black Special #4	1936
1047	B	KM-11	1936
1048	B	KM-21	1936
1049	B	KG-21	1936
1050	B	KG-31	1936
1051	B	KG-31	1936
1052	B	KG-21	1936
1053	B	L-30 & L-37	1936

1936 FON Series (continued)

FON		Model	Production Year
1054	B	A-00	1936
1055	B	RK #1285	1936
1056	B	Kraftsman 34-S	1936
1057	B	A-1	1936
1058	B	ES-150	1936
1059	B	KG-31	1936
1060	B	KG-31	1936
1061	B	KG-31	1936
1062	B	KG-21	1936
1063	B	KG-21, RK #1115 & RK #1281	1936
1064	B	KTG-21	1936
1065	B	KG-14	1936
1066	B	KG-31, KTG-31, KHG-31 & Cromwell TG-4	1936
1067	B	KTG-21 & Capital TG-2	1936
1068	B	KG-21	1936
1069	B	KG-31	1936
1070	B	Advanced Jumbo	1936
1073		EH-150 "special"	1936
1074	B	KG-14	1936
1078	B	J-35	1936
1080	B	L-50	1936
1081	B	L-00	1936
1082	B	KG-21 & KHG-21	1936
1083	B	KG-21, RK #1115 & RK #1281	1936
1084	B	KG-14 & RK #1281	1936
1085	B	KG-21 & RK #1285	1936
1086	B	KG-21	1936
1087		MB-11	1936
1088	B	KG-21 & RK #1228	1936
1089	B	RK #1228	1936
1091	B	RK #1270	1936
1092	B	RK #1254	1936
1093	B	RK #1254	1936
1094	B	KG-14 & Kraftsman 225-S	1936
1098	B	ES-150	1936
1099	B	KG-21 & RK #1281	1936
1100	B	KG-14	1936
1101	B	KG-14	1936
1102	B	Black Special	1936
1103	B	L-30	1936
1104	B	KG-21	1936
1105	B	KG-31	1936
1107	B	Advanced Jumbo	1936
1108	B	L-75	1936

FON		Model	Production Year
1109	B	TB-1	1936
1119	B	RK #1115	1936
1120	B	KG-14	1936
1121	B	A-00	1936
1122	B	A-Century	1936
1123	B	L-00	1936
1124	B	L-30	1936
1125	B	L-37	1936
1126	B	HG-00 "3/4"	1936
1127	B	KG-21 & RK #1254	1936
1128	B	RK #1254	1936
1129	B	KG-21 & RK #1285	1936
1130	B	RK #1285	1936
1132	B	Kraftsman 225-S	1936
1134	B	Kraftsman 38-S & 48-S	1936
1135		Kraftsman 36-S	1936
1136	B	ES-150	1936
1137	B	ES-150	1936
1138	B	KH-21 "mandola"	1936
1143	B	Kraftsman 34-S	1936
1146	B	A-00	1936
1149	B	KG-14	1936
1150	B	KG-21	1936
1152	B	Cromwell G-4, Capital & Coast Wholesale CW-4	1936
1153	B	KG-14	1936
1154	B	Cromwell G-5 & Capital J-3	1936
1155	B	KJ "mando-bass"	1936
1158	B	KG-21 & RK #1228	1936
1159	B	KG-21	1936
1162	B	KM-11	1936
1163	B	KG-21	1936
1164	B	KM-21	1936
1165	B	KHG-11	1936
1168	B	KG-21	1936
1169	B	KG-21	1936
1173	B	EH-100	1936
1174	B	A-1	1936
1175	B	TG-50	1936
1176	B	KG-21	1936
1177	B	KG-21	1936
1178	B	KG-14 & RK #1254	1936
1180	B	Kraftsman 225-S	1936
1182	B	Kraftsman 36-S	1936
1183	B	KG-21 & Kraftsman 36-S	1936

1936 FON Series (continued)

FON		Model	Production Year
1186	B	Kraftsman 36-S & ETG-150	1936
1187	B	RK #1254	1936
1193	B	RK #1254	1936
1195	B	L-5	1936
1196	B	ES-150	1936
1197	B	ES-150	1936
1199	B	L-50	1936
1228	B	RK # 1254	1936
1256	B	KG-31	1936
1288	B	RK #1228	1936
1367	B	KG-31	1936
1418	B	TG-37	1936
1432	B	Kraftsman guitars	1936
1466		MB-2	1936
1480	B	Kraftsman guitars	1936
1824	B	KG-31	1936
1907	B	KG-11	1936

PLEASE REMEMBER

When ordering Guitars to always state whether Wire or Gut Strings are wanted

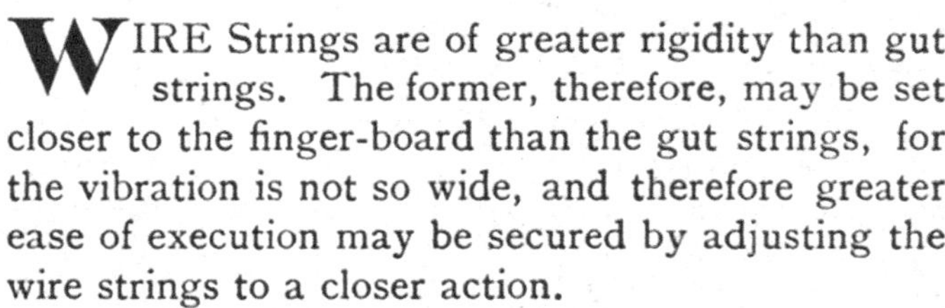

WIRE Strings are of greater rigidity than gut strings. The former, therefore, may be set closer to the finger-board than the gut strings, for the vibration is not so wide, and therefore greater ease of execution may be secured by adjusting the wire strings to a closer action.

Furthermore, due to the elasticity of the gut strings, as well as the high action necessitated, the bridge and nut are high. When changing to gut strings, it usually necessitates moving the bridge forward possibly a quarter of an inch in order that the scale be absolutely true in all positions on all strings.

Generally speaking, other manufacturers split the difference, so that for neither stringing are the tones true in all positions.

The Gibson Mandolin-Guitar Co. Kalamazoo Michigan

A humorous reminder to dealers, circa 1910's
Steve Huber Collection

1937 FON Series

During 1937 Gibson used FON's between 1 and 1400, with a few isolated numbers being higher. The addition of a letter suffix "C" occurred at the start of 1937, but only some models were singled out for that distinction. The rationale for the "C" suffix is not clear. No duplication of numbers is seen between FON with a letter suffix "C" and those without. This suggests that the letter suffix was added later on the production floor and was not part of the original pre-printed form used in the weekly production meetings. Some 1936 FON's with a letter "B" suffix (like 584-B) were carried over into 1937, and the 1937 instruments then received a "C" suffix (becoming 584-C.) This seems to be the case where production of a batch occurred at the end of 1936 and was prolonged into 1937. Some FON's from this period remain to be discovered, and the following table is not meant to be all inclusive. Data for this table was taken mainly from shipping ledgers.

FON		Model	Production Year
1	C	KG-21	1937
2	C	A-1	1937
3	C	KG-31	1937
4	C	KG-21	1937
5	C	Black Special & Black Special #4	1937
6	C	L-50	1937
8	C	TG-50	1937
9	C	L-30, TG-30, L-37 & TG-37	1937
10		RB-3 & TB-3	1937
11	C	KM-11	1937
12	C	KG-11	1937
13	C	KG-31, Cromwell G-4 & Coast Wholesale CW-4	1937
16	C	KK-31 "mando-cello"	1937
18	C	KG-31, Cromwell G-4	1937
19	C	KG-31, Cromwell G-14, Capital J-2, J-16 & Coast CW-4	1937
20	C	KG-21, KTG-21 & RK #1285	1937
21	C	KM-21 & RK #1642	1937
23	C	L-5 "Special"	1937
24	C	TB-00	1937
25	C	ES-150	1937
26	C	L-30 & L-37	1937
27	C	ETG-150	1937
28	C	KG-21	1937
29	C	KG-21 & KTG-21	1937
30	C	L-00	1937
31	C	Advanced Jumbo	1937
32	C	L-30 & L-37	1937
33	C	L-30 & L-37	1937
34	C	L-30, L-37 & TG-37	1937
35	C	L-50 & ES-150	1937
36	C	L-30 & KG-31	1937
37	C	KM-21 & RK #1642	1937
38	C	KG-21 & RK #1228	1937
41	C	Cromwell GTG-4 & Capital J-TG	1937
42	C	RK #1285	1937

1937 FON Series (continued)

FON		Model	Production Year
43	C	RK #1270	1937
44	C	Super 400	1937
45	C	KG-31	1937
46	C	Francis Day & Hunter "special"	1937
47	C	RK #1285	1937
49	C	KG-31	1937
50	C	L-00	1937
51	C	EM-150	1937
54	C	L-0	1937
56		RB-3 & PB-3	1937
57	C	EM-150	1937
58	C	KG-31 "Special," Capital J-2, RK #1123 & RK #1228	1937
59	C	Cromwell GTG-4, Capital J-2 & Coast Wholesale TG-CW-4	1937
60	C	L-50	1937
61		EH-100	1937
62	C	KG-11	1937
65	C	RK #1270	1937
66	C	L-30 & L-37	1937
67	C	A-1	1937
68		TB-1	1937
70	C	ES-150	1937
71	C	KM-21	1937
73	C	KHG-11 "Morris King Special"	1937
78	C	J-35	1937
80	C	L-00	1937
81	C	RK #1115	1937
82	C	Cromwell G-2	1937
83	C	RK #1228	1937
85	C	RK #1228	1937
86	C	KG-21 & L-30	1937
87	C	Cromwell G-6	1937
88	C	KG-21	1937
89	C	KG-21 & KTG-21	1937
90	C	L-5	1937
91	C	J-35	1937
93	C	L-5	1937
94	C	L-7	1937
95	C	EH-150	1937
96	C	KG-21	1937
97	C	Cromwell G-5 & Capital J-3	1937
98	C	KG-21 & Cromwell G-6	1937
99	C	A-00	1937
100	C	KG-21	1937
101	C	A-Century	1937

FON		Model	Production Year
102	C	L-75 & ES-150	1937
103	C	ES-150	1937
104	C	L-37	1937
105	C	RK #1124	1937
106	C	KG-21	1937
107	C	L-00 3/4	1937
108	C	KG-21	1937
109	C	KG-21	1937
110	C	RK #1115	1937
111	C	RK #1115	1937
113	C	TG "Special"	1937
114	C	RK #1127 & RK #1270	1937
115	C	KG 3/4	1937
116	C	RK #1124	1937
118	C	Cromwell G-4, Capital J-2, J-16 & Coast CW-4 & CW-5	1937
119	C	L-47	1937
121	C	L-5	1937
122	C	KG-31	1937
123	C	HG-00	1937
124	C	J-35	1937
125	C	L-Century	1937
126	C	KG-21	1937
128	C	KG-21	1937
129	C	KG-14	1937
133	C	RK #1228	1937
134	C	RK #1228	1937
136	C	KG-31	1937
138	C	RK #1124	1937
141	C	ES-150	1937
142	C	EM-150	1937
145	C	KTG-21 & KHG-21	1937
146	C	TG-75	1937
149	C	L-5 "Special"	1937
150	C	RK #1123	1937
151	C	KM-11	1937
153	C	ES-150	1937
154	C	L-30	1937
155	C	RK #1123	1937
156	C	KG 3/4	1937
158	C	ES-150	1937
161	C	TG-50	1937
162		TB-75 & TB-3	1937
163	C	Black Special	1937
164	C	TG-50	1937

1937 FON Series (continued)

FON		Model	Production Year
165	C	L-50	1937
166	C	KM-21	1937
168	C	Black Special	1937
169	C	Black Special	1937
170	C	HG "double neck"	1937
171		HG "double neck"	1937
172	C	ETG-150	1937
174	C	A-00	1937
176	C	A-Century	1937
177	C	L-00	1937
178	C	Advanced Jumbo	1937
180	C	KG-21	1937
181		PB-75 & PB-3	1937
182		RB-75	1937
183	C	RK #1123 & RK #1228	1937
184	C	RK #1123 & RK #1228	1937
185	C	RK #1124	1937
186	C	KK-31 "mando-cello"	1937
188	C	KG-31	1937
189	C	KG-21 & KTG-21	1937
191	C	KG-11	1937
192	C	Cromwell G-5 & EG-5	1937
193	C	EGH	1937
194	C	EM-100	1937
196	C	L-75	1937
198	C	Cromwell G-5 & Capital J-3	1937
199	C	KG-21	1937
200	C	Cromwell EG-5 & ETG-5	1937
201	C	H-0	1937
202	C	HG-00	1937
203	C	L-00	1937
204	C	L-00 3/4	1937
205	C	L-37	1937
206	C	L-50	1937
211	C	RK #1123	1937
213	C	Cromwell EG-5 & RK #1012 & #1124	1937
214	C	Cromwell EG-5 & RK #1012 & #1124	1937
216	C	KM-11	1937
217	C	KG-21	1937
218	C	KHG-14	1937
219	C	KG 3/4	1937
223		RK #1129	1937
224		RK #1129	1937
225	C	L-30 & L-37	1937

FON		Model	Production Year
227		EH-150	1937
230	C	Black Special	1937
231		TB-1	1937
232	C	ES-150	1937
233	C	Cromwell EG-5 & RK #1127	1937
234	C	ES-150	1937
237		EH-150	1937
238	C	Cromwell G-6 & RK #1012	1937
240	C	TG-50	1937
241		EG-H	1937
242	C	L-30	1937
243	C	L-30, Black Special & L-37	1937
244	C	L-50	1937
245	C	KG-21	1937
246	C	EM-125 & EM-150	1937
248	C	L-37	1937
249	C	TG-50	1937
250	C	KG-31 & RK #1123	1937
251	C	KG-11	1937
252	C	L-30	1937
253		GB-1	1937
254	C	Cromwell GTG-4 & Coast Wholesale TG-CW-4	1937
255	C	L-4	1937
256	C	KG-31 & Black Special #2	1937
258	C	L-Century	1937
259	C	L-00	1937
262	C	ES-150	1937
263	C	Cromwell G-6	1937
264	C	Cromwell G-6 & KG-31	1937
265	C	KG 3/4	1937
266	C	L-75	1937
267	C	EH-150	1937
268	C	TG-30, L-30 & L-37	1937
269	C	Cromwell G-5	1937
270	C	A-Century	1937
271	C	KG-21	1937
272	C	L-50	1937
273	C	L-Century	1937
276	C	L-5 “Special”	1937
278		EH-150	1937
279		EH-150	1937
280		EH-100	1937
281		EG-H	1937
282		EG-H	1937

1937 FON Series (continued)

FON		Model	Production Year
283	C	KHG-14	1937
284	C	KG-11	1937
285	C	KM-11	1937
286	C	F-5	1937
287	C	Cromwell G-4, Capital J-16, Coast CW-4 & CW-5	1937
288	C	KG-21	1937
289	C	KG-21	1937
290	C	Black Special	1937
293	C	KTG-21	1937
294	C	ES-150	1937
295		EH-100	1937
297		EH-150	1937
300	C	EM-100	1937
302	C	L-5	1937
304	C	RK #1115	1937
305	C	RK #1136	1937
307	C	"Special Banjo"	1937
310	C	L-0	1937
311		EH-100	1937
312		EH-100	1937
313	C	Black Special	1937
314	C	RK #1127	1937
315	C	A-50	1937
317	C	L-00	1937
318	C	L-37	1937
319	C	L-30	1937
320	C	L-50	1937
322	C	RK #1115	1937
323	C	RK #1115	1937
324	C	RK #1123 & KG-21	1937
325	C	KG-31, Cromwell G-4, Capital J-16 & Coast Wholesale CW-4	1937
326	C	L-30	1937
327	C	L-75	1937
329		EH-150	1937
330		EH-150	1937
331		EH-150 "new model"	1937
332		EH-150	1937
333	C	Cromwell G-5	1937
336	C	KG-31	1937
337	C	L-0	1937
339	C	L-30 & L-37	1937
340	C	L-37 & TG-37	1937
341	C	ES-150 & Francis Day & Hunter "special"	1937
342	C	RK #1127 & RK #1128	1937

FON		Model	Production Year
343	C	S-1	1937
345	C	S-1	1937
346		TB-7	1937
347		TB-12	1937
348		TB-18	1937
349	C	RK # 1012, #1127 & #1128	1937
350	C	Cromwell G-5, G-6, KG-31 & Capital J-18	1937
351	C	Cromwell G-5 & Capital J-17	1937
352	C	Coast Wholesale CW-6	1937
353	C	RK #1124	1937
354	C	H-0	1937
355	C	A-1	1937
356	C	A-50	1937
357	C	L-00	1937
358	C	L-75	1937
360	C	RK #1115	1937
361	C	L-50	1937
362	C	Advanced Jumbo	1937
363	C	KG-14	1937
364	C	L-Century	1937
365		EH-150	1937
366		EH-150	1937
367	C	KG-31	1937
369	C	KM-11	1937
370	C	EH-150	1937
371	C	EH-150	1937
372	C	A-75	1937
373	C	L-50	1937
374	C	L-0	1937
375	C	L-00	1937
376	C	J-35	1937
377	C	J-35	1937
378	C	Advanced Jumbo	1937
379	C	Black Special & Black Special #4	1937
380	C	L-30, Black Special & L-37	1937
381	C	L-50 & Black Special	1937
382	C	RK #1228	1937
383	C	RK #1124	1937
384	C	KG-21	1937
385	C	KG-11	1937
386	C	KG-11	1937
387	C	KG-14 & RK #1136	1937
388	C	KG-31	1937
389	C	L-30 & KG-31	1937

1937 FON Series (continued)

FON		Model	Production Year
390		TB-7	1937
391		TB-12	1937
392		TB-18	1937
393	C	KTG-21	1937
394	C	RK #1110	1937
396	C	KG-21	1937
397	C	HG-00	1937
398	C	L-Century	1937
399	C	L-30 & Black Special	1937
400	C	L-37	1937
401	C	L-50	1937
402	C	ES-150	1937
403	C	Black Special #2	1937
404	C	L-75	1937
406	C	KG-21	1937
407		EH-150	1937
408		EH-150	1937
411	C	L-37	1937
413		RB-18	1937
414		PB-18	1937
416		TB-75	1937
418	C	L-30, Black Special & Black Special #2	1937
419	C	L-37	1937
420	C	L-30	1937
421	C	L-00	1937
422	C	L-00	1937
423	C	L-0	1937
424	C	L-0	1937
425	C	L-50	1937
428	C	RK #1129	1937
429	C	L-30	1937
430	C	L-30	1937
434	C	ES-150 & ETG-150	1937
436	C	KG-31	1937
437	C	KG-21	1937
438	C	KHG-11	1937
439	C	KHG-14	1937
440	C	ES-150	1937
441	C	Francis Day & Hunter "Special"	1937
442	C	J-35	1937
443	C	S-1	1937
445		RB-75	1937
446		EG-H	1937
447	C	KG-11	1937

FON		Model	Production Year
448	C	KG-21	1937
449	C	KG-21	1937
450	C	KG-31	1937
451	C	KG-31	1937
452	C	RK #1124	1937
454	C	L-30	1937
455	C	L-75	1937
456		RK #1129	1937
457	C	TU	1937
459	C	J-35	1937
460	C	L-50	1937
463	C	A-1	1937
464	C	L-00	1937
465	C	L-00	1937
466	C	J-35	1937
468	C	Black Special & Black Special #2	1937
469	C	Black Special & Black Special #4	1937
470	C	L-30 & L-37	1937
471	C	L-30, L-37 & Black Special	1937
480		EH-100	1937
481		EH-100	1937
482	C	Black Special #2	1937
484	C	L-50	1937
485	C	L-0	1937
486	C	Black Special #2	1937
487	C	KG-21	1937
488	C	KM-11	1937
489	C	KG-21	1937
490	C	KG-21	1937
491	C	KG-14 & RK #1115	1937
492	C	Black Special & Black Special #2	1937
493	C	Black Special & Black Special #2	1937
494	C	A-00	1937
495	C	ES-150	1937
496	C	L-5	1937
497	C	L-5	1937
498	C	Black Special & Black Special #2	1937
499		HG "double neck"	1937
500		EH-150	1937
501		EH-150	1937
502		EH-100	1937
503		EH-100	1937
506	C	KG-11	1937
508	C	KG-14	1937

1937 FON Series (continued)

FON		Model	Production Year
509	C	KG-14	1937
511	C	Black Special #4	1937
512	C	L-00	1937
513	C	Black Special & Black Special #4	1937
514	C	L-50	1937
515	C	EM-150	1937
518		RB-75	1937
520	C	L-75	1937
521	C	L-5	1937
522	C	L-0	1937
526	C	A-1	1937
527	C	L-0	1937
528	C	L-0	1937
529	C	L-00	1937
530	C	Black Special & Black Special #2	1937
532		TB-75	1937
533	C	KG-11	1937
536	C	KG-31	1937
537	C	Jumbo	1937
539	C	RK #1115	1937
540	C	RK #1123	1937
541	C	Francis Day & Hunter "Special"	1937
542	C	RK #1127 & RK #1128	1937
543	C	RK #1127 & RK #1128	1937
545	C	L-5	1937
547	C	ES-150	1937
549	C	L-75	1937
551	C	RK Jumbo	1937
552	C	Black Special #2	1937
553	C	RK #1124 & Francis Day & Hunter "Special"	1937
554	C	KHG-11	1937
556		EH-100	1937
557	C	Black Special & Black Special #2	1937
558	C	A-1	1937
560	C	Black Special #4	1937
561	C	Black Special & Black Special #4	1937
562		EHG "10-string"	1937
563	C	RK #1115	1937
564	C	L-00	1937
565	C	L-50	1937
569	C	J-35	1937
570	C	Cromwell G-5	1937
571	C	Black Special & Black Special #4	1937
572	C	Black Special & Black Special #2	1937

FON		Model	Production Year
573	C	Advanced Jumbo	1937
574	C	KM-11	1937
576	C	KG-31 & Cromwell G-5	1937
577	C	ETG-150	1937
578	C	S-2	1937
579	C	RK #1124	1937
580	C	KG-31, Black Special & Black Special #2	1937
581	C	Black Special & Black Special #4	1937
584	C	L-30	1937
585	C	L-37	1937
587	C	KG-14	1937
588	C	RK #1134	1937
589	C	RK #1135	1937
590	C	RK #1136	1937
591	C	RK #1137	1937
592	C	RK #1123	1937
593	C	RK #1124	1937
594	C	RK #1139	1937
595	C	RK #1111	1937
598	C	RK #1124	1937
599	C	L-0	1937
600	C	L-50	1937
601		TB-Florentine	1937
602	C	L-37	1937
603	C	Black Special & Black Special #4	1937
604	C	RK #1111	1937
610	C	L-0	1937
611	C	S-1	1937
612	C	L-00	1937
613	C	L-50 & TG-50	1937
614	C	Black Special	1937
615	C	ES-150	1937
618	C	TG-50	1937
619	C	Black Special & Black Special #2	1937
621	C	RK #1144, RK #1127 & RK #1012	1937
624	C	KG-21	1937
626	C	A-00	1937
629	C	L-00	1937
633	C	RK #1144, RK #1127 & RK #1012	1937
636	C	L-30	1937
637	C	KHG-14	1937
639	C	KG-31	1937
640	C	TG-2	1937
642	C	KM-11	1937

FON		Model	Production Year
643		TB-Florentine	1937
644	C	A-1	1937
645	C	HG-0	1937
647	C	TG-00	1937
648	C	TG-30	1937
649	C	TG-37	1937
650	C	ES-150	1937
651	C	L-30 & Black Special	1937
653	C	A-75	1937
657	C	KG-31	1937
658	C	HG "double neck"	1937
659	C	KG-31	1937
660	C	Kalamazoo "Sport"	1937
661	C	Francis Day & Hunter "Special"	1937
662	C	L-37	1937
663	C	Cromwell G-4 & Coast Wholesale CW-4	1937
669	C	KHG-11	1937
671	C	KG-21	1937
673	C	KG-31	1937
674	C	RK #1137 & RK #1138	1937
675	C	L-0	1937
678	C	L-30 & Black Special	1937
679	C	L-50	1937
680	C	KG-31	1937
682	C	ES-150	1937
683		EH-150	1937
686		RB-1	1937
687	C	KHG-14	1937
688	C	L-5 "Special"	1937
690	C	L-0	1937
691	C	S-1	1937
692	C	HG-00	1937
694	C	RK #1110, #1111 & #1140	1937
695	C	Kalamazoo "Sport"	1937
696	C	L-30	1937
698	C	EPG-150 & ETG-150	1937
699	C	L-Century	1937
700		EH-150 "8 string"	1937
702	C	ES-150	1937
703	C	EM-150	1937
704	C	Montgomery Ward guitar	1937
706	C	KG-11	1937
707	C	KG-11	1937
710	C	L-50	1937

FON		Model	Production Year
712	C	KG-11	1937
713	C	Kalamazoo "Sport"	1937
714	C	KG-21 & KHG-21	1937
715	C	KG-11 & KHG-11	1937
716	C	KG-31 "Special"	1937
736	C	KG-31	1937
746		EH-150	1937
754		HG "double neck"	1937
761	C	KG-14	1937
764	C	KG-21	1937
768	C	KG-11	1937
770	C	Advanced Jumbo	1937
773		EHG "10-string"	1937
774	C	KG-21	1937
780	C	Black Special	1937
783	C	RK #1140	1937
787	C	KHG-11	1937
788	C	KHG-14	1937
804	C	RK #1115	1937
806		TB-3	1937
815	C	A-50	1937
819	C	L-30	1937
821	C	RK #1012	1937
822	C	L-00	1937
824	C	KG-21	1937
825	C	KG-21	1937
850	C	KG-31	1937
851	C	L-30	1937
859	C	KG-31	1937
875	C	Cromwell G-4	1937
877	C	J-35	1937
878	C	L-30	1937
880	C	L-37	1937
882	C	ES-150	1937
885	C	RK #1127	1937
888	C	KG-31	1937
890	C	KG-21	1937
892	C	Black Special #2	1937
894	C	RK #1110 & #1111	1937
909	C	TB-4	1937
918	C	Black Special #2	1937
920	C	MB-1	1937
925	C	L-30	1937
936	C	Advanced Jumbo	1937

1937 FON Series (continued)

FON		Model	Production Year
940	C	KG-21	1937
942	C	L-7	1937
950	C	L-7	1937
951	C	L-7	1937
976	C	J-35	1937
978	C	Advanced Jumbo	1937
990		PB-1	1937
996		EH-150	1937
997		EH-150	1937
998		EH-150	1937
1001	C	KG-21	1937
1002	C	KG-21	1937
1004	C	KG-21	1937
1008	C	KG-21	1937
1057		MB-11	1937
1071	C	J-35	1937
1090	C	RK #1128 & RK #1270	1937
1109		TB-11 & MB-11	1937
1112		RB-2	1937
1113		EH-150	1937
1114		EH-150	1937
1115		TB-1	1937
1117		MB-1	1937
1123		TB-3	1937
1156		TB-1	1937
1166		PB-1	1937
1167		RB-1	1937
1176		RB-1	1937
1178	C	KG-31	1937
1188		EH-150	1937
1190	C	KG-11	1937
1192	C	KG-14	1937
1193	C	KHG-11	1937
1194	C	L-00	1937
1199	C	L-50 or L-00?	1937
1200	C	L-30	1937
1201	C	L-37	1937
1202	C	TG-50	1937
1203	C	A-00	1937
1205	C	A-1	1937
1208	C	ES-150	1937
1209	C	L-30	1937
1210	C	L-37	1937
1211	C	L-Century	1937

FON		Model	Production Year
1212	C	L-75	1937
1213	C	KG-14	1937
1214	C	KG-14	1937
1215	C	L-00	1937
1217	C	KG-21 & KG "Special"	1937
1218	C	Reznick Radio Special	1937
1219	C	KG-11	1937
1221		EH-150 "double neck"	1937
1223		TB-3	1937
1224	C	Advanced Jumbo	1937
1226	C	KG-21	1937
1227	C	ETG-150	1937
1229	C	A-1	1937
1230	C	L-37	1937
1231	C	L-30 & Black Special	1937
1232	C	L-50	1937
1233	C	TG-50	1937
1234	C	Coast Wholesale CW-4	1937
1235		EH-100	1937
1236		EH-100	1937
1237		EH-150	1937
1238		EH-150	1937
1239		EH-150	1937
1240	C	KM-11	1937
1241	C	KG-14	1937
1243	C	KG-11	1937
1244	C	Cromwell G-4, Capital J-2 & Coast Wholesale CW-4	1937
1247	C	ES-150	1937
1250	C	KJ "mando-bass"	1937
1251	C	KG-11 "Reznick Radio Special"	1937
1252	C	L-30 & L-37	1937
1253	C	L-37	1937
1254	C	L-50	1937
1255	C	TG-50	1937
1256	C	KG-31 "Special"	1937
1258	C	L-Century	1937
1259	C	L-00	1937
1260	C	L-00	1937
1261	C	L-30	1937
1262	C	L-50	1937
1263	C	KG-31	1937
1265	C	L-30	1937
1266	C	Black Special #4	1937
1267	C	KG-31	1937

1937 FON Series (continued)

FON		Model	Production Year
1268	C	KG-31 & KTG-31	1937
1269	C	L-00	1937
1270	C	L-00	1937
1271	C	L-30	1937
1272	C	L-37	1937
1274	C	Cromwell G-4, Capital J-2 & Coast Wholesale CW-4	1937
1277	C	"custom guitars"	1937
1280	C	A-00	1937
1281	C	KG-21	1937
1282	C	A-50	1937
1283	C	S-1	1937
1284	C	J-35	1937
1285	C	L-30 & Black Special #2	1937
1286	C	L-50	1937
1287	C	KG-31, Cromwell G-4 & G-14, Capital J-2, J-16 & Coast CW-4	1937
1288		RB-3	1937
1289		TB-3	1937
1290	C	KG-14	1937
1291	C	KG-21	1937
1294	C	L-00	1937
1302	C	A-00	1937
1303	C	A-Century	1937
1304	C	HG-00	1937
1306		MB-3	1937
1308	C	KG-14	1937
1309	C	KG-14	1937
1310	C	KG-21	1937
1315		RB-1	1937
1317	C	KG "Special"	1937
1318		EH-100	1937
1319		EH-150	1937
1321	C	L-00	1937
1322	C	L-00	1937
1323	C	J-35	1937
1324	C	L-30 & Black Special	1937
1325	C	L-37	1937
1326	C	KG-21	1937
1327	C	ETG-150	1937
1330	C	KG-11	1937
1331	C	PG-37	1937
1332	C	RK #1285	1937
1336	C	ES-150	1937
1337	C	A-00	1937
1341	C	L-30	1937

FON		Model	Production Year
1344	C	L-50	1937
1345		S-1 or TB-3?	1937
1346	C	L-00	1937
1347	C	Black Special	1937
1348	C	L-30 & L-37	1937
1349	C	L-50	1937
1350	C	TG-50	1937
1352	C	L-37	1937
1353		MB-1	1937
1356	C	KG-31	1937
1357	C	EM-150	1937
1359	C	L-Century	1937
1362	C	L-50	1937
1363	C	KG-11	1937
1366	C	KG-14	1937
1367	C	KG-31	1937
1368	C	KG-21	1937
1370	C	KM-21	1937
1371	C	A-00	1937
1372	C	L-30	1937
1373	C	L-30 & L-37	1937
1374	C	TG-30 & Capital J-16	1937
1377	C	L-00	1937
1379	C	L-00 & L-1	1937
1387	C	L-00	1937
1388	C	Black Special	1937
1389	C	L-50	1937
1391	C	RK #1129	1937
1392		TB-7	1937
1393		TB-12	1937
1394		TB-18	1937
1396	C	L-5	1937
1398	C	PG-4	1937
1399	C	L-5	1937
1548	C	L-7	1937
1630	C	KG-31	1937
1709		MB-11	1937
1800	C	L-30	1937
1810	C	KG-21	1937
1824	C	L-30	1937
1825	C	L-37	1937
1867	C	KG-31	1937
1868	C	KG-21	1937
1872	C	L-30	1937

1937 FON Series (continued)

FON		Model	Production Year
1873	C	L-37	1937
1886	C	ES-150	1937
1896	C	L-5	1937
1962	C	L-Century	1937
1963	C	KG-31	1937
2549	C	Reznick Radio Special	1937

Jazz guitar greats, and Gibson endorsers, Dick McDonough and Carl Kress, circa 1934

John Post Collection

1938 FON Series

During 1938 Gibson used FON's between 1 and 1000, with a few isolated numbers being higher. The addition of a letter suffix "D" occurred at the start of 1938, but only some models were singled out for that distinction. The rationale for the "D" suffix is not clear. No duplication of numbers is seen between FON's with a letter suffix "D" and those without. This suggests that the letter suffix was added later on the production floor and was not part of the original pre-printed form used in the weekly production meetings. Some 1937 FON's with a letter "C" suffix (like 563-C) were carried over into 1938 and the 1938 instruments then received a "D" suffix (becoming 563-D.) This seems to be the case where production of a batch occurred at the end of 1937 and was prolonged into 1938. Many FON's from this period remain to be discovered, and the following table is not meant to be all-inclusive.

FON		Model	Production Year
4	D	L-37 & L-75	1938
6	D	L-Century	1938
7	D	L-75	1938
11	D	GS-35 (gut-string guitar)	1938
13	D	SJ-200	1938
14	D	H-0	1938
15	D	SJ-200	1938
22	D	L-Century	1938
26	D	RK #1128	1938
28	D	S-1	1938
34	D	RK #1123 & Washburn #5246 (Tonk Brothers)	1938
35	D	Black Special	1938
37	D	L-4	1938
38	D	Black Special	1938
39	D	L-75	1938
40	D	GS-85 (gut-string guitar)	1938
41	D	GS-35 (gut-string guitar)	1938
44	D	SJ-200	1938
59	D	Advanced Jumbo	1938
63	D	S-1	1938
74	D	Cromwell G-5	1938
76	D	SJ-200	1938
77	D	S-1	1938
78	D	L-Century	1938
79	D	L-Century	1938
89	D	J-35	1938
90	D	Advanced Jumbo	1938
93	D	Advanced Jumbo	1938
94	D	Small-body special	1938
98	D	Advanced Jumbo	1938
100	D	TG-0	1938
109	D	TG-50	1938
116	D	SJ-200	1938
128	D	Black Special	1938
133		TB-1	1938

1938 FON Series (continued)

FON		Model	Production Year
134		TB-75	1938
137	D	L-37	1938
138	D	RK #1027	1938
141	D	ETG-100	1938
158	D	Black Special	1938
176	D	L-37	1938
183	D	RK #1110	1938
187	D	Advanced Jumbo	1938
191	D	L-37	1938
256	D	Black Special	1938
267	D	Cromwell G-5	1938
269	D	Cromwell G-5	1938
291	D	TG-30	1938
312	D	RK #1171 (M-5)	1938
326	D	Cromwell G-6	1938
328	D	Cromwell G-5	1938
340	D	KG-21	1938
376	D	L-37	1938
382	D	EM-150	1938
409		RB-7	1938
410		PB-7	1938
411		RB-12	1938
412		PB-12	1938
439	D	Advanced Jumbo	1938
441		TB-1 & PB-1	1938
444		PB-4	1938
447	D	Cromwell G-4	1938
461	D	KG-21	1938
470	D	KGN-12	1938
502		EHG "10-string"	1938
524	D	KHG-11	1938
534	D	RK #1115	1938
563	D	RK #1115	1938
569	D	Cromwell G-5	1938
570	D	J-35	1938
575	D	Cromwell G-5	1938
583	D	Black Special	1938
585	D	Cromwell G-4	1938
592	D	RK #1123	1938
593	D	RK #1123	1938
595	D	RK #1010, #1110 & #1140	1938
611	D	ETG-150	1938
622	D	ES-150	1938
627	D	L-30, L-37 & Special #3	1938

FON		Model	Production Year
631	D	KG-21	1938
634	D	Black Special	1938
637	D	Black Special	1938
654		PB-75	1938
655	D	UB-4	1938
663	D	Advanced Jumbo	1938
664		TB-75	1938
666		RB-7	1938
667		RB-12	1938
668		RB-18	1938
677	D	H-0	1938
681	D	KG-21	1938
685	D	Black Special	1938
687	D	Black Special	1938
693		RB-1	1938
703	D	RK #1110	1938
704	D	RK #1137	1938
708	D	A-50	1938
709	D	L-Century	1938
711	D	L-37	1938
713	D	Kalamazoo "Sport"	1938
716	D	Kalamazoo "Sport"	1938
718	D	RK #1136	1938
719		EH-100	1938
723	D	L-Century	1938
726	D	RK #1134	1938
728	D	Black Special	1938
729	D	ES-150	1938
730	D	TG-37	1938
735	D	Black Special	1938
736	D	L-30	1938
737	D	L-37	1938
740	D	TG-37	1938
741	D	TG-30	1938
743		RB-1	1938
744		RB-18	1938
747	D	Cromwell G-4, Coast Wholesale CW-4 & Capital J-16	1938
751	D	L-37	1938
752		RB-75	1938
755	D	Kalamazoo "Sport"	1938
756	D	L-50	1938
757	D	HG-00	1938
758	D	Black Special & Special #3	1938
760	D	TG-37	1938

1938 FON Series (continued)

FON		Model	Production Year
761	D	KG-21	1938
764		TB-18	1938
765	D	L-50	1938
766	D	KTG-14	1938
767	D	KG-21	1938
770		PB-12	1938
774	D	L-50	1938
775	D	L-30, Black Special & Special #3	1938
776	D	L-37 & Black Special #2	1938
779	D	KHG-14	1938
781	D	L-37	1938
782	D	RK #1009	1938
783	D	RK #1010, #1110, #1111, #1127 & #1140	1938
785	D	Black Special	1938
786	D	L-30	1938
787	D	Cromwell TG-4 & RK #1137	1938
788	D	Black Special	1938
789	D	ES-150	1938
790	D	L-30 & Black Special #2	1938
791	D	L-37 & Black Special	1938
800	D	UB-4	1938
801	D	F-5	1938
804	D	Advanced Jumbo	1938
808	D	H-0 “12-string”	1938
809	D	L-50	1938
811	D	ETG-150	1938
812	D	Francis Day & Hunter “Special”	1938
814	D	RK #1136	1938
822	D	ES-150	1938
826	D	KK-31 “mando-cello”	1938
833		TB-1	1938
835	D	L-75	1938
836		MB-3	1938
837	D	Special 3	1938
838	D	KTG-14	1938
839	D	ETG-150	1938
840	D	L-75	1938
844	D	A-1	1938
858	D	Cromwell G-4	1938
860	D	RK #1127 & RK #1128	1938
861	D	KG-21	1938
865	D	SJ-200 “Special”	1938
866	D	Cromwell G-4	1938
871	D	RK #1012, RK #1127 & RK #1128	1938

FON		Model	Production Year
879	D	Gibson Special Flattop	1938
882	D	EM-150	1938
883	D	Advanced Jumbo	1938
885	D	RK #1127 & RK #1128	1938
886	D	Capital J-16 & Cromwell G-4	1938
887	D	Advanced Jumbo	1938
888	D	RK #1123	1938
892	D	EM-150	1938
893	D	Coast Wholesale CW-4, Cromwell G-4 & Capital J-16	1938
894	D	KM-21	1938
895	D	A-1 & RK #1010	1938
899	D	J-35	1938
900	D	Capital JTG-20 & Cromwell TG-4	1938
902	D	HG-00	1938
904	D	Advanced Jumbo	1938
905	D	A-50	1938
906	D	S-1	1938
910	D	KTG-21	1938
912		PB-7	1938
914	D	RK #1124	1938
917	D	Capital J-20 & Cromwell TG-4	1938
924	D	H-0	1938
925	D	KHG-11	1938
940	D	KTG-11 & KTG-21	1938
941	D	L-00	1938
950	D	RK #1123	1938
952	D	EM-150	1938
958	D	EM-150	1938
959	D	A-1	1938
961	D	RK #1124	1938
975	D	A-1	1938
981	D	SJ-200	1938
983	D	L-75	1938
985	D	EM-150	1938
987		RB-2	1938
998		RB-75	1938
999	D	SJ-200	1938
1063	D	Cromwell TG-4	1938
1666	D	KTG-31	1938
1737	D	L-37	1938

1939 FON Series

During 1939 Gibson used FON's between 1 and 980, with a few isolated numbers being higher. The addition of a letter suffix "E" occurred at the start of 1939, but only some models were singled out for that distinction. The rationale for the "E" suffix is not clear. No duplication of numbers is seen between FON with a letter suffix "E" and those without. This suggests that the letter suffix was added later on the production floor and was not part of the original pre-printed form used in the weekly production meetings. Many FON's from this period remain to be discovered, and the following table is not meant to be all inclusive. Data in this table was obtained mostly from shipping ledgers. Very few 1939 FON's are presented because by that time Gibson's shipping clerks were not recording as much information about the instruments.

FON		Model	Production Year
145	E	TG-50	1939
149	E	L-4	1939
171	E	Special #3	1939
200		EM-100	1939
201	E	L-Century	1939
206	E	SJ "Special - Experimental"	1939
211	E	L-75	1939
218	E	Advanced Jumbo	1939
232	E	ES-150	1939
269	E	Advanced Jumbo	1939
419		EH-100	1939
423	E	SJ-100	1939
490	E	KG-21	1939
500		RB-18	1939
546	E	SJ-100	1939
550	E	J-35	1939
589	E	KG-22	1939
595	E	KG-12	1939
597	E	RK #1127	1939
612	E	J-35	1939
615	E	Special #5	1939
655	E	Special #5	1939
763		TB-7 & PB-7	1939
856		TB-18	1939
857		PB-18	1939
926	E	ES-100	1939
936	E	ES-100	1939
938		PB-7	1939
981		RB-1	1939
1218	E	Advanced Jumbo	1939
2446	E	KG-31	1939

1940-1945 FON Series

The FON's used by Gibson during the period 1940-1945 appear to be all one continuous set and range between 1 and 7900, with a few isolated numbers being higher. The addition of a letter suffix continued with "F" being used at the start of 1940, "G" at the start of 1941, and "H" used from 1942 through 1945. Inexplicably, other batches during the same period received a letter *prefix* of "E", "F" or "G" seemingly without regard to the production year. Some batches continued to receive no letter at all (prefix or suffix.) No duplication of numbers is seen for those with a letter or without. This suggests that the letter suffix (or prefix) was added later on the production floor and was not part of the original pre-printed form used in the weekly production meetings. Many FON's from this period remain to be discovered, and the following table is not meant to be all-inclusive. The data in this table was mainly extracted from shipping ledgers. A date range (i.e. 1940-44) indicates that no specific year could be determined.

FON			Model	Production Year
	5	F	MEH	1940
	29	G	L-00	1941
	30	G	L-00	1941
	84	G	L-30	1941
	91	F	ES-150	1940
E	103		ETB	1940-44
	123	G	HG-00	1941
	166	F	J-55	1940
	167	F	SJ-100	1940
	168	F	SJ-200	1940
	200	G	EM-100	1941
	203	F	KM-12	1940
E	215		ES-100	1940-44
E	229		TB-11	1940-44
	247	F	Special #3	1940
	248	F	Special #5	1940
	249	G	TG-50	1941
G	251		J-55	1940-44
	264	F	KG-22	1940
	265	F	RK #1121	1940
F	289		KEH	1940-44
F	298		KEHR & MEH	1940-44
	303	F	KGN-32	1940
	304	F	KGN-12	1940
	305	F	KMN-12	1940
F	312		Console Grande	1940-44
	314	G	A-1	1941
E	317		RB-00	1940-44
	320		J-45	1940-45
F	321		EH-150	1940-44
F	322		Console Grande	1940-44
	328	F	RK #1114	1940
	331	F	L-47	1940
	339	F	Special #3	1940
	366		Southerner Jumbo	1940-45

1940-1945 FON Series (continued)

FON			Model	Production Year
	372		Southerner Jumbo	1940-45
F	380		UB-4 & UB-5	1940-44
	393	G	KG-22	1941
E	397		KTB	1940-44
F	397		KTB	1940-44
F	398		KRB	1940-44
	399	F	Special #3	1940
	400	G	KES	1941
	428	G	KG-12	1941
F	440		MB-11	1940-44
F	441		RB-11	1940-44
F	442		PB-11	1940-44
	444	F	A-50 & EM-150	1940
	449	F	ES-100	1940
	451	F	L-0	1940
F	453		RB-75	1940-44
E	454		PB-75	1940-44
	466		LG-2	1940-45
	480	G	J-35	1941
	483		J-45	1940-45
	499		EH "Double Neck"	1940-45
	501	F	TG-50	1940
	515	F	KGN-32	1940
	521	F	J-35	1940
	522	F	J-55	1940
F	532		EH-150 & EH-185	1940-44
	552	F	ES-150	1940
F	552		ES-150	1940-44
F	559		RB-00	1940-44
F	560		TB-00	1940-44
	561		Southerner Jumbo	1940-45
	561	F	ES-100	1940
	564	F	Special #5	1940
	565	F	F-4	1940
	577	G	ES-150 (TG)	1941
	584	G	L-30	1941
	607	F	J-35	1940
	610	F	L-0	1940
F	611		EH-185	1940-44
F	612		EH-100	1940-44
F	614		RB-1	1940-44
	630	F	L-50	1940
	633		Southerner Jumbo	1940-45
	642		LG-2	1940-45

FON			Model	Production Year
F	649		Console Grande	1940-44
F	662		TB-7	1940-44
F	663		MB-11	1940-44
	666	F	A-00 & EM-150	1940
F	668		TB-11	1940-44
	668	G	KGN-32	1941
	669	F	SJ-100	1940
	682	F	J-35	1940
	683	F	SJ-100	1940
F	685		KM-12	1940-44
	686	F	Super 400	1940
F	688		TB-11	1940-44
F	689		EPB-150	1940-44
F	690		RB-7	1940-44
F	691		EH-185	1940-44
F	692		EH-185	1940-44
	692	F	ES-150	1940
	693	F	KM-22	1940
	695	F	KMN-12	1940
	696	F	SJ-100	1940
	711	F	SJ-200	1940
	711	G	J-50	1941
	720	H	ES-125	1942-45
	730	F	L-50	1940
	744	F	ES-150	1940
	746	F	EM-150	1940
	749	F	SJ-100	1940
	754	F	J-55	1940
	757	F	A-50	1940
	758	F	J-55	1940
	759	F	ES-100	1940
	760	F	L-50 & ES-150	1940
F	761		RB-00	1940-45
F	762		TB-7 & PB-7	1940-45
	766	F	J-35	1940
F	771		KEH & KEHR	1940-45
	773	H	L-50	1942-45
E	780		EPB-150	1940-45
E	781		EPB	1940-45
	785	F	J-35	1940
	797	F	L-5	1940
	799	F	Special #3	1940
	801	F	ES-100	1940
	802	F	L-00 & Special #5	1940

1940-1945 FON Series (continued)

FON			Model	Production Year
	803	F	A-00, EM-125 & EM-150	1940
	805	F	H-0	1940
	808	F	J-55	1940
	812	F	ES-100	1940
F	813		EH-150	1940-44
	813	F	ES-100 & ES-125	1940
	814	F	ES-150	1940
	816	F	EM-150	1940
	819	F	L-50	1940
	824	F	ES-100	1940
F	826		EH-185	1940-44
	831	F	HG-00	1940
F	832		EH-150 & EH-185	1940-44
	834	F	ES-100	1940
	839	G	L-37	1941
F	871		TB-75	1940-44
	874	F	L-5	1940
F	881		MB-00	1940-44
	883	F	ES-150	1940
	883	G	ES-150	1941
	888		LG-2	1940-45
	888	F	ES-150	1940
	893	F	RK #1137	1940
	894	F	RK #969	1940
	896	F	SJ-100	1940
F	897		EH-100	1940-44
F	899		EH-100	1940-44
	902	F	KG-12	1940
	903		L-50	1940-45
	904	F	KGN-12	1940
	905		L-50	1940-45
F	906		RB-75	1940-44
F	907		Console Grande	1940-44
	909	F	Special 3 & Special 5	1940
F	910		SJ-100	1940-44
	911	F	KG "Sport"	1940
	911	G	KG "Sport"	1941
	912	F	ES-150	1940
	914		Southerner Jumbo	1940-45
	916		J-45	1940-45
	918	F	TB-12 & PB-12	1940
	920	F	RK #1028	1940
F	924		EH-100	1940-44
F	925		EH-150	1940-44

FON			Model	Production Year
	926	F	ES-100	1940
	927	F	RK #1028	1940
	929	F	RK #1101	1940
	933	F	RK #1137	1940
	934	F	RK #1127	1940
	935	F	Black Special	1940
	936	G	L-75	1941
	937	F	L-50 & ES-150	1940
	942	F	RK #1052	1940
F	943		TB-75	1940-44
	943	F	RK "Ray Whitley"	1940
	944	F	J-35	1940
	945	F	L-5	1940
	946	F	A-00	1940
F	961		EH-185	1940-44
	961	F	ES-100	1940
F	963		TB-7	1940-44
	963	F	A-50	1940
	965	F	L-00	1940
	966	F	J-35	1940
	966	G	J-45	1941
F	967		MB-00	1940-44
E	968		EH-150 "new style"	1940-44
F	968		EH-150 "new style"	1940-44
	969		EH-100	1940-45
F	969		EH-100	1940-44
	973	F	KN-12	1940
	982	F	J-35	1940
	998	F	ES-125	1940
F	1011		KEH & KEHR	1940-44
F	1037		EH-185	1940-44
F	1048		EH-185	1940-44
F	1049		EH-185	1940-44
	1079	F	L-37	1940
	1084	F	J-35	1940
F	1100		KEHR	1940-44
F	1101		EH-100	1940-44
	1102	G	SJ-200	1941
F	1108		Console Grande	1940-44
	1117	F	KG-22	1940
	1119	F	KG "Sport"	1940
E	1120		TB-1	1940-44
	1120	F	M "Special Haw."	1940
	1121	F	ES-125	1940

1940-1945 FON Series (continued)

FON			Model	Production Year
	1124	F	SJ-200	1940
	1158	F	KM-12 & KMN-12	1940
F	1159		TB-00	1940-44
F	1162		EH-185, EH-250 & EH-275	1940-44
	1217	F	L-30, ES-100 & ES-125	1940
	1218	F	SJ-100	1940
	1219	F	J-35	1940
	1220	F	L-00	1940
	1221	F	L-0	1940
F	1222		ETB-150	1940-44
	1225	F	Kalamazoo Oriole	1940
	1225	H	J-35	1942-45
	1227	F	KGN-12	1940
	1231	F	L-5	1940
	1233	F	L-50 & ES-150	1940
	1285	G	J-55	1941
	1330	F	KGN-12	1940
	1340	F	KGN-12	1940
	1342	F	A-00	1940
	1355	F	EM-150	1940
	1405	F	Special #5	1940
F	1408		Console Grande	1940-44
	1410	F	KGN-32	1940
	1411	F	KG-12	1940
	1423	F	KGN-12	1940
F	1426		EH-100	1940-44
F	1428		MEH	1940-44
F	1429		MEHG & KEHR	1940-44
	1446	F	ES-100	1940
	1446	G	ES-125	1941
	1447	F	ES-100 & ES-125	1940
	1448	F	L-30 & ES-100	1940
	1449	F	L-30 & ES-125	1940
	1449	G	ES-100	1941
	1450	F	L-50 & ES-150	1940
	1451	F	ES-150	1940
	1453	F	L-50 & ES-150	1940
	1454	F	ES-150	1940
	1457	F	KG-12	1940
	1461	F	Special #5	1940
	1462	F	Special #3	1940
	1463	F	J-35	1940
	1464	F	J-35 "Blonde Natural"	1940
	1465	F	J-35	1940

FON			Model	Production Year
	1466	F	L-0	1940
	1469	F	H-0	1940
	1479	F	ETG-150	1940
E	1480		EH-185	1940-44
F	1480		EH-185	1940-44
F	1481		EH-150	1940-44
G	1507		KEH & KEHG	1940-44
F	1552		Console Grande	1940-44
E	1585		EH-185	1940-44
	1695	F	L-47	1940
F	1699		MB-11	1940-44
F	1700		RB-00	1940-44
	1701	F	KGN-32	1940
	1702	F	M "Special Haw."	1940
G	1705		EH-185	1940-44
F	1763		EH-150	1940-44
F	1776		EH-100	1940-44
F	1783		RB-11	1940-44
E	1784		PB-00	1940-44
F	1784		PB-00	1940-44
E	1785		EH-185	1940-44
G	1785		EH-185	1940-44
G	1786		EH-100	1940-44
	1787	F	KES	1940
E	1788		RB-11	1940-44
F	1801		KRB	1940-44
	1823	F	KMN-12	1940
F	1871		TB-7	1940-44
F	1872		RB-7	1940-44
E	1915		KEH	1940-44
	1930	F	L-50 & ES-150	1940
F	1932		EH-150	1940-44
E	1950		KEHG, MEHG & Werlein "Special"	1940-44
F	1950		KEHG, MEHG & Werlein "Special"	1940-44
F	1954		EH-185	1940-44
F	1969		EH-150	1940-44
	1993	F	A-50	1940
	1994	F	J-35	1940
	1995	F	Special #3	1940
E	1996		Console Grande	1940-44
F	1996		Console Grande	1940-44
	1997	F	KMN-12	1940

1940-1945 FON Series (continued)

FON			Model	Production Year
	1998	G	KG-32	1941
F	2000		EH-185	1940-44
	2002		L-50	1940-45
	2003		Southerner Jumbo	1940-45
	2004		J-45	1940-45
	2005		Southerner Jumbo	1940-45
	2006		LG-2	1940-45
	2007		L-50	1940-45
F	2008		MB-00	1940-44
	2009		ES-125	1940-45
	2019		Southerner Jumbo	1940-45
	2022		Southerner Jumbo	1940-45
	2029		L-50	1940-45
	2030		L-50	1940-45
F	2031		ETB-150	1940-44
	2032		L-50	1940-45
F	2046		UB-2	1940-44
F	2047		EH "11-string"	1940-44
	2059		LG-2	1940-45
E	2088		ETB-150	1940-44
	2089	F	KG-32	1940
F	2099		EH-185	1940-44
	2109		J-45	1940-45
	2110		Southerner Jumbo	1940-45
	2111		LG-2	1940-45
	2119		Southerner Jumbo	1940-45
	2130		LG-2	1940-45
	2132		L-50	1940-45
	2139		Southerner Jumbo	1940-45
	2142		J-45	1940-45
	2143		J-45	1940-45
	2144		KM-11	1940-45
	2148		LG-2	1940-45
	2149		J-45	1940-45
	2150		Southerner Jumbo	1940-45
	2150	F	KG-12	1940
	2153	F	KMN-12	1940
	2168		LG-2	1940-45
	2177	G	L-0	1941
	2191		LG-2	1940-45
	2192		J-45	1940-45
	2193		LG-2	1940-45
F	2199		EH-275	1940-44
	2209		L-50	1940-45

FON			Model	Production Year
	2210		L-50	1940-45
	2211		L-50	1940-45
	2219		LG-2	1940-45
	2220		J-45	1940-45
	2221		J-45	1940-45
	2222		J-45	1940-45
	2224		Southerner Jumbo	1940-45
	2225		Southerner Jumbo	1940-45
	2238		A-1	1940-45
	2240	F	KG-12	1940
E	2241		KEH	1940-44
E	2242		Werlein "Special"	1940-44
E	2243		MEHG & Werlein "Special"	1940-44
F	2243		MEHG & Werlein "Special"	1940-44
E	2244		MEHG & KEH	1940-44
F	2244		MEHG & KEH	1940-44
F	2258		TB-11	1940-44
F	2259		RB-00	1940-44
	2261	F	KG "Sport"	1940
G	2285		ETB-150	1940-44
	2287	G	L-00	1941
	2288		TB-11	1940-45
	2289	G	Special #5	1941
	2290	G	ES-100 & ES-125	1941
	2291	G	L-37	1941
	2292	G	ES-150	1941
E	2295		RB-00	1940-44
G	2297		TB-00	1940-44
E	2298		TB-11	1940-44
E	2299		RB-11	1940-44
	2300	G	KES	1941
	2301	G	KG-22	1941
	2302	G	KHG-12	1941
G	2306		KRB	1940-44
E	2310		KEH	1940-44
	2313		LG-2	1940-45
	2314		J-45	1940-45
	2315		J-45	1940-45
	2316		J-45	1940-45
	2317		Southerner Jumbo	1940-45
	2318		Southerner Jumbo	1940-45
	2322		ETB	1940-45
	2353		PB-18	1940-45
	2363		L-50	1940-45

1940-1945 FON Series (continued)

FON			Model	Production Year
	2364		J-45	1940-45
E	2371		EH-150	1940-44
F	2371		EH-150	1940-44
	2372	G	KGN-12	1941
	2375	G	KM-12	1941
	2376	G	L-37 & ES-125	1941
	2377	G	L-30 & ES-125	1941
	2380	G	L-0	1941
	2381	G	L-00	1941
	2385		Southerner Jumbo	1940-45
	2395		LG-2	1940-45
	2396		LG-2	1940-45
	2405		L-50	1940-45
	2407		J-45	1940-45
	2408		J-45	1940-45
	2409		J-45	1940-45
	2411		LG-2	1940-45
	2412		LG-2	1940-45
	2414		L-50	1940-45
F	2418		KEH & MEHG	1940-44
	2420		J-45	1940-45
	2424		Southerner Jumbo	1940-45
	2426		Southerner Jumbo	1940-45
	2431		Southerner Jumbo	1940-45
	2447	G	L-37	1941
	2454		J-45	1940-45
	2455		J-45	1940-45
E	2465		EH-150	1940-44
	2476		RB-00	1940-45
	2500	G	KES	1941
	2505	G	L-30, L-37 & Special #3	1941
	2506	G	A-1 & EM-150	1941
	2507	G	ES-150	1941
	2509	G	KG-22	1941
	2513		J-45	1940-45
	2515		J-45	1940-45
F	2518		EH-100	1940-44
E	2538		EH-185	1940-44
F	2538		EH-185	1940-44
	2539		A-50	1940-45
F	2544		EH-100 & KEH	1940-44
	2549		J-45	1940-45
	2550		J-45	1940-45
	2551		A-50	1940-45

FON			Model	Production Year
	2553		J-45	1940-45
	2554	G	Special #7	1941
	2555	G	Special #7	1941
	2556		J-50	1940-45
	2558		J-45	1940-45
	2565		J-45	1940-45
	2569		J-45	1940-45
E	2570		MEHG	1940-44
	2576	G	KG-22	1941
	2577	G	KES	1941
	2578	G	KES	1941
	2580		A-50	1940-45
	2583	G	KG-12	1941
	2585	G	L-47	1941
	2586	G	J-35	1941
	2587	G	J-35	1941
	2588	G	J-35 "Natural"	1941
	2621		LG-2	1940-45
	2633		Southerner Jumbo	1940-45
	2649		LG-1	1940-45
	2650		LG-1	1940-45
	2652		A-50	1940-45
	2655		J-45	1940-45
	2667		J-45	1940-45
	2669		LG-2	1940-45
	2670	G	J-55	1941
	2671	G	SJ-100	1941
E	2672		TB-7	1940-44
	2678		LG-2	1940-45
	2681		J-45	1940-45
	2684		J-45	1940-45
	2685		Southerner Jumbo	1940-45
	2686		A-50	1940-45
	2697		LG-2	1940-45
	2711		A-50	1940-45
	2712		J-45	1940-45
	2719		National	1940-45
	2727	G	H-1	1941
	2730		J-45	1940-45
	2732		J-45	1940-45
	2735		Southerner Jumbo	1940-45
	2739	G	L-00	1941
	2740		LG-2	1940-45
E	2744		EH-150	1940-44

1940-1945 FON Series (continued)

FON			Model	Production Year
	2745		Southerner Jumbo	1940-45
E	2750		MEH	1940-44
E	2753		TB-18	1940-44
	2755		ES-125	1940-45
	2756		TB-7	1940-45
	2758		RB-75	1940-45
	2762		J-45	1940-45
	2776		L-50	1940-45
	2777		L-50	1940-45
	2778	G	Special #3	1941
	2779	G	Special #5	1941
	2780	G	ES-125	1941
	2781	G	ES-100 & ES-125	1941
	2782	G	L-50 & ES-150	1941
	2783	G	ES-150	1941
	2785	G	L-50	1941
E	2788		TB-75 & RB-75	1940-44
E	2789		RB-00	1940-44
E	2790		RB-11	1940-44
E	2791		RB-7	1940-44
	2792	G	KM-12	1941
	2793	G	KM-12	1941
	2794	G	KM-12	1941
	2801	G	KGN-12	1941
	2804		KTB	1940-45
	2806		KRB	1940-45
	2816		LG-2	1940-45
	2827		Southerner Jumbo	1940-45
	2841		KRB	1940-45
	2860	G	ES-150	1941
	2868		LG-2	1940-45
	2886		RB-7	1940-45
	2890		J-45	1940-45
	2904		J-45	1940-45
	2907		J-45	1940-45
E	2914		EH-150	1940-44
F	2914		EH-150	1940-44
E	2915		KEH	1940-44
E	2923		MB-11	1940-44
	2924	G	mandolin	1941
	2928	G	L-0	1941
	2929		L-50	1940-45
	2938		LG-2	1940-45
	2943		J-50	1940-45

FON			Model	Production Year
	2944		J-45	1940-45
	2959		J-45	1940-45
	2961		LG-2	1940-45
	2967		TB-75	1940-45
	2972		J-45	1940-45
	2981		Southerner Jumbo	1940-45
E	2988		ETB-150	1940-44
	2999	G	L-0	1941
	3000	G	L-00	1941
	3001	G	J-35	1941
	3002	G	J-55	1941
E	3003		TB-00	1940-44
E	3004		MB-00	1940-44
	3005	G	KM-12	1941
	3006	G	KM-12	1941
	3009	G	KGN-12	1941
	3012	G	KGN-32	1941
E	3015		KRB	1940-44
	3067	G	Mastertone Special "Haw."	1941
	3082	G	L-50 & ES-150	1941
E	3120		TB-11	1940-44
E	3121		PB-11	1940-44
E	3122		RB-11	1940-44
	3167		TB-11	1940-45
	3168	G	SJ-200	1941
E	3171		RB-00	1940-44
F	3171		RB-00	1940-44
E	3210		KEH	1940-44
	3216	G	KGN-12	1941
	3221	G	KMN-12	1941
	3222	G	KMN-12	1941
	3223	G	ES-125	1941
	3224	G	J-35	1941
	3225	G	J-35	1941
	3226	G	EM-125 & EM-150	1941
E	3280		EH-185	1940-44
E	3281		PB-7	1940-44
	3285	G	J-55	1941
	3299	G	J-50	1941
	3301	G	KES	1941
	3303	G	L-30	1941
	3304	G	A mandolin	1941
E	3307		KEH	1940-44
E	3317		TB-1	1940-44

1940-1945 FON Series (continued)

FON			Model	Production Year
E	3347		TB "Spc.," TB-75 & TB-Florentine	1940-44
	3357		RB-00	1940-45
	3369	G	ES-300	1941
E	3370		KTB	1940-44
	3371	G	KM-12	1941
	3372	G	A-00 & EM-125	1941
E	3374		RB-00	1940-44
	3377	G	EM-125	1941
	3378	G	ES-125	1941
	3379	G	L-50	1941
	3380	G	L-50	1941
E	3381		EH-150	1940-44
	3383	G	GS-85	1941
	3462	G	EM-150	1941
	3463	G	Black Special #4 & #5	1941
	3464	G	HG-00	1941
	3465	G	L-0	1941
E	3515		KRB	1940-44
E	3521		MEHG	1940-44
F	3521		MEHG	1940-44
	3522	G	J-35	1941
E	3526		EH-150	1940-44
	3529	G	L-30	1941
	3570	G	J-55	1941
C	3674		TB-11 & PB-11	1940-44
E	3674		TB-11 & PB-11	1940-44
F	3674		TB-11 & PB-11	1940-44
E	3675		MB-00	1940-44
	3681		J-45	1940-45
	3706	G	J-35	1941
E	3741		EH-150	1940-44
	3742	F	L-00	1940
	3743	G	J-35	1941
	3749		Southerner Jumbo	1940-45
E	3790		RB-11	1940-44
E	3791		MB-11	1940-44
E	3792		RB-00	1940-44
F	3793		TB-11	1940-44
E	3794		TB-7 or TB-75 or TB-18	1940-44
E	3795		TB-11	1940-44
E	3796		TB-00	1940-44
	3799	G	J-35	1941
	3814	G	A-00	1941
E	3815		EH-125	1940-44

FON			Model	Production Year
E	3829		EH-150 "8 string"	1940-44
	3837	G	KES	1941
	3839	G	L-30	1941
	3840	G	L-30	1941
	3842	H	Non-Gibson mandolin	1942-45
E	3847		TB "Special"	1940-44
	3860	G	ES-150	1941
E	3861		KRB	1940-44
	3881	G	KGN-32	1941
	3885	G	KG-12	1941
	3887	G	J-35	1941
	3888	G	J-35	1941
	3908		LG-2	1940-45
	3958	G	Special #5	1941
	3959	G	KG-12	1941
	3983		KTB	1940-45
	3999	G	L-0	1941
	4043		J-50	1940-45
	4044	G	L-0	1941
E	4085		EH-125	1940-44
	4090	G	A-50	1941
	4090	H	F-5	1942-45
	4091	G	F-5	1941
	4093	G	KM-12	1941
	4097	G	J-35	1941
	4098	G	SJ-100	1941
	4099	G	ES-150	1941
	4100	G	L-50	1941
	4102	G	SJ-200	1941
	4130		A-50	1940-45
E	4141		Electraharp	1940-44
	4158		TB-75	1940-45
	4160	G	TG-00	1941
	4217	H	J-35	1942-45
F	4227		EH-185	1940-44
	4228	G	L-50	1941
	4229	G	KM-12, KM-22 & KH-22	1941
	4235	G	J-45	1941
	4237		TB-00	1940-45
E	4256		TB-75	1940-44
	4258	G	L-0	1941
	4259	G	L-0	1941
	4260	G	J-55	1941
	4261	G	SJ-200	1941

1940-1945 FON Series (continued)

FON			Model	Production Year
	4262	G	ES-125	1941
E	4266		TB-75	1940-44
F	4266		TB-75	1940-44
	4268	G	KG-12	1941
	4305	G	J-35	1941
	4317		TB "Custom"	1940-45
	4363		EH-185	1940-45
	4364		EH-185	1940-45
	4365	G	J-35	1941
	4366	G	Special #5	1941
E	4370		RB-75	1940-44
	4372		Southerner Jumbo	1940-45
E	4396		RB-00	1940-44
	4409	G	EM-150	1941
E	4414		RB-00	1940-44
E	4415		RB-11	1940-44
	4419		MEHG	1940-45
	4420		MEHG	1940-45
E	4423		EH-125, EH-150 & EH-275	1940-44
	4442		A-50	1940-45
	4443		A-50	1940-45
	4467	G	SJ-100	1941
	4473	G	A-00	1941
E	4507		EH-185 "10-string"	1940-44
	4519	G	Southerner Jumbo	1941
	4520	G	Southerner Jumbo	1941
	4525	G	L-30	1941
	4526	G	ES-150	1941
	4527	G	ES-150	1941
	4528		EH-150	1940-45
	4530	G	KMN-12	1941
	4532	G	KG-12	1941
	4534	G	KG-12	1941
	4535	G	KG-12	1941
	4537	G	ES-125	1941
	4539	G	KG "Sport"	1941
E	4651		EH-150	1940-44
E	4652		EH-125 & EH-275	1940-44
F	4652		EH-125	1940-44
G	4652		EH-125	1940-44
E	4653		KRB	1940-44
	4657	G	L-00	1941
	4659	G	J-35	1941
	4660	G	J-35	1941

FON			Model	Production Year
	4690		Black Special #4	1940-45
F	4712		TB-7	1940-44
F	4713		TB-7	1940-44
	4799	G	A-00	1941
	4802	G	J-35	1941
	4803	G	J-45	1941
	4804	G	SJ-200	1941
	4935	G	J-55	1941
E	4936		RB-00	1940-44
F	4936		RB-00	1940-44
E	4937		RB-00	1940-44
	5005	G	SJ-200	1941
	5020	G	F-5	1941
	5022	G	KG-16	1941
	5036		RB-00	1940-45
	5068	G	A-1	1941
	5091		Electraharp	1940-45
	5123	G	ES-125	1941
	5126	G	L-0	1941
	5127	G	L-0	1941
	5129	G	J-35	1941
	5130	G	J-35	1941
	5131	G	J-35	1941
F	5133		KRB	1940-44
	5150	F	KG-32	1940
	5155	G	SJ-100	1941
	5220	G	F-5	1941
	5221	G	H-0	1941
	5224	G	L-00	1941
	5225	G	J-35	1941
	5226	G	J-35	1941
	5227	G	J-55	1941
	5228	G	Special #5	1941
	5229	G	Special #5	1941
	5231	G	L-30	1941
	5232	G	L-50	1941
	5234	G	KMN-12	1941
	5235	G	KES	1941
	5237	F	KGN-32	1940
	5283	G	L-00	1941
	5285	G	J-55	1941
	5291	H	A-50	1942-45
E	5300		MB-00	1940-44
	5302		RB-7	1940-45

1940-1945 FON Series (continued)

FON			Model	Production Year
E	5304		MB-00	1940-44
	5323		EH-125	1940-45
	5324		EH-125	1940-45
F	5325		EH-125	
F	5326		EH-100	
	5326	G	BR-1	1941
	5327	G	J-35	1941
	5328		EH-125	1940-45
	5328	G	GS-85	1941
	5332	G	KG-12	1941
	5333	G	KES	1941
	5335	G	KHG-12	1941
	5363		RB-00	1940-45
	5370		KTB	1940-45
	5462		TB-00	1940-45
	5479	H	EM-150	1942-45
	5526	G	J-35	1941
	5543	G	KM-12	1941
	5544	G	KM-12	1941
	5550	H	KG-22	1942-45
	5571	H	TG-50	1942-45
F	5634		MB-00	1940-44
E	5635		MB-11	1940-44
F	5635		MB-11	1940-44
F	5636		RB-00	1940-44
F	5637		TB-75	1940-44
	5638		TB-75 or PB-75	1940-45
F	5639		RB-00	1940-44
	5749	H	A-1, EM-125, EM-150	1942-45
	5754	H	KGN-12	1942-45
	5768	H	KGN-12	1942-45
	5795		TB-11	1940-45
	5814	H	S-1	1942-45
F	5815		TB-11	1940-44
F	5816		RB-75 or PB-75	1940-44
F	5818		MB-00 or MB-11	1940-44
	5820		RB-7	1940-45
	5835		PB-1	1940-45
	5878	H	ES-125	1942-45
	5880	H	A-50	1942-45
	5882		PB-7 or RB-7	1940-45
F	5883		RB-75	1940-44
	5920	H	A-1	1942-45
	5921	H	A-50	1942-45

FON			Model	Production Year
	5922	H	J-35	1942-45
F	5924		TB-11	1940-44
F	5925		MB-11	1940-44
F	5926		MB-11	1940-44
	5937		TB-75 or PB-Florentine	1940-45
	5964	H	KM-22	1942-45
	5998		TB-7	1940-45
E	6163		EH-185	1940-44
E	6348		TB-11	1940-44
F	6914		KRB	1940-44
	7017	H	Special #5	1942-45
	7029	H	KES	1942-45
	7038		EH-125	1940-45
	7039		EH-125	1940-45
	7081	H	LG-2	1942-45
	7082	H	LG-3	1942-45
	7089	H	L-0	1942-45
	7095	H	ES-150	1942-45
	7099	H	J-35	1942-45
	7102	H	L-30	1942-45
	7103	H	L-50	1942-45
	7109	H	LG-2	1942-45
	7111	H	LG-1	1942-45
	7112	H	LG-3	1942-45
	7113	H	LG-3	1942-45
	7114	H	J-45	1942-45
	7115	H	J-45	1942-45
	7116	H	J-50	1942-45
	7117	H	J-50	1942-45
	7118	H	J-50	1942-45
	7119	H	J-50	1942-45
E	7172		RB-00	1940-44
	7200	H	ES-125	1942-45
	7202	H	ES-125	1942-45
	7209	H	L-00	1942-45
	7212	H	L-00	1942-45
	7214	H	L-0	1942-45
	7216	H	L-0	1942-45
	7217	H	J-35	1942-45
	7218	H	J-35	1942-45
F	7221		EH-125	1940-44
F	7298		MEHG	1940-44
F	7299		EH-125	1940-44
F	7311		KEH	1940-44

1940-1945 FON Series (continued)

FON			Model	Production Year
F	7312		MEHG	1940-44
F	7313		KEH & MEHG	1940-44
F	7314		MEHG	1940-44
F	7315		EH-150	1940-44
F	7316		EH-125	1940-44
F	7317		EH-125	1940-44
F	7318		EH-125	1940-44
	7337		TB-00	1940-45
F	7370		EH-150	1940-44
F	7371		MEHG	1940-44
	7380	H	ES-150	1942-45
	7429	H	L-0	1942-45
	7430	H	L-0	1942-45
	7431	H	J-35	1942-45
	7432	H	J-35	1942-45
	7433	H	J-45	1942-45
	7434	H	J-45	1942-45
	7458	H	L-0	1942-45
	7460	H	L-00	1942-45
	7462	H	J-45	1942-45
	7463	H	J-45	1942-45
	7464	H	Special #3	1942-45
	7465	H	Special #3	1942-45
	7466	H	L-30 & L-37	1942-45
	7469	H	ES-125	1942-45
	7471	H	ES-150	1942-45
	7472	H	ES-150	1942-45
	7473	H	ES-150	1942-45
	7474	H	L-50	1942-45
	7476	H	KG-12	1942-45
	7477	H	KG-12	1942-45
	7478	H	KG-12	1942-45
	7480	H	KES	1942-45
	7488	H	KGN-12	1942-45
	7513		KEH	1940-45
	7515		EH-150	1940-45
	7597		ES-125	1940-45
	7612		MEHG	1940-45
	7691		EH-185	1940-45
	7702	H	J-45	1942-45
	7703	H	LG-1	1942-45
	7704	H	LG-1	1942-45
	7706	H	LG-1	1942-45
	7707	H	LG-1	1942-45

FON			Model	Production Year
	7711	H	LG-3	1942-45
	7712	H	LG-2	1942-45
	7714	H	LG-2	1942-45
	7717	H	J-50	1942-45
	7720	H	J-45	1942-45
	7721	H	J-50	1942-45
	7727	H	L-0	1942-45
	7730	H	L-50	1942-45
	7731	H	L-50	1942-45
	7732	H	L-50	1942-45
	7733	H	L-50	1942-45
	7734	H	L-50	1942-45
	7735	H	L-50	1942-45
	7737	H	Special #7	1942-45
	7931	H	KM-12	1942-45
	7941	H	A-1	1942-45
	7943	H	A-1	1942-45
	7946	H	A-1	1942-45
	8074	H	SJ	1942-45
E	8096		TB-75	1940-44
E	8928		TB-75	1940-44
E	8952		RB-1	1940-44
E	8975		PB-1	1940-44

Early mandolin orchestra

Centerstream Archives

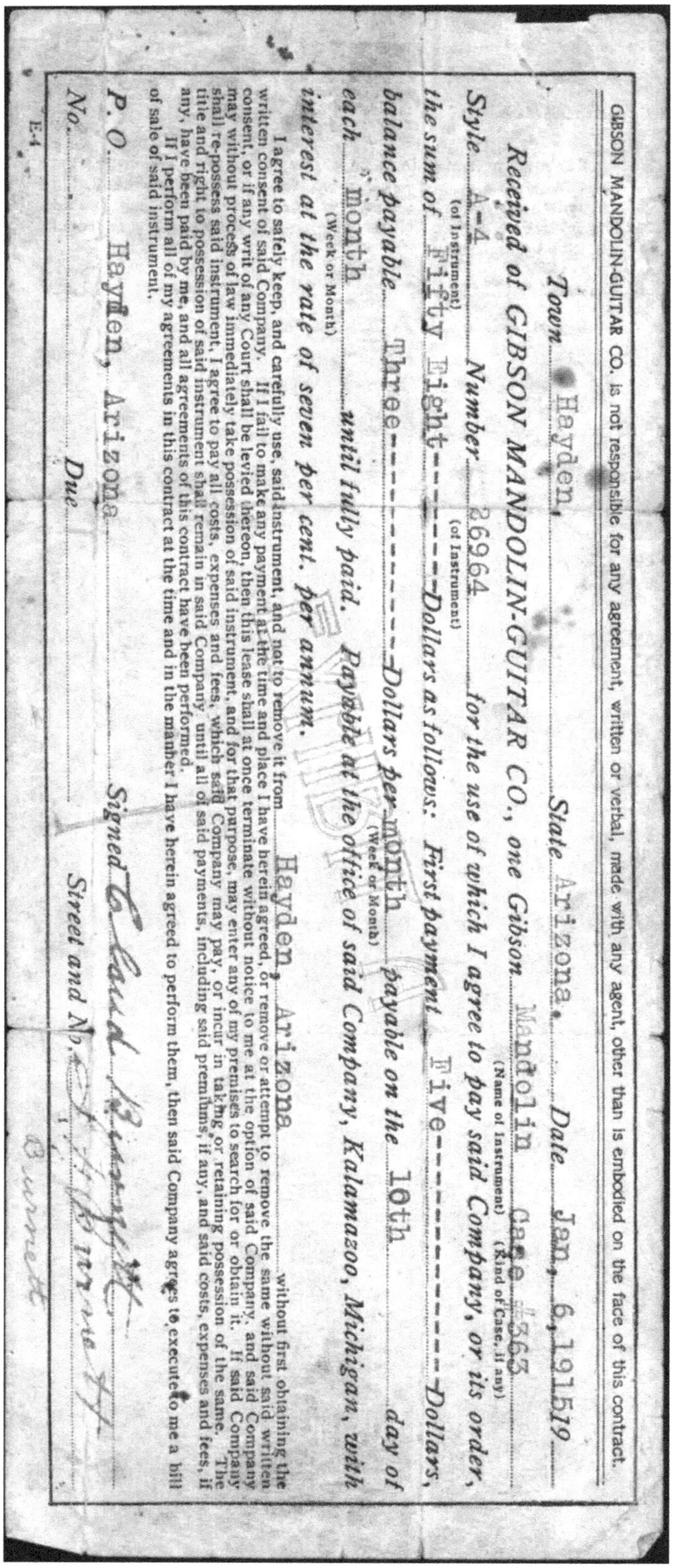

GIBSON MANDOLIN-GUITAR CO. is not responsible for any agreement, written or verbal, made with any agent, other than is embodied on the face of this contract.

Town Hayden, *State* Arizona. *Date* Jan. 6, 1915 19

Received of GIBSON MANDOLIN-GUITAR CO., one Gibson Mandolin (Name of Instrument) Case #363 (Kind of Case, if any)

Style A-4 (of Instrument) *Number* 26964 (of Instrument) *for the use of which I agree to pay said Company, or its order,*

the sum of Fifty Eight---------*Dollars as follows: First payment* Five-----------*Dollars,*

balance payable Three-----------*Dollars per* month (Week or Month) *payable on the* 10th *day of*

each month (Week or Month) *until fully paid. Payable at the office of said Company, Kalamazoo, Michigan, with interest at the rate of seven per cent. per annum.*

I agree to safely keep, and carefully use, said instrument, and not to remove it from Hayden, Arizona without first obtaining the written consent of said Company. If I fail to make any payment at the time and place I have herein agreed, or remove or attempt to remove the same without said written consent, or if any writ of any Court shall be levied thereon, then this lease shall at once terminate without notice to me at the option of said Company, and said Company may without process of law immediately take possession of said instrument, and for that purpose, may enter any of my premises to search for or obtain it. If said Company shall re-possess said instrument, I agree to pay all costs, expenses and fees, which said Company may pay, or incur in taking or retaining possession of the same. The title and right to possession of said instrument shall remain in said Company until all of said payments, including said premiums, if any, and said costs, expenses and fees, if any, have been paid by me, and all agreements of this contract have been performed.

If I perform all of my agreements in this contract at the time and in the manner I have herein agreed to perform them, then said Company agrees to execute to me a bill of sale of said instrument.

P.O. Hayden, Arizona *Signed* [illegible]

No. *Due* *Street and No.* [illegible]

E-4

This bill of sale for an A-4 mandolin (serial # 26964) shows that the instrument was produced before January 6th, 1915. Many other documents of this type were used to revise the serial number index included in this chapter.
Collection of Ron Middlebrook

Chapter 5 - Serial Numbers

Overview

During the pre-World War II period, Gibson used a separate serial number system in addition to the factory order number system covered in the preceding chapter. These two numbering systems are often confused with one another, even by knowledgeable vintage instrument experts. All Gibson instruments received a factory order number at the beginning of the production process, but not all Gibson instruments received a serial number. Higher-end guitars and mandolins received them consistently from 1902 onward. Gibson serial numbers are the best indicator of when an instrument was *shipped*, while factory order numbers are the best indicator of when an instrument was *manufactured*.

Serial Number Assignment

Serial numbers are *not* a good indicator of production date because many instruments that qualified for one did not receive it until final inspection, just prior to being shipped. Thus, any delay between completion of an instrument and its subsequent shipping created disparities in the chronology of the factory order number and the serial number. The possible exception to this rule were Loar's "Master Model" instruments, the earliest Nick Lucas Special guitars, and some other higher-priced models which may have had serial numbers reserved in advance of production. The process of final inspection included stringing, casing, and placement of the paper serial number label. This final inspection did not occur until shipping was imminent. While most instruments were manufactured and shipped within a fairly short, contiguous timeframe, others were completed and then hung around the factory for years before being shipped. The latter paradigm produced instruments with older features and newer serial numbers. The reverse situation also occurred when instruments were manufactured and labeled with all expectation of being shipped, but then did not ship or were later returned to the factory on dealer exchange. These older instruments were occasionally "updated" with newer bridges, tuners, etc., and then shipped, producing an instrument with an older serial number and newer features!

Back Inventory

In a 2009 interview with Adrian Glerum Jr. (son of long-time Gibson employee Adrian Glerum Sr.), he stated that when an order reached the factory floor it was understood that the order would be slightly "over-built" to account for any instruments that were deemed unsuitable for sale by reason of constructional faults (known as spoilage). This was true regardless of whether Gibson was building a batch for inventory or filling a direct order. Multiple eyewitness accounts indicate that this practice resulted in "extra" instruments which were kept in stock at the factory, sometimes for many years. If and when these instruments finally did ship, they would each receive a current serial number, if they qualified for one. One ex-Gibson employee who worked at the factory from 1938 to 1940 stated that by the time he was hired, this process had resulted in "hundreds of completed instruments of all types and models sitting around in the racks."

Serial Number Systems

Gibson used at least three different systems of serial numbering before World War II. The earliest system was a simple counting number that rose incrementally as the years progressed. This first system *was in continuous use* from 1902 through 1947. The second system was begun in 1938 and consisted of a two- or three- letter prefix, followed by a number (e.g., DA-5086 or EGE-4302). Inexplicably, this second system was used at the same time as the first system. It was discontinued in 1940. A third and separate series of serial numbers was used on Gibson banjos in 1919 and 1920. Beginning in 1921 this system was dropped, and banjos simply had their factory order number die stamped in the rim. Why banjos were treated differently remains unclear. In 1938 Gibson returned to a policy of placing serial numbers on banjos using the second system (e.g., DA-5091) instead of a factory order number. The company then reverted to using only factory order numbers on banjos in 1941. Some instruments like ukuleles and lower-quality guitars and mandolins never received serial numbers at all.

Serial Number Placement

For the vast majority of pre-World War II Gibson guitars and mandolins having serial numbers, they may be found in one of two places on the instrument: handwritten on a paper label that is glued inside the body or stamped into the back of the peghead. During the brief period (1938-1940) when banjos received serial numbers, they were also stamped into the back of the peghead in the form of two letters followed by a number (e.g., DA-5118). These serial numbers are easy to confuse with the late-style factory order numbers that were also stamped into the back of banjo pegheads during 1941-1945. These FON's appear as a hyphenated number with a single letter prefix (e.g., E4256-23).

Revision of Numerical Serial Number Index

The following chart represents a major revision of the accepted Gibson numerical serial number chronology. It is based on actual sales receipts, shipping ledgers, production totals, and other original factory records. In using this chart *it is important to remember that a pre-war Gibson serial number is not a good indicator of the production date*. This is because many instruments were delayed in shipping and because under normal conditions the numerical serial numbers were not applied until just prior to shipping. The best guide to a production date for any pre-World War II Gibson instrument is its factory order number in combination with a close examination of its construction features. As an example of this disparity, this chart shows Loar-signed F-5 mandolins with serial numbers from the 1928 period. Of course, those mandolins were manufactured prior to Loar's departure from the company in 1924, but they did not ship until four years later.

Numerical Serial Number Index: 1905-1947

First Number	Shipping Year
3400	1905
5100	1906
6700	1907
7200	1908
7650	1909
9100	1910
11600	1911
14700	1912
18800	1913
23780	1914
27000	1915
32940	1916
37600	1917
44360	1918
51120	1919
57900	1920
62340	1921
66800	1922
71800	1923
75000	1924
77350	1925
79300	1926
80800	1927
82500	1928
84000	1929
85400	1930
86800	1931
88500	1932
89460	1933
90200	1934
91400	1935
92718	1936
94025	1937
95093	1938
95754	1939
96000	1940
96579	1941
97382	1942
97665	1943
97810	1944
98151	1945
98602	1946
99322	1947

Letter Prefix Serial Number Index: 1938-1940

Letter Prefix	Shipping Year	Brand Name
DA	1938	Gibson
DC	1938	Cromwell
DG	1938	Gibson
DGE	1938	Gibson (electric)
DK	1938	Kalamazoo
DKE	1938	Kalamazoo (electric)
DW	1938	Montgomery Ward
DWE	1938	Montgomery Ward (electric)
EA	1939	Gibson
EC	1939	Cromwell
EG	1939	Gibson
EGE	1939	Gibson (electric)
EK	1939	Kalamazoo
EKE	1939	Kalamazoo (electric)
EW	1939	Montgomery Ward
EWE	1939	Montgomery Ward (electric)
FA	1940	Gibson
FG	1940	Gibson
FGE	1940	Gibson (electric)
FK	1940	Kalamazoo
FKE	1940	Kalamazoo (electric)
FW	1940	Montgomery Ward
FWE	1940	Montgomery Ward (electric)

Chapter 6 - Dealers and Wholesalers

A large display of Gibson instruments in the front window at Lyon & Healy, Chicago, circa 1936
Steve Huber Collection

Overview

Gibson's network of music store dealers was initiated in 1924 by general manager Harry L. Ferris. Prior to that point, Gibson marketed their instruments through "teacher-agents" who sold Gibson instruments to their students for a percentage of the profit. The change in sales methodology to a dealership network was announced by Ferris to the music industry in a *Music Trade Review* magazine article dated January 8, 1924.

In another *Music Trade Review* article dated March 8, 1924, Ferris explained some of the terms upon which Gibson would grant a dealership: "To back up our large national advertising campaign, we have launched a drive to secure a number of dealer representatives who are primarily interested in small goods selling, and who will actively cooperate with us in fretted instrument sales promotion. The product will not be sold through jobbers, although we do permit some of the largest retail accounts to establish sub-agents. Protection of franchises for the sale of Gibson instruments will be given everywhere and more than one account will be opened only in the larger cities. Teacher connections are considered desirable for the dealer in the promotion of the sale of Gibson instruments." In spite of Ferris's proscription against using wholesalers (jobbers) to sell Gibson brand

instruments, within five years Gibson would be using firms like Continental Music Company to do exactly that. The principle of not granting more than one dealership within a specific town would also fall to the wayside. By 1935, the small town of Newark, Ohio had two Gibson dealers and a Gibson teacher-agent!

The change to a network of music store dealers was not an easy one because of Gibson's reputation for making high-quality, and equally high-priced, instruments. The music store dealers simply did not believe they could sell Gibson instruments. With hard work and a promotional budget, Ferris showed them that they could and in the process doubled the number of Gibson's sales accounts to over 500. Gibson still sold instruments through teachers after 1924, but the era of the Gibson retail dealerships had begun.

Distribution Warehouses

By 1928 Gibson had established their eastern distribution headquarters in New York City at 71 West 23rd Street. Gibson used this site to hold a limited inventory for quick transfer to locations in the northeastern part of the country. This quasi-warehouse had been moved to a building owned by the New York Band Instrument Company at 1166 6th Avenue by 1936. A smaller, but similar operation was set up in Philadelphia in the Real Estate Trust Company building on the corner of Broad and Chestnut streets. Gibson's west coast warehouse was located in San Francisco.

Other Brands

The production of Gibson-built instruments bearing a name other than Gibson on the peghead (e.g., Cromwell, Kel Kroydon, Fascinator, etc.) began in 1927 with the Oriole brand banjos. The idea expanded in 1929 with instruments built for Montgomery Ward and J.W. Jenkins. But the practice did not become a significant portion of Gibson's production until after 1933.

Nontraditional Dealer Locations

A full 90% of Gibson's pre-World War II dealership locations were traditional, stand-alone music stores, dealing in a variety of keyboard, band, and fretted instruments. However, the remaining 10% revealed a creative bent in Gibson's sales force. At locations mainly in the Central Plains and southeastern part of the country, a Gibson dealership was often co-located with an unrelated business. In 1935 Gibson had 56 dealers whose primary concern was selling jewelry. Another 45 locations were furniture or hardware stores, these being primarily found in the southeastern part of the country. Another 20 sales outlets were represented by pawn brokers and loan offices.

Dealer Net and Retail Pricing

Very little evidence has come to light which would thoroughly explain Gibson's net pricing structure for dealerships. Available documents seem to indicate that net pricing for "teacher-agents" was consistent for all of them, no matter how often, how many, or what type of instruments they ordered. However, it is likely that net pricing for dealerships would have varied considerably, depending on size, order volume, and order content. There may have been a general "tiered" system, or it may have been negotiated on a case-by-case basis. In the instance of instruments built by Gibson for Montgomery Ward, the markup was 66% on regular items and as much as 70% on big sellers like the model #926 Carson Robison guitar. However, this doesn't tell us anything about the markup on Gibson brand instruments because Montgomery Ward set their own retail prices.

Some indication of the markup on Gibson brand instruments may be deduced from the data in Appendix C. It shows that Gibson generally set their retail prices between three and five times the cost of production. For example, the production cost of a TB-11 banjo constructed during 1941 was $18.04. The retail list price of that instrument was $68.25, roughly four times the cost to build it. This bit of evidence fits well with the preceding example of the Montgomery Ward instruments. Gibson may have *generally* set their "dealer net" halfway between the production cost and their retail price. Gibson always saved money when possible. One factory document dated 1941 states that the company had cut 84 cents from the production cost of a PB-11 banjo by "using obsolete necks and fingerboards."

Evidence shows that Gibson adjusted their retail price list at will, not following any consistent schedule. In 1929 they issued three updates (January, May, and September), but the corresponding three updates for 1930 fell on totally different months (February, June, and December). By way of comparison, there seems to have been only one retail price list issued in 1925 and 1926, respectively.

"Six Months - Same As Cash"

In 1930 Gibson actively encouraged their dealers to sell instruments using a "same-as-cash" scheme. For the same price as an immediate, "paid-in-full" cash transaction, a customer could make a partial down payment and then pay the balance due in monthly installments. They even provided dealers with a handy chart showing the down-payment amount and the subsequent monthly payment for each type of instrument they sold. The terms offered were: 25% down on instruments selling for $100 or less and the balance due in six monthly installments. For instruments selling at a retail value of more than $100, the requirement was 20% down and the balance due in ten monthly installments. There is evidence that Gibson had been directing their teacher-agents to sell instruments on similar terms since at least 1913. The extension of this policy to include dealers in 1930 may have been an initial symptom of the national financial crisis precipitated by the stock market crash of October 1929.

Account Collection

Factory records show that before World War II Gibson usually shipped instruments to their larger and mid-level dealers in advance of payment, with expectation of the invoice being paid in full within 30 days. Smaller dealers were generally handled on a C.O.D. basis. Accounts more than 90 days in arrears were referred to collections. Gibson outsourced some of their bad debt collection work to the Bradstreet Company of Detroit, Michigan. Records from 1937 through 1939 reveal that Gibson charged off less than 2% of total sales to bad debt.

In a 1940 report to the board of directors, general manager Guy Hart gave a specific recap of eight dealers who were more than 90 days in arrears. These are interesting because they show the various ways in which Gibson dealt with account collections. The C.J. Angell Music Company of Mocksville, North Carolina owed Gibson $102.53 and is described by Hart as, "another one of those good-but-slow accounts, and we are now concentrating to get this balance – then will notify him that he is to be C.O.D." By contrast, the Amarillo Band House of Amarillo, Texas owed Gibson $273.76 and had clearly crossed a line. Hart summarizes this situation by stating, "This fellow sort of put one over on us. We had been dealing with him quite a while in a small way. He came to the factory and made arrangements to get a display of instruments for a county fair held in Amarillo. He sold the instruments and has never paid us. We have started suit against him."

In this 1937 photo, Gibson salesmen "Doc" Caldwell and George Post are entertaining customers gathered outside the display window at Wittich's Music Store in Reading, Pennsylvania. The "gig" was booked by the music store owner without the prior knowledge of Caldwell and Post, who showed up for a regularly scheduled sales appointment and found out they were the stars of the show! Unfortunately, Post knew very little about playing the guitar, so he talked a lot, strummed a few simple chords, and bluffed his way through the performance.
John Post Collection

Return–Exchange Policy

The existing Gibson shipping ledgers clearly reveal that the company had a dealer return policy in place which allowed the exchange of unsold Gibson merchandise for other instruments of comparable or lower value. Many entries for shipment of new instruments are noted as "exchange" items. Also, throughout the ledgers of the late 1930's there were older models being shipped which obviously did not represent current production models. Among others, these items included many guitars, harp-guitars, and mandolin family instruments with older serial numbers. Certainly, some of these represented "new-old-stock" which was finally being cleared out, but others must have represented dealer returns.

Warranty Repairs

Gibson maintained a full-time department at the Kalamazoo factory to handle warranty issues and general repairs. The shipping ledgers reveal that most persons sent their faulty instruments back to Gibson through their local dealers. Gibson's warranty policy was rather liberal, with the famous Mastertone banjo guarantee stating, "Any defect in material or workmanship, except heads, strings and pegs, will be repaired free of charge or replaced with another of same style or value, if returned to our factory, charges prepaid." An earlier version of this same warranty stated, "The head and strings are highest quality available, but as they are not manufactured by Gibson Mandolin-Guitar Company, they cannot be included in the guarantee." The warranty for guitars and mandolins was worded in a slightly different way: "Guaranteed against faulty workmanship or material. Should this instrument, with proper care and usage, go wrong, we agree to repair it free of charge, at our factory, or to replace it with another of same style or value." The Gibson warranty evidently stayed with the instrument, as no mention is made of restriction to the original owner.

Some Gibson instruments were more prone to warranty returns than others. A 1933 batch of style L-00 guitars, manufactured under factory order number 777, seems to have been a particular problem. Over two dozen members of this specific batch were returned for repair before World War II. All of Gibson's flattop guitar models are well represented in the shipping ledgers as repair returns. This may have been due to problems in keeping the bridge glued to the top using the products then available. Mandolins manufactured prior to the addition of truss rods in 1921 also populated the repair shop in abundance. In passing, it should be noted that Gibson sometimes repaired instruments built by other companies, including guitars by C.F. Martin & Company. Of course, these do not fall under the category of warranty repair.

Montgomery Ward

The importance of Montgomery Ward to Gibson in the decade of the 1930's can hardly be overstated. Throughout the last half of that period, Montgomery Ward was consistently Gibson's largest retail outlet, even if the instruments they sold did not bear the Gibson name. In 1935 a full 12% of all shipping went to Montgomery Ward. By comparison, in that year it would have required the combined business of the next four largest Gibson retailers to match the volume of Montgomery Ward alone.

Gibson began building instruments for Montgomery Ward in 1929. The earliest of these were banjos of the Mastertone design bearing the names "Recording King" and "Studio King." The main difference between these Montgomery Ward banjos and actual Gibson Mastertones of the period was the absence of an adjustable truss rod in the neck. Gibson reserved that important innovation only for instruments bearing the company name. The first Gibson-built guitar sold by Montgomery Ward debuted in the 1930 Fall-Winter catalog as their model #807, a Recording King imitation of the Gibson "Nick Lucas Special" model.

Gibson built very few instruments for Montgomery Ward in 1932, and that year represented the lowest point in Gibson's production generally during the Great Depression. However, the hiatus was brief, with several Gibson-built models appearing in the 1933-34 Fall-Winter catalog, including for the first time Recording King mandolins. The Gibson-Montgomery Ward relationship prospered through 1940 when it abruptly ended. Montgomery Ward had always carried instruments built by a variety of musical instrument companies and continued to do so even after their break with Gibson in 1940. The reasons for the cessation of the relationship are not clear.

J.W. Jenkins Music Company

The J.W. Jenkins Music Company of Kansas City, Missouri was probably Gibson's most important true dealership. They consistently accounted for a significant portion of Gibson's total sales, for example 4% of 1935 alone. The company was founded about 1881 by John Woodward Jenkins Sr. in

a room rented from a sewing machine and wallpaper shop. His son John Wesley Jenkins (1864-1932) expanded the business to locations in Oklahoma City, Tulsa, Topeka, Wichita, and many other places in Oklahoma, Texas, and Arkansas. One hallmark of the company's customer service policy was to provide instruments that left the stores tuned and ready to play. In April of 1932 Jenkins Music opened a purpose-built, modern, eight-story structure at 1217 Walnut Street in Kansas City as their new home location. Entire floors were devoted to pianos, band instruments, stringed instruments, sheet music, and even a printing division for their annual catalog. A 250-seat auditorium was available for concerts and recitals. Seven months later John W. Jenkins was killed in a car accident. His will disbursed more than $20,000 to be divided among 120 long-time employees of his stores. After the death of his father, Paul W. Jenkins Sr. continued the operation, and he was succeeded by his son Paul W. Jenkins Jr. The business was eventually purchased by Hal Cowen. It was then acquired by Schmitt Music Company of Minneapolis, Minnesota in November 1997 when Cowen retired.

Besides selling the complete line of Gibson products, Jenkins Music Company is also notable for being the major distributor of the Kel Kroydon line of budget instruments. Gibson began building guitars and banjos for Jenkins using the Kel Kroydon name in 1929. None of them featured the adjustable truss rod, but in other aspects they are easily identifiable as Gibson-made instruments. The experiment was short-lived, and no musical instruments bearing the Kel Kroydon brand were produced after 1931. Gibson reused the name on a line of wooden toys which they produced in 1931-1933.

A display window of the J.W. Jenkins Company, circa 1926.
Steve Huber Collection

New York Band Instrument Company

The New York Band Instrument Company was one of the largest music stores in the country and one of Gibson's most important accounts. They easily rivaled the J.W. Jenkins Company in sales of Gibson instruments and variety of inventory on hand. The company was in business by 1925 at 111 E. 14th Street, near Union Square in New York City. The top floor of their building had rental studios for music teachers. A New York University dormitory now sits on the former site of the New York Band Instrument Company. It is interesting that the company largely avoided selling instruments bearing Gibson's in-house, budget-brand name "Kalamazoo." Instead, they sold the exact same Gibson-built product under the "Cromwell" brand name. This line was also marketed through the C.G. Conn organization through their Continental Music Company outlets.

Grossman Music Company

Anyone familiar with the retail musical instrument business of the 21st century is familiar with the Grossman Music *Corporation* as a wholesale vendor of parts and accessories. It is now generally forgotten that the Grossman Music *Company* once ran a retail storefront in Cleveland, Ohio, with the present-day corporation being a lineal descendant of the 20th century company. This one store accounted for more than 3% of Gibson's shipping in the 1930's, a fact that places it easily in the top five pre-World War II Gibson retailers. Grossman carried the entire spectrum of Gibson products in their retail store but did not sell them in their wholesale catalogs. They also shunned the Gibson "Kalamazoo" budget-brand product, opting instead to carry the Gibson-built "Cromwell" line.

Continental Music Company

The Continental Music Company was founded in 1923 as a wholesale division of the C.G. Conn retail store in Chicago. They published an annual catalog and quickly became one of the largest wholesale distributors of musical instruments in the United States, a position they maintained up into the 1950's. They had major warehouses in both Chicago and San Francisco. Continental accounted for 3% of Gibson's business in 1935. They carried the entire Gibson product line and preferred to deal in "Cromwell" budget-brand instruments, instead of Gibson's in-house brand "Kalamazoo." Continental owned the Carl Fisher music catalog at one time as well as the "Tonk Brothers" brand of instruments.

Grinnell Brothers Inc.

Grinnell Brothers of Detroit, Michigan went out of business in 1981 after almost 100 years of retail music store operations. The company was founded in 1882 by Ira L. and Clayton A. Grinnell. They originally concentrated on keyboard instruments and by 1903 were even going so far as to produce their own line of pianos. When fretted instruments became popular at the turn of the 20th century, the company adapted, bringing in both Gibson and Martin products. In 1908 they built a huge store at 1515 Woodward Avenue in Detroit. The structure was designed by Albert Kahn (1869-1942), the renowned "daylight factory" architect. The multi-floor building still stands today.

From an early date Grinnell Brothers began opening satellite stores around the state of Michigan. By 1935 they had locations in Ann Arbor, Bay City, Flint, Grand Rapids, Jackson, Kalamazoo, Lansing, Midland, Monroe, Pontiac, Port Huron, River Rouge, Royal Oak, Saginaw, Wyandotte, and Ypsilanti. Expansion continued over the next decades with new stores in Ohio, Kentucky, New York, and Ontario, Canada. By 1965 they were the largest retail musical merchandiser in the US. The Detroit

riots of 1967 resulted in an extended period of urban flight from downtown Detroit. This situation in combination with the bankruptcy of their piano manufacturing division sounded the beginning of the end for Grinnell Brothers. Their stores entered a period of slow decline, culminating in the closure of the business in 1981.

Grinnell Brothers carried an especially rich selection of Gibson products. It would clearly have been an excellent choice for the prospective Gibson owner before World War II. They were perhaps Gibson's largest client for the budget-brand "Kalamazoo" instruments.

International Retailers

Shipping of Gibson instruments overseas dates back at least as far as 1908 when teacher-agent Aladar de Vekey was purchasing products for his students in Bournemouth, England. Canadian music stores were included from the beginning of Gibson's dealership program in 1924. Companies like Archambault Musique in Quebec and Beare & Sons of Toronto were both strong Gibson dealers. The first overseas dealerships were opened up under the guidance of Guy Hart in about 1926. A decade later Gibson was shipping to Australia, Aruba, the West Indies, South Africa, New Zealand, Brazil, and Curacao in the Antilles Islands. In Europe locations in London, Amsterdam, Antwerp, Rotterdam, Gothenburg, and Stockholm all sold Gibson products. In the Far East a Gibson was "good enough" in Calcutta, Bangkok, Osaka, Kobe, Shanghai, Manila, and Hong Kong.

H. Polliack & Company Ltd.

H. Polliack & Company, Ltd. was one of Gibson's largest overseas dealers. The company founder was Herman Polliack, born September 17, 1888 in Kovna, Lithuania. He was a Russian Jew whose family emigrated to Capetown, South Africa before 1907. By 1922 Polliack was operating a store in Johannesburg selling appliances, pianos, "gramophones" (record players), and popular recordings. The Polliack store became a Gibson dealership after Herman made a buying trip to New York City in 1926. The relationship quickly prospered with Polliack making return trips in 1929, 1931, 1933, 1936, and 1947. Gibson sold their complete line of merchandise to Polliack, including guitars, banjos, and mandolins. Interest in these fretted instruments is explained by the prevalence of "Boeremusiek,"a type of folk music played by the immigrant Dutch families or "Boers" of South Africa. It greatly resembled American country music of the period and was performed as a dance music at similar venues, i.e., community gatherings, barn dances, schoolhouses, etc.

POLLIACKS for EVERYTHING MUSICAL and ELECTRICAL

Sole Distributors for:

Norge Refrigerators - His Master's Voice Radio - Columbia Gramophones and records - Crosley Radio and Refrigerators - Westinghouse Electric Ranges, Lamps and Appliances - Pianos by the World's Best Makers - Musical - Instruments of every description. -

H. Polliack & Co., Ltd.

P.O. Box 3008. JOHANNESBURG

CAPETOWN and PRETORIA

Trade Enquiries particularly requested

Gibson Dealers: Circa 1935

The following table partially reconstructs Gibson's pre-war dealership base with over 1,000 locations represented. It was compiled from Gibson shipping ledgers and other external sources. The location of a dealership and its owner are shown if the data could be ascertained with reasonable certainty. Company names are presented "as-found." The list is not intended to be comprehensive and certainly varied from time to time over the pre-war years.

Dealership Name	Location		Owner
Abernathy, Clarkson & Wright	Burlington	VT	
Ackerman Piano Company	Marion	OH	Henry Ackerman
Adams Music Company	Peoria	IL	
Adams Piano Company			
Adams Richards Furniture Company			
Aegerter & Odland Music			
Aegerter Music House	Menno	SD	E.A. Aegerter
Aegerter Stephens Music			
Akers Music Shop	Lebanon	IN	
Akins Music Shop			
Akron Inst of Music	Akron	OH	
Albemarle Music Store	Albemarle	NC	D.A. Lipe
Alberni Music Company			
Alberts Loan Office	Bristol	TN	
Alexander Music House	Spartanburg	SC	A.M. Alexander
Allgood Music Company			
Allington Music Store	Freeport	IL	G.W. Allington
Alton Music Shop			
Altone Music Sales			
Amarillo Band House	Amarillo	TX	
American Beauty Music House	Rockford	IL	
Anderson Music Company Ltd.			
Anderson Music House	Charles City	IA	
Andrews Music Company	Charlotte	NC	Edgar M. Andrews
Andrus & Company Music Store	Williamsport	PA	Daniel S. Andrus
Anita Music Shop			
Angell Music	Mocksville	NC	Charlie J. Angell
Anthony Gibbs & Company	Melbourne	Australia	
App's Music House	Burlington	IA	
Arace Brothers			
Archambault Musique	Montreal	Canada	Edmond Archambault
Armitage Music & Novelty			L. Armitage
Armstrong Music House	Towanda	PA	
Arnold Jewelry			
Arts Music Shop			
Aschbaueher Music Store			
Ashley Music Company			
Atlas Grocery Company			
Ault Music Company	Fort Worth	TX	
Austin Music Company			

Gibson Dealers: Circa 1935 (continued)

Dealership Name	Location		Owner
Avery Music Company	Concord	NH	William H. Avery
Bailey's Music Rooms	Burlington	VT	
Baltimore Music Company	Baltimore	MD	
Baltin Music Company Inc.			
Barnes Music Company			
Barters Music Shop	Rutland	VT	
Barth Feinberg Inc.	New York City	NY	
Bashams Jewelry & Music Store	Salem	IL	
Bates & Company	Meadville	PA	Edward T. Bates
Baylor Nelms Furniture Company	Kingsport	TN	
Beare & Son	Toronto	Canada	
Beasley Music Company	Texarkana	AR	H.V. Beasley
Becker Music House	Grand Island	NE	
Beckert & Perks Music Company			
Beckley Music Store	Beckley	WV	
Beedle Piano Company	Keene	NH	Charles C. Beedle
Beerman Music House	Muskegon	MI	
Beers Music Store	Clearfield	PA	A. Charles Beer
Beesley Music Company	Salt Lake City	UT	Alvin A. Beesley
Bell Music & Stationery Company			
Bellson Music Company	Kewanee	IL	Louis Bellson
Bellson Music Company	Moline	IL	Louis Bellson
Bellson Music Company	St. Paul	MN	Louis Bellson
Bender Music Service	Clinton	IA	Arthur J. Bender
Bendersky & Son			I. Bendersky
Bendix Music & Electric Shop	Walla Walla	WA	
Bennett Music Company			J.E. Bennett
Berinage Music Store			
Bermans Jewelry Store			
Berniers Music Shop			
Bevon & Company	Calcutta	India	T.E. Bevon
Bickmore Music Store & Photo Studio			
Bidinger Music House			
Biekarck Music House	Warren	PA	Rex F. Biekarck
Biermans Music Store	Northfield	MN	
Billy Barnes Music			
Biloxi Music Store	Biloxi	MS	
Blanchetts Music Shop	Slough	England	
Blanchetts Piano Shop			
Bock Music Company			
Bolin Music House	Geneva	NY	
Bollinger Music & Jewelry Company	Oskaloosa	IA	Mary B. Bollinger
Bollinger Music Company	Ft. Smith	AR	R.C. Bollinger
Boltin Music Company	New Brunswick	NJ	

Dealership Name	Location		Owner
Bond Furniture Company			
Border Music Supplies			
Bothner Music	Cape Town	South Africa	Charles Bothner
Bourghaltzer Drug Company			
Boxberger Music Shop	Fort Wayne	IN	Harry M. Boxberger
Bradshaw Music Company	Fitzgerald	GA	
Braga Music Company			J.C. Braga
Braimon Jewelry Company			
Bramans Music Company	Virginia	MN	
Branch Hardware Company			C.M. Branch
Branders Music Shop	Duluth	MN	
Brannans Music Company			
Brannons Jewelry Company			
Braswell Hardware Company	Demopolis	AL	
Braxton Music Company	Raleigh	NC	S.A. Braxton
Brays Furniture Store			
Brehmer Music Store			
Brewer Music Company			
Bristow & Son	Petersburg	VA	R.C. Bristow
Brockman Music Company			
Brown Music Company	Manhattan	KS	R.H. Brown
Broyles Piano Company	Shreveport	LA	
Brunswick Music Shop	Terre Haute	IN	
Bryan Music Store			
Buchanan Music Company			
Buchanan Music Shop	Rockford	IL	
Budds Music House	Lansing	MI	
Bunch Furniture Company Inc.	Statesville	NC	
Bunn Music Company			T.O. Bunn
Bunns Sweet Shop			
Burgers Music House	Lancaster	PA	
Burns Melody Shop	Waco	TX	
Burri Stores			J. Burri
Butler Music Company	Marion	IN	
Butlers Music & Furniture			
Byerly Brothers Music Company	Davenport	IA	George & Eldred Byerly
Byerly Brothers Music Company	Peoria	IL	George & Eldred Byerly
Byerly Brothers Music Company	Springfield	IL	George & Eldred Byerly
Cabbon Music Company			
Cable Piano Company	Atlanta	GA	
Cable Piano Company	Lansing	MI	
Caldwell Music Store			R.W. Caldwell
Candioto Piano Company	Lexington	KY	Joseph Candioto
Cannon Furniture & Music Store			R.E. Cannon

Gibson Dealers: Circa 1935 (continued)

Dealership Name	Location		Owner
Canton Music Shop	Canton	OH	
Carlson Music			
Carolina Loan Office			
Carpenters Furniture Company			
Carter The Music Dealer	Charlottesville	VA	George P. Carter
Carter the Music Man			
Casa Mexicano de Musica	Mexico City	Mexico	
Casa Mexiranada			
Casey Music Store	Olean	PA	
Central Music Company			
Central Pawnbrokers Outlet			
Chalmers Music Company			
Chandler Music Store	Chillicothe	OH	B.F. Chandler
Chatham Jewelry & Optical			
Chattanooga Loan Office	Chattanooga	TN	
Chears Jewelry Store	Sanford	NC	W.F. Chears
Citizens Loan Office			
City Music Shop			
City Book & Office Supply			
City Music Company			
Clark Music Company	Syracuse	NY	L.B. Clark
Clayson Brothers Music Company	Burlington	IA	
Cleveland Music House			
Clifford Jewelry & Music Company	Norwich	CT	
Clifford Jewelry & Music Company	South Norwalk	CT	
Cline Music Company Inc.	Dallas	TX	
Cloutier Jewelry			H.N. Cloutier
Coast Wholesale Music	Los Angeles	CA	
Coast Wholesale Music	San Francisco	CA	
Cocroft Music Company	Thomasville	GA	C.C. Cocroft
Coffins Music Shop			
Collins Piano Company	Portland	OR	J.J. Collins
Colonial Radio & Sporting Goods			
Colorado Springs Music Company	Colorado Springs	CO	
Columbia Jewelry Company			
Columbia Music Company			
Conine Music Store			
Conlons Jewelry & Music			
Conn Ltd. Retail Store	New York City	NY	C.G. Conn
Connally Drug Company	Denton	TX	
Connelly Music & Radio Company			
Continental Music Company	Chicago	IL	
Continental Music Company	San Francisco	CA	
Cooper Brothers			

Dealership Name	Location		Owner
Copeland Jewelry			
Copp Music Shop	South Bend	IN	John & Chester Copp
Covells Music Store			
Cox Music Company			
Cranes Music Store			
Cumberland Music Company	Cumberland	MD	
Cumberland Valley Music & Machine Company	Harlan	KY	
Cumming Music Company			A.L. Cumming
Cut Rate Music Company	Kalamazoo	MI	
Dalton Music Company			
Daly Music Company	Grand Rapids	WI	F.P. Daly
Daniels Music Company			
Danielson Music House			
Danmuellers Music			
Davis Smith Shop			
Davitt & Hanser Music Company	Cincinnati	OH	
Dawson Music Company			J.W. Dawson
Day Company			L.S. Day
Days Music Store	Elyria	OH	
Dazey Music Store			J.W. Dazey
De Forest Music House	Sharon	PA	W.C. DeForest
Deacon Music			D.Erina Deacon
Deans Music House			
Deland Music Shop			
Denman Music Company	Brownwood	TX	
Denton, Cottier & Daniels	Buffalo	NY	
Desautels Music House	Manchester	NH	
Dewey Roush Loan			
Dickinson Music Shop			
Dickinson Piano Company	Missoula	MT	
Dietz Music House	Lincoln	NE	G.J. Dietz
DiVito Music Company			
Dixie Music & Jewelry Company			
Dixie Music Company	Orlando	FL	
Dodds Jewelers			
Doorak Music Company			J.M. Doorak
Dorn & Kirschner	Union	NJ	
Drake Jewelry Company			
Dreibelbis Music Company	Butte	MT	Louis Dreibelbis
Drum Shop & Temple of Music			
Duesler Music House	Fort Wayne	IN	
Duffield Music House	Chambersburg	PA	
Duncan Music Store			
Duncanson Brothers			

Gibson Dealers: Circa 1935 (continued)

Dealership Name	Location		Owner
Dunhams Music House	Asheville	NC	
Dunlap Music Company			
Durden Music Company	Athens	GA	P.H. Durden
Durham Jones Pharmacy			
Durlauf Music Shoppe	Louisville	KY	A.F. Durlauf
Easman & Company Inc.			
Eastern Musical Supply	Falmouth	ME	
Edgley Music Shop	Dallas	TX	George M. Edgley
Edmund Gram Music House	Milwaukee	WI	
Elbel Brothers	South Bend	IN	
Elk River Coal & Coke	Widen	WV	
Elk River Coal & Lumber Company	Widen	WV	
Elkins Music Company			
Ellis Machine & Music Company	Burlington	NC	
Ellis Music Company	Burlington	NC	Charles B. Ellis
Engle & Sons	Winchester	IN	A.T. Engle
Englehardt Music Company			
Enterprise Loan Company			
Eschbach Music House	Ames	IA	Arthur H. Eschbach
Eshelman Music House	St. Joseph	MO	Walter L. Eshelman
Evans Jewelry Store			
Evans Music House			
Evans Piano House			
Evanston Floral & Music			
Fabregas Music Store	Houma	LA	
Fairalls Music Store	Newark	OH	Perley J. Fairall
Fauchen Parks Furniture Company			
Fawley Music Company	Morgantown	WV	O.B. Fawley
Fayette Music House	Aberdeen	WA	
Felty Music Store	Lebanon	PA	Boyd R. Felty
Ferguson Music Store	San Jose	CA	
Fiddle Shop			
Fieldale Furniture & Hardware Company	Fieldale	VA	
Fife Music	Hollywood	CA	Harold C. Fife
Finkelstein Company			H. Finkelstein
Finley Davidson Company	Middletown	OH	
Finley Music Company			
Fisher Hardware			
Fisher Music Company			
Fisher Music Store			
Fisher Musical Instruments Inc.	New York City	NY	Carl Fisher
Fishmans Sporting Goods Company	Auburn	AL	
Flanner Hafsoos Music House	Milwaukee	WI	Joseph Flanner
Flasters Music Shop			

Dealership Name	Location		Owner
Fleming Music Company			
Fleming Music Store			
Fletcher Brothers Music Inc.			
Flieth-Ehlers Mercantile Company	Cornucopia	WI	
Floyds Music & Jewelry Shop			
Folsom Music Company	Brainerd	MN	Walter Folsom
Folsom Music Company	Little Falls	MN	Walter Folsom
Folsom Music Company	Brainerd	MN	
Forbes & Son Piano Company	Decatur	AL	E.E. Forbes
Forbes & Son Piano Company	Anniston	AL	E.E. Forbes
Forbes & Son Piano Company	Birmingham	AL	E.E. Forbes
Forbes Radio & Refrigerator Company	Birmingham	AL	
Force Music House	Vandalia	OH	E.A. Force
Ford Green Music Company			
Foster Music Company			
Foster Schumaker & Company			
Francis Day & Hunter	London	England	
Frankhuizen Piano & Radio Company	San Mateo	CA	Pieter Frankhuizen
Franklin Music House	Newark	NJ	
Frelinger Music House	Lafayette	IN	
Fremont Music Center	Fremont	CA	
Frick Brothers Music Center			
Friedmans Music Shop	Newark	NJ	
Fuller Music Company	New Bern	NC	
Gadsden Loan Office			
Gage Musical Instrument Company			
Galperin Music Company	Charleston	WV	
Galveston Piano Company	Galveston	TX	
Ganus Brothers	Birmingham	AL	
Garehime Music Company	Las Vegas	NV	
Garinos Household Appliances			
Garner Music Store	Garner	NC	
Gartman Music			
Gartner Sweet Music Company	Ravenna	OH	
Garza's Furniture & Music	San Antonio	TX	
Gashill Music Company			
Gaston Music & Furniture Company	Hastings	NE	
Georges Music Shop	Schenectady	NY	
Gibson Music Company			
Gibson Music House			
Gibson Music Shop			
Gilman Music Company			
Gilmore Jewelry			
Ginsberg Music Company	Roswell	NM	

Gibson Dealers: Circa 1935 (continued)

Dealership Name	Location		Owner
Glen Brothers Music Company	Ogden	UT	
Glen Brothers Music Company	Salt Lake City	UT	
Globe Music Company	Chicago	IL	
Goggan Music Company	San Antonio	TX	Thomas Goggan
Goodin Drum Furniture Company	Maiden	NC	
Gorton Music Company	Benton Harbor	MI	L.B. Gorton
Gourlie Music Company	Tampa	FL	
Grand Island Music Company	Grand Island	NE	
Grant Jewelry Company			W.A. Grant
Graves Music Company	Corpus Christi	TX	
Green Music House	Dallas	TX	Elmer Green
Greene Music Company	Toledo	OH	J.W. Greene
Greene Piano Company			J.H. Greene
Greens Music Company			
Greens Music Store	Canton	OH	
Greensboro Music Company	Greensboro	NC	
Greensburg Piano Company			
Gregory's Music Shop	Plainfield	NJ	
Gressett Music House	Meridian	MS	A. Gressett
Gretsch & Brenner	Manhattan	NY	Walter Gretsch, Wm Brenner
Grigware Music House	Midland	MI	P.M. Grigware
Grillo Music Company			A.J. Grillo
Grim Brothers Music Store			
Grinnell Brothers	Ann Arbor	MI	Ira & Clayton Grinnell
Grinnell Brothers	Bay City	MI	Ira & Clayton Grinnell
Grinnell Brothers	Kalamazoo	MI	Ira & Clayton Grinnell
Grinnell Brothers	Detroit	MI	Ira & Clayton Grinnell
Grinnell Brothers	Flint	MI	Ira & Clayton Grinnell
Grinnell Brothers	Grand Rapids	MI	Ira & Clayton Grinnell
Grinnell Brothers	Jackson	MI	Ira & Clayton Grinnell
Grinnell Brothers	Lansing	MI	Ira & Clayton Grinnell
Grinnell Brothers	Midland	MI	Ira & Clayton Grinnell
Grinnell Brothers	Monroe	MI	Ira & Clayton Grinnell
Grinnell Brothers	Pontiac	MI	Ira & Clayton Grinnell
Grinnell Brothers	Port Huron	MI	Ira & Clayton Grinnell
Grinnell Brothers	River Rouge	MI	Ira & Clayton Grinnell
Grinnell Brothers	Royal Oak	MI	Ira & Clayton Grinnell
Grinnell Brothers	Saginaw	MI	Ira & Clayton Grinnell
Grinnell Brothers	Toledo	OH	Ira & Clayton Grinnell
Grinnell Brothers	Wyandotte	MI	Ira & Clayton Grinnell
Grinnell Brothers	Ypsilanti	MI	Ira & Clayton Grinnell
Groom Music Company			Edward Groom
Groom Music Company			William Groom
Grossman Music Company	Cleveland	OH	

Dealership Name	Location		Owner
Groves Music Company	LaSalle	IL	
Guisinger Music House	Fayetteville	AR	
Gurley Claesgen Music Company			
Guttenberger Music Shop	Macon	GA	
Hall Music Company	Abilene	TX	
Hall Music Company	Warren	OH	
Halls Music Company			
Halls Music House	Trail	Canada	
Halls Music Shop	Middletown	CT	
Hallum Furniture Company	Aberdeen	NC	
Hallum Furniture Company	Hamlet	NC	
Hallum Furniture Company	Laurinburg	NC	
Hallum Furniture Company	Wadesboro	NC	
Halsted Music Shop	Chicago	IL	
Hanger Brothers Music			
Hanks Brothers Music Company			
Hank's Furniture & Loan			
Hanschild Music Company	Victoria	TX	
Hanson's Music Store Inc.	Kane	PA	
Harbours Jewelry			
Harding & Miller Music Company	Evansville	IN	
Hardman Music Company			
Hardt Music Company			
Hardy Music Company	Bay City	MI	
Harper Music Shop	Detroit	MI	
Harrington Brothers	Cortland	NY	
Harris Brothers			
Harris Company			A. Harris
Harris Music House			
Hart Drug Company	High Point	NC	
Harvey's Music Parlors	St. Johnsbury	VT	
Harwood Wilson Inc.			
Hawken & Son Inc	Springfield	OH	Earl K. Hawken
Hazels Jewelry & Music			
Hazels Music Shop			
Heatons Music Store	Columbus	OH	Otto B. Heaton
Heims Music Store	Danbury	CT	
Heintzman & Company Ltd.	Toronto	Canada	
Hellsterns Music Store	Cambridge	OH	Albert A. Hellstern
Henchman Music Store			
Hendrick Music House	Santa Barbara	CA	
Henike Music Shop			
Henry County Furniture Company	Martinsville	VA	Benjamin M. Townes
Henton Knecht Music Company	Philadelphia	PA	

Gibson Dealers: Circa 1935 (continued)

Dealership Name	Location		Owner
Hermers Music Store			
Hermes Company			
Hert Music Company			
Heyde & Son Music Company	Marion	IL	J.B. Heyde
Hickeys Lyceum Music Store	Ithaca	NY	Joseph Hickey
Hickok Music Company	Poughkeepsie	NY	Charles H. Hickok
Hill Music Company			
Hillikers Music Store			
Hiltbrunner Music Company	Cedar Rapids	IA	C.O. Hiltbrunner
Hirzels Music Service	Lewiston	ID	
Hoelle Music Company	Trenton	NJ	John W. Hoelle
Hoffman Brothers Music Company			
Hollenberg Music House	Hot Springs	AR	
Homeyer & Company	Boston	MA	Charles W. Homeyer
Hood Music Company	Muncie	IN	
Hookers Chocolate Shop			
Hoover Music Company	Springfield	MO	H.L. Hoover
Hospe Company	Omaha	NE	A. Hospe
Houber Jewelry			
Houck Music	Memphis	TN	O.K. Houck
House Music Company	Steubenville	OH	Chauncey A. House
House Music Company	Fairmont	WV	Chauncey A. House
House Music Company	Wheeling	WV	Chauncey A. House
Houston Band House	Houston	TX	
Houston Band Instrument Company	Houston	TX	
Hudson's Bay Company	Winnepeg	Canada	
Huff Music Store	Bethlehem	PA	A.C. Huff
Hunleth Music Company	St. Louis	MO	
Hunt Jewelry			
Hurst Music Store Ltd.			
Ideal Furniture Company	Hazard	KY	
Imfeld Music Company	Hamilton	OH	Ferdinand Imfeld
International Musical Supply Company			
Irvings Music Shop			
Isa & Company			D. Isa
Italian Emporium of Music			
Jacobs Music House	Fort Wayne	IN	George Jacobs
James Music Company			Will James
Jamison Music Company			
Jean & Son			A.J. Jean
Jenkins Music Company	Joplin	MO	J.W. Jenkins
Jenkins Music Company	Kansas City	MO	J.W. Jenkins
Jenkins Music Company	Oklahoma City	OK	J.W. Jenkins
Jenkins Music Company	Topeka	KS	J.W. Jenkins

Dealership Name	Location		Owner
Jenkins Music Company	Tulsa	OK	J.W. Jenkins
Jenkins Music Company	Wichita	KS	J.W. Jenkins
Jenkins Music Company	Bartlesville	OK	J.W. Jenkins
Jenkins Music Company	Seminole	OK	J.W. Jenkins
Jenkins Music Shop			
Jesse French Company Inc.	Mobile	AL	Jesse French III
Jesse French Company Inc.	Montgomery	AL	Jesse French III
Johnson Music Company			
Jonas Carlson Music Store	Cadillac	MI	Jonas Carlson
Jones Furniture Company			
Jones Music Company			
Jones Music House			
Jones Smith Furniture Company			
Joosten Piano Company	Peoria	IL	E.J. Joosten
Julius Music House	York	PA	
Kahns Jewelry & Music	Bay City	MI	
Kalamazoo Musical Instrument Company	Kalamazoo	MI	Charles Martelle
Karlberg Music Shop			
Kastning Music Store	Santa Fe	NM	
Kauffman & Son	Lewistown	PA	B.W. Kauffman
Kaufman Music House			
Kays Music Store			
Keely Guitar Shop			
Keene Inc.			H. Keene
Kelleman Music Company			
Kellers Music Store	Easton	PA	
Kelly & English Music Shop			
Kelso Music Company	Cleveland	OH	
Kenny Music Company	Huntington	WV	
Keoun Music & Furniture Company	Marshall	TX	T.H. Keoun
Kerbel Jewelry Company	Longview	TX	Sam Kerbel
Kesselman-O'Driscoll Company	Milwaukee	WI	
Kidd-Frix Music & Stationery Company	Charlotte	NC	
Kienles Music Company			
Kimbell Music Company			
Kings Music Shoppe			
Kitt Company			H.L. Kitt
Kittenger's	Christiansburg	VA	
Kling Music Company	Rochester	MN	Vincent Kling
Kloepfers Music Store	Galion	OH	
Kluck Music House	Waterloo	IA	
Knight Campbell Music Company	Denver	CO	
Knight Campbell Music Company	Trinidad	CO	
Koontz Music Store			

Gibson Dealers: Circa 1935 (continued)

Dealership Name	Location		Owner
Kornblum Brothers Music Company	St. Louis	MO	Bernard & David Kornblum
Korzinek Music Shop	Manitowoc	WI	
Kraft Music Company	Frankfort	IN	
Kramer Music Company	Gary	IN	C.J. Kramer
Kreichgauer Piano Company			
Kring Music Company			
Kroh Music Company	Muskogee	OK	H.A. Kroh
La Bean Music Store			
La Fleur Music Company	Williston	ND	I.F. LaFleur Sr.
La Grange Jewelry & Arms Company			
Laconia Music Store	Laconia	NH	
Landaus Brothers			
Lang Brothers Music			
Langs Music Shop			
Large Music Company			
Larimans Music			
Larsens Music Shop			
Larson Cycle Company			
Laterneaus Music Store			J. Laterneaus
Lauders Music Shop			
Laumans Music Shop			
Lefavour Music House	Salem	MA	
Lehman Furniture Company			
LeRoy Music Company			C. LeRoy
Levis Music Store	Rochester	NY	
Levy Page Company Inc.	Portsmouth	VA	
Lewis & Palmer Music Company			
Lewis Music House			
Lexington Music Shop			
Lillians Music Shop			
Lincoff Jewelry	Weirton	WV	
Lindamood Music Company	Helena	MT	
Linnemans			
Linquist Musical Instrument Company	Minneapolis	MN	
Lion Music & Jewelry Company	Bastrop	TX	
Lion Music & Jewelry Company	Laredo	TX	
Livingston & Company			H. Livingston
Logan Music Shop	Larned	KS	
Loser's Music	Lebanon	PA	
Lott Furniture Company			
Louis Loan Company			
Louis Musical Store			
Lowenstein Music Company			
Lowensteins Loan Company			

Dealership Name	Location		Owner
Loyal Music Store			
Ludwig Music House	St. Louis	MO	
Luge Music Shop			Louis Luge
Lukes Music Store			
Lutz Furniture Company	Lenoir	NC	O.P. Lutz
Lynch Jewelry Shop			
Lynchs Music Store			
Lynn Sheely Company	Bristol	TN	Lynn Sheely
Lynn Sheely Company	Greenville	TN	Lynn Sheely
Lynn Sheely Company	Johnson City	TN	Lynn Sheely
Lynn Sheely Company	Morristown	TN	Lynn Sheely
Lyon & Healy Inc.	Chicago	IL	
M. Doyle Marks & Son Inc.	Elmira	NY	M.Doyle Marks
Madison Jewelry Company			
Mahan Music Store			
Main & Day Music House			
Main Loan Office			
Main Music Shop			
Major Music Company			
Major Music Shop			
Malone Furniture Company			
Manlove & Son	Connersville	IN	Emory Manlove
Marcellus Roper Company	Worcester	MA	
Mariner Music House			J.D. Mariner
Marion Music Company	Indianapolis	IN	
Marlick Piano			
Marsh Music House			
Marshall Music Company			
Mart Music Store			
Maruca Wallpaper & Music Company			
Marx Music Store	Sacramento	CA	Ellas Marx
Mason Furniture Company			
Mason Jewelry			M.E. Mason
Mass Music Company			L. Mass
Massillon Music Company	Massillon	OH	
Mathis & Youmans Company	Valdosta	GA	
Max Flaster Music Shop			
Maxwell Jewelry Company			
May Company			
Mayer Music Company			H.P. Mayer
Maynard Music Company	Raleigh	NC	
Maynard Music Company	Salisbury	NC	
Mays Music Company			
McClister Music Company	Bristol	TN	
McClister Music Company	Kingsport	TN	

Gibson Dealers: Circa 1935 (continued)

Dealership Name	Location		Owner
McCoys House of Music			
McCoys Inc.	Torrington	CT	
McCoys Inc.	Waterbury	CT	
McCoys Music & Electric	Norristown	PA	
McCoys Music House			
McCoys Music Shop	Norristown	PA	
McCreary Music Company			
McFayden Music Store			
McIntosh Music House	Kalispell	MT	
McKenzie Music Company	Janesville	WI	
McKim Music Company	Cincinnati	OH	
McLean Music Company			
McWhorter Music Company			
Megarity Music	Beaumont	TX	Charles B. Megarity
Meiklejohn Company			
Melody Haven Inc.	Roanoke	VA	Charles A. Rowe Sr.
Melody Music Company			
Melody Music Shop			
Melody Shoppe	Punxsutawney	PA	
Mendel Music House			
Metropolitan Loan Company			
Meyer Music Store	Kalamazoo	MI	A.R. Meyer
Meyer Seeger Music Company	Appleton	WI	
Meyerholtz Music Company	Sidney	OH	Lawrence J. Meyerholtz
Meyers Music House	Grand Haven	MI	
Meyers Music House	Holland	MI	
Meyers Music Shop	Kokomo	IN	
Meyers Music Store	Minerva	OH	
Midwest Music Shop	Kalamazoo	MI	
Midwest Music Supply Company			
Midwest Radio Company	Cincinnati	OH	
Miffins Book & Music Store			
Miles Music Store	Knoxville	TN	T.A. Miles
Milhollan Music	Oklahoma City	OK	J.B. Milhollan
Miller Furniture Company			
Miller Music Company	Kankakee	IL	J.Bert Miller
Miller Music Company	Ft. Worth	TX	C.C. Miller
Miller Music Company	Lebanon	PA	
Millsams			
Minot Music Company	Minot	ND	
Mizzi Music Mart			
Modern Music Company			
Modern Music Shop			
Modesto Music Store	Modesto	CA	

Dealership Name	Location		Owner
Moe's Jewelry Store			
Mollers Jewelry Store			
Monaghan Jewelry			
Monroe Music Company			
Montgomery Jewelry Company			
Montgomery Ward & Company	Albany	NY	
Montgomery Ward & Company	Baltimore	MD	
Montgomery Ward & Company	Chicago	IL	
Montgomery Ward & Company	Denver	CO	
Montgomery Ward & Company	Ft. Worth	TX	
Montgomery Ward & Company	Kansas City	MO	
Montgomery Ward & Company	Oakland	CA	
Montgomery Ward & Company	Portland	OR	
Montgomery Ward & Company	St. Paul	MN	
Morgans Jewelry & Music Shop	High Point	NC	
Morris Music House	Eugene	OR	
Morton Lines Music Company	Springfield	MO	
Moses & Company	Richmond	VA	Walter D. Moses
Muncys Music Store			
Murphey The Jeweler	Tyler	TX	
Murray Company	Durham	NC	W.R. Murray
Muscatine Music House	Muscatine	IA	W.J. Burnett
Musholt Music Company	Quincy	IL	
Music Box Company			
Music Mart	Sandusky	OH	
Music Shop	Burlington	?	
Music Shop	Hagerstown	MD	
Music Shop	Laurel	MS	
Music Shop	Mansfield	OH	
Music Shop	Oak Hill	WV	
Music Shop	Paris	IL	
Music Shop	Trenton	NJ	
Music Shop	Wausau	WI	
Music Shop	Wooster	OH	
Musicians Supply Shop	Boston	MA	
Mygrant Band & Orchestra House	Kokomo	IN	Alton S. Mygrant
Myhres Watch Shop			
National Book & Music			
National Music Company			
National Music Shop			
National Musical Supply Company Inc.			
Nave Music Store			
Navenshegg's Music Store	East Conemaugh	PA	Victor E. Navenshegg
Navratil Music House	Brenham	TX	

Gibson Dealers: Circa 1935 (continued)

Dealership Name	Location		Owner
Needles Music Company			
Needles Music House			
Nelsons Music House	Algona	IA	
Nerhaugen Music Shop			
Ness Music Company			
New Era Radio Company			
New Music Store			
New Rochelle House of Music	New Rochelle	NY	
New York Band Instrument Company	New York City	NY	
Newtons Music Store			
Nicholson Ltd.	Fremantle	Australia	
Nicholson Ltd.	Perth	Australia	
Nicomede Music Company	Altoona	PA	Joseph Nicomede
Niles Music & Radio Shop			
Niles Music Company			
Niles Music Shop			
Nutting Inc.	Nashua	NH	William L. Nutting
Nye Music Shoppe			
Ogren Music House	Rockford	IL	A.G. Ogren
Olsen Music Store	Michigan City	IN	
Olsen's Music Store	Conway	AR	
Olson Music House			
Ongs China Shop			
Oppleman Jewelry, Music & Pawn	Lynchburg	VA	L. Oppleman
Orendorff Music Shop	Bloomington	IL	
Orlando Music Company	Orlando	FL	
Oscar Hall Music Company			
O'Shea Music Store			
Owens Jewelry Shop			
Paige & Company Inc.	Terre Haute	IN	W.H. Paige
Paling Ltd.	Sydney	Australia	W.H. Paling
Paplin Piano Company			
Parker Music Company	Dallas	TX	Charles Parker
Parker-Miller Jewelry Company	Lexington	NC	H. Calvin Miller
Parker's Music House	Harrisburg	PA	Lloyd L. Parker
Parks Music House Company	Hannibal	MO	
Parrott Furniture Company	Newport	TN	
Pasco Music Company			
Pauls Calaiainne Music Store			
Pauls Music Store			
Paynes For Music	Greenville	SC	
Pearson Company Inc.	Anderson	IN	
Pearson Company Inc.	Indianapolis	IN	
Pearson Company Inc.	Muncie	IN	

Dealership Name	Location		Owner
Pearson Company Inc.	New Castle	IN	
Pearson Company Inc.	Richmond	IN	
Peat's Music House	Utica	NY	
Pence Radio & Electric	Flat	AK	Lee T. Pence
Pendleton Music House	Pendleton	OR	
Penewell Music Company	Madison	Wisconsin	Jack Penewell
Penman & Company	St. John's	Canada	A.M. Penman
Peoples Home Furniture Company			
Perlmutter Inc.	Hartford	CT	Louis I Perlmutter
Perrin Music Store	Waseca	MN	D.E. Perrin
Perry Music Store			
Petty Music Company	Pittsburghh	PA	W.E. Petty
Peyer Music Company	St. Paul	MN	Joseph I. Peyer
Phelps Dodge Mercantile		AZ	
Philip-Werlein Ltd.	New Orleans	LA	Parham Werlein
Phillips Music Company	Morgantown	WV	S.A. Phillip
Phillips Music Company	Pueblo	CO	D.Z. Phillips
Philpitt & Son	Jacksonville	FL	S.Ernest Philpitt
Philpitt & Son	Miami	FL	S.Ernest Philpitt
Philpitt & Son	St. Petersburg	FL	S.Ernest Philpitt
Philpitt & Son	Tampa	FL	S.Ernest Philpitt
Philpitt & Son	Washington	DC	S.Ernest Philpitt
Picketts House of Music	Charleston	SC	
Pifer Music Shop			
Pink Music Company			
Pinks Music House			
Pittsburg Music Repair Company			
Place Music Company			William Place
Platt Music Company	Los Angeles	CA	Benjamin Platt
Pletchers Jewelry Store			
Ploumus Company			W. Ploumus
Plunker Chord Company			
Polangin Music Shop	Farrell	PA	William Polangin
Polk Music & Supply			
Polk Music Company			
Polk Musical Supply Company	Atlanta	GA	
Polliack & Company Ltd.	Johannesburg	South Africa	Herman Polliack
Polliack & Company Ltd.	Capetown	South Africa	Herman Polliack
Popma Music Company			
Poppler Piano Company	Grand Forks	ND	J.A. Poppler
Popps Music Store & Studios	Dayton	OH	Ed Popp
Porter & Son Company	Lima	OH	B.S. Porter
Porter & Son Company	Findley	OH	B.S. Porter
Porter Music & Furniture Company	Galax	VA	W.L. Porter

Gibson Dealers: Circa 1935 (continued)

Dealership Name	Location		Owner
Porter Company	Worcester	MA	W.L. Porter
Porters Jewelry Store			
Porters Music Shop			
Prescotts Sporting Goods			
Prices Soda Shop			
Public Pawn Shop			
Pyron Jewelry	Spray	NC	J.C. Pyron
Quart Music Store			P.T. Quart
Radio & Music Supply Company			
Raiford Stores Inc.			
Ramas Music Company			
Reed Music Company	Austin	TX	J.R. Reed
Reeder Music House			
Reidling Music Company	Albuquerque	NM	
Reidsville Jewelry Company	Reidsville	NC	
Reiland Loan			Al Reiland
Renders Brothers Company			
Reniers Music House	Dubuque	IA	Ralph Renier
Resnick's Music	Winston-Salem	NC	
Rexburg Music Company	Rexburg	ID	
Reynolds Music House			
Rhein Music Company	Belleville	IL	Walter L. Rhein
Rhodes Day Furniture Company	North Wilkesboro	NC	
Rinaldo's Music Shop	Middletown	CT	
Ritter Music Company	Atlanta	GA	
Ritter Music Company	Indianapolis	IN	
Roat Music Company	Battle Creek	MI	Charles E. Roat
Robert Simpson Company Ltd.	Toronto	Canada	
Roberts Music Company			
Roberts Music Store			G.W. Roberts
Robinson & Son			
Robinson Music Company			
Robinson Photo Music Company			
Rocano & Son Sporting Goods	Danbury	NY	
Rolla Radio Company			
Rose Music Company	Minneapolis	MN	B.A. Rose
Rosemary Furniture Company			
Ross Music Store	Akron	OH	
Rowensteins			
Rudicks Music & Jewelry Company	Akron	OH	Joseph Rudick
Rudman Music Company			
Russ Brothers			
Russells Music Store	Oxford	England	
Rutz Music Company	Mobile	AL	

Dealership Name	Location		Owner
Salak Brothers Piano Company	Racine	WI	
Salter's Music Shop	Wilmington	DE	
Sampson Music Company	Boise	ID	C.B. Sampson
Sampson Music Company	Buhl	ID	C.B. Sampson
Sampson Music Company	Nampa	ID	C.B. Sampson
Sampson Music Company	Pocatello	ID	C.B. Sampson
Sampson Music Company	Twin Falls	ID	C.B. Sampson
Sampson Music Company	Weiser	ID	C.B. Sampson
San Antonio Music Company	San Antonio	TX	
Sandee Music Company			
Sandel Music Company			
Sanders Music Shop			
Santa Rosa Furniture Company	Milton	FL	
Sarphite The Jeweler			
Sarver's Music Store	Piqua	OH	P.F. Sarver
Sarver's Music Store	Sidney	OH	P.F. Sarver
Sarver's Music Store	Waupakonata	OH	P.F. Sarver
Sauer Music Company	Lorain	OH	Arthur B. Sauer
Sawkins Music House	Alma	MI	
Sawkins Music House	Ithaca	MI	
Sawkins Music House	St. Louis	MI	
Schafer Music Shop	Waterloo	IA	A.C. Schafer
Schenley Jewelry	Schenley	PA	
Schiller Brothers Inc.			
Schmoller & Mueller Piano Company	Omaha	NE	
Schonfield Music & Hawaiian			
Schultz Music Store			
Schweitzirs			
Scotts Music Shop			
Seaton Piano Company	Aurora	IL	J.C. Seaton
Seder's Music Company	Worcester	MA	Carl Seder
Seiberling & Lucas Music	Portland	OR	Frank Lucas
Sell Brothers			
Senerchia Brothers Music Store			
Shanks & Adams Jewelry Company	Waterloo	IA	
Sheets Piano House			
Sheffer Music Company	Dayton	OH	
Shepanski Music Shop			
Sheppard Company			B.J. Sheppard
Sherman Clay & Company	Oakland	CA	
Sherman Clay & Company	San Francisco	CA	
Sherman Clay & Company	Portland	OR	
Sherman Clay & Company	Sacramento	CA	
Sherman Clay & Company	San Jose	CA	

Gibson Dealers: Circa 1935 (continued)

Dealership Name	Location		Owner
Sherman Clay & Company	Santa Rosa	CA	
Sherman Clay & Company	Seattle	WA	
Sherman Clay & Company	Vallejo	CA	
Sherman Sporting Goods Store			
Shumaker Music Store			
Siegling Music House Inc.	Charleston	SC	Rudolph Siegling
Sikking Company	Springfield	IL	A.W. Sikking
Silvers Piano Company	Tacoma	WA	
Smart's Music Store	Mansfield	OH	Eugene Smart
Smith & Phillips			
Smith Music Company			A. Smith
Smith Music Company			C. Smith
Smith Music House			H.R. Smith
Smith Music Store			
Soo Music Shop			
Soriano's Music & Electric	Niles	OH	Nickolas Soriano
Sorkin Music Company	Philadelphia	PA	Louis Sorkin
Souders Music Shop	Muncie	IN	
South Plains Music Company	Lubbock	TX	
Southeastern Music Company	Miami	FL	
Southern Loan & Jewelry Company			
Southern Music Company	Jacksonville	FL	
Southern Sales Company			
Southwestern Music Corporation	Dallas	TX	
Southwestern Music Shop	Corsicana	TX	
Spaniard Piano Company	Maysville	KY	Richard Spaniard
Sparks Music Company			J.B. Sparks
Spaulding Furniture Company	Rutland	VT	
Spears & Son			
Spears Music House Inc.	Rome	NY	
Spence Music Company	Zanesville	OH	
Spencer Radio Shop			
Spiegel, May, Stern & Company	Chicago	IL	
Sproesser Jewelry Company	Watertown	WI	William D. Sproesser
Squires Music House	Shippensburg	PA	Fred C. Squires
St. Charles Music House	St. Charles	MO	
St. Joseph Music House	Benton Harbor	MI	
St. Louis Band House	St. Louis	MO	
St. Louis Band Instrument Company	St. Louis	MO	
St. Louis Music & Supply Company	St. Louis	MO	
Stallsmith Music Store	Gettysburg	PA	P.W. Stallsmith
Star Jewelers Inc.			
Star Loan Company			
Stark Piano Company	Bellingham	WA	E. Oberlatz

Dealership Name	Location		Owner
Staunton Furniture Company	Staunton	VA	
Stenger Music House			
Stephens Music Company			
Stephens Music Shop			
Stephens Music Store			
Stephenson Music & Sporting Company			
Stephenson Music Company	Raleigh	NC	C.H. Stephenson
Sterchi Brothers Stores Inc.	Kingsport	TN	
Sterchi Brothers Stores Inc.	Knoxville	TN	
Sterchi Brothers Stores Inc.	Chattanooga	TN	
Sterlings Music Store			
Stickhill Music Company			H.E. Stickhill
Stifels Music Store	Loveland	CO	A.V. Stifel
Stoner Piano Company	Des Moines	IA	
Stout's Music House	Kirksville	MO	Russell Stout
Strahls Music Store			
Straube Piano Company	Hammond	IN	
Strobels Music Store	Nashville	TN	Robert W. Strobel
Stromberg Music Company			
Stroudsberg Music Company	Stroudsberg	PA	
Suddarth & Company	Gallatin	TN	B. D. Suddarth
Summers & Son	Chillicothe	OH	H.C. Summers
Summers & Son	Athens	OH	H.C. Summers
Summers & Son	Jackson	OH	H.C. Summers
Summers & Son	Portsmouth	OH	H.C. Summers
Superior Music Company	Superior	WI	
Swingle Music Store	Newark	OH	B.S. Swingle
Szalay Music Store	Trenton	NJ	Edward Szalay
Targ & Dinner Inc.	Chicago	IL	
Tarpley Music Store	Pampa	TX	
Tate Radio Company	Harrisburg	IL	
Tattersdill Music House	Camden	NJ	
Tavis Music Company	Bismark	ND	A.R. Tavis
Taylor Musical Instruments	Columbia	MO	
Temple Music Company	Memphis	TN	
Temple Music House			
Temple Music Shop	Temple	TX	
Temple of Music			
Terminal Loan Office	San Francisco	CA	
Terry & Sons Inc.			H.L. Terry
Textile Jewelry Company			
Thatcher Music Company	Logan	UT	Brigham G. Thatcher
The Colonial			
The Fiddle Shop			

Gibson Dealers: Circa 1935 (continued)

Dealership Name	Location		Owner
The Music Box			
The Music House			
The Music Mart	Salisbury	NC	
The Music Shop	Burlington	?	
The Music Shop	Columbus	OH	
The Music Shop	Cottonwood	AZ	
The Music Shop	Hagerstown	MD	
The Music Shop	Huron	SD	
The Music Shop	Kewanee	IL	
The Music Shop	Nashville	TN	
The Music Shop	Oak Hill	WV	
The Music Shop	Paris	IL	
The Music Shop	Wausau	WI	
The Music Shop	Prescott	AZ	
The Music Store	Superior	WI	
The Pass Music Store			
The Pompilio Music House			
The Post Exchange			
The Song Shop			
The Violin Shop			
Thearle Music Company	San Diego	CA	
Theis Furniture Exchange			
Thomas Music Company			
Thomas Music House			
Tolzien Music Store	Amarillo	TX	
Tom Berry Music Company			
Toms Guitar Shop			
Tonk Brothers Company	Chicago	IL	
Tosi Music Company	Boston	MA	
Tri State Music Company			
Troup Brothers	Harrisburg	PA	Abraham & Lewis Troup
Troup Music House	Harrisburg	PA	John H. Troup
Troup Music House	Lancaster	PA	John H. Troup
Truitt Music House	Pittsburgh	PA	H. Russell Truitt
Truman & Monn			
Tucker Music Shop			W.H. Tucker
Turbeville Music Company	Gainesville	TX	F.H. Turbeville
Turners Music Shop	Wallace	ID	
Turners Variety House			
Uncle Normans			
Uncle Sam's Loan Office	Bristol	TN	
United Music Company	Brockton	MA	
Universal Radio Company	Philadelphia	PA	
Valero Music Company	Tampa	FL	Joaquin Valero

Dealership Name	Location		Owner
Valley Music Company			
Valley Music Store			
Valpo Music House			
Van Why's Music Store	East Stroudsburg	PA	Norman Van Why
Van Zeeland Music Company	Appleton	WI	
Vance Music Company	Mason City	IA	John D. Vance
Vancouver Music Company	Vancouver	Canada	
Vernon Music Company			
Vernon Piano Company			
Vestal Music & Machine Company	Sherman	TX	Hugh A. Vestal
Volkwein Brothers	Pittsburgh	PA	
Waas Time Shop			
Wagners Music Store			
Wagoner Furniture Company	Hickory	NC	
Wainwright Music Company	Marietta	OH	
Waite Melody Shop			
Walberg & Auge	Worcester	MA	Barney Walberg
Waldon Music Shop	Allentown	PA	
Walker Music	Baltimore	MD	Fred Walker
Wallace & Schwartz Music Company			
Ward-Brodt Music Company	Madison	WI	T.Lane Ward
Ware Music Company			
Warlick Piano Company	Bluefield	WV	
Warren Music Company	Portland	OR	
Warren Music Store	Warren	OH	
Watson Music Company	Mt. Vernon	IL	Fred P. Watson
Watson Music Shop			
Weaver Music Company			L.C. Weaver
Webber Music Company			
Webbers Music Shop			
Weber Jewelry & Music	St. Cloud	MN	
Weber Music & Radio Company			
Weeks & Dickenson	Binghamton	NY	E.R. Weeks
Welch Furniture Company			C.C. Welch
Wellers Store			
Wells Music Company	Casper	WY	Charles E. Wells
Wells Music Company	Denver	CO	Charles E. Wells
Weltys			
Werner Cycle Shop			
Wernsman Music Company	LaSalle	IL	A.F. Wernsman
Wert Music House			
West End Music Company			
West Music House			W.W. West
West Music House	Greensboro	NC	Harvey West

Gibson Dealers: Circa 1935 (continued)

Dealership Name	Location		Owner
West Side Music House			
Westmorelands			
White Jewelry Store			
White Music Company			
White Music Store			
Whited & Son			C.A. Whited
Whitehead Music Company			
Whiteman Music Company			
Whitley Jewelry Company			
Whitlock Music Company	Enid	OK	
Whitman Music Company			
Wichita Music Company			
Wilbur Music Company			
Wiley Dry Goods Company			
Williams Music Company			R.E. Williams
Wilson & Sons Ltd.	Quebec	Canada	H.C. Wilson
Wilson & Sons Ltd.	Sherbrooke	Canada	H.C. Wilson
Wilson Music Company	Oshkosh	WI	
Winfields Music Store			
Winfields Stationers			
Wing On Company Ltd.	Hong Kong	China	
Winnipeg Musical Supply Company	Winnepeg	Canada	
Winnipeg Musical Supply Company	Edmonton	Canada	
Winnipeg Piano Company	Winnepeg	Canada	
Wiscott Music House			
Wiswell Music Store	Chicago	IL	L.C. Wiswell
Wittich's Music House	Hazelton	PA	Arthur & Otto Wittich
Wittich's Music House	Reading	PA	Arthur & Otto Wittich
Wolffe Violin Shop			J.C. Wolffe
Woodman Furniture Company			
Woodson Furniture & Undertaking Company	Jackson	AL	
Workman Green Company			
Worth Jewelry			
Wrights Music Store			
Yahrling-Rayner Music Company	Youngstown	OH	Charles H. Yahrling
Yates Music Company	Auburn	AL	
Ye Brunswick Shoppe	Dubuque	IA	
Ye Music Shoppe			
Young Music Company			W. Young
Zenders Music Company	Lima	OH	Tony Zender

Chapter 7 - Teacher-Agents

Gibson teacher-agent Betty Reichenbach circa 1932, holding her Gibson Granada tenor banjo
Joy Musselman Collection

Overview

The teacher-agent was an important factor in selling Gibson instruments throughout the pre-World War II period. These individuals worked from their homes or music studios, purchasing instruments directly from the factory at wholesale prices and then selling them at a profit. This method of product marketing predated the formation of the company in 1902, as Orville Gibson also sold instruments this way. But even afterwards, it was strongly supported by the company's first general manager, Sylvo Reams, and the first sales manager, Lewis A. Williams. Both of them had experience in selling instruments as Reams had formerly been a partner in a retail music store and Williams had been a music teacher in New York State. Gibson continued to support the teacher-agent system even after the inception of a retail dealership network in 1924.

Company Support

Gibson originally provided ongoing support to their teacher-agents via the *Sounding Board Salesman* magazine. This monthly periodical was published by Gibson and contained sales tips, slogans, and generally the latest news about Gibson instruments. *Mastertone Magazine* replaced the *Sounding Board Salesman* in November 1926 with a more general content which appealed to dealers as well as teacher-agents. It was published for 14 years.

The company also invested considerable resources in producing a wide variety of teacher supplies. Official student award certificates, graduated teaching methods, student scheduling books, and financial ledgers were readily available to the Gibson teacher-agent. Instrument selling tips were also distributed, especially during the period in which Lewis A. Williams worked for the company. Gibson encouraged teacher-agent membership in the American Guild of Banjoists, Mandolinists and Guitarists by attending their national conventions and printing their rhetoric in some catalogs.

Proportion of Sales

The 1935 Gibson shipping ledger lists over 1,000 teacher-agents, each of whom on average purchased fewer than five instruments in a year. The total accounted for perhaps 20% of all sales, making the teacher-agent market much smaller than that of the authorized dealerships in the mid-1930's. Because the number of instruments sold per teacher-agent was low, it was essential to keep a high number of teacher-agents in play to make this scheme profitable. Also, after factoring in the inescapable overhead costs for the teacher-agents of sales, marketing, billing, etc., Gibson's return on investment was considerably reduced. The company continued to work with a few teacher-agents up into the 1950's, but by and large this inefficient method of selling products died out with the onset of World War II.

From some teacher-agents even slow payments were acceptable. In 1940 long-time Gibson teacher-agent Eugene E. Claycomb owed the company $93.34. General manager Guy Hart told the board of directors that Claycomb was "an old and valued teacher-agent, who has given us lots of business; he is on C.O.D. and pays a little from time to time on the old account." In the case of Luella Allen of Omaha, Nebraska, who owed $72.29, Hart noted, "an old Gibson teacher, also stockholder in the company, now on C.O.D."

Geographical Distribution

The Gibson teacher-agent paradigm seems to have taken hold more strongly in the northeastern and midwestern regions of the country. Pennsylvania, New York, Ohio, Illinois, and Michigan in particular were the strongest states for this marketing scheme. Because the teacher-agent relationship developed during the earliest years of the company, it could be that this quirk of geographical distribution was simply a function of the nation's population distribution at that time. It clearly required a somewhat denser, settled population and worked better in small to medium-size towns, where the teacher-agent had ready access to people with disposable income and an inclination towards culture.

William B. McMichael

William B. McMichael was one of the most successful Gibson teacher-agents and in many ways typifies the genre. He was born on February 17, 1908 in Cleveland, Ohio and attended high school in Youngstown, graduating in 1927. McMichael learned to play the plectrum banjo as a high school student and performed as a member of the Rayen School Orchestra. He also played a variety of other instruments, including tenor banjo, guitar, Hawaiian guitar, mandolin, bass, and accordion. He began his career as a Gibson teacher-agent at Youngstown in 1927 and continued to work there until moving to Newark, Ohio in 1932. In 1933 at the age of 25, he was elected to the board of directors for the American Guild of Banjoists, Mandolinists and Guitarists, the youngest man ever to receive this honor. McMichael married Miss Florence Lindsey in 1934 and promptly taught her to play the mandolin. They would work together teaching music for the rest of their lives.

A master organizer, McMichael lost no time in creating a variety of student bands in Newark. He understood the value of involving the local community by creating business sponsorships. A surviving scrapbook shows that he relentlessly used the newspapers to promote his student concerts. These events varied from lavish stage productions to something as simple as marching in a Newark parade. A typical local concert consisted of various student groups performing pieces in appropriately themed costumes. Usually, the teacher-agent (in this case McMichael) would personally end the program with a strong solo performance. Another alternative was to bring in a performer from another town to provide the show's closing act. By 1938 McMichael's efforts had resulted in a whopping 90 students, as reported in Gibson's *Mastertone Magazine*. Some Gibson teacher-agents in the same era had as many as 150 students.

Somehow, in the depths of the Great Depression, McMichael even found a way to take his students to American Guild competitions all over the country. The first convention they attended was held in 1933 at the Century of Progress Fair in Chicago. In 1934 they traveled to Holyoke, Massachusetts, in 1935 to Lawrence, Massachusetts, then to Minneapolis in 1936, on to Detroit in 1937, St. Joseph, Missouri in 1938, and finally the World's Fair at New York City in 1939! The cost of transportation was underwritten by local business sponsors and by the payment of weekly dues (15 cents) from each student. At the conventions the students took part in configurations such as: string quartets, banjo clubs, junior ensembles, Hawaiian orchestras, and solo competitions. McMichael's students consistently took top national honors.

William B. McMichael died at Newark on December 10, 1969. His wife Florence continued to run their teaching studio well into the 1980's. She died in 1990 after more than 50 years as a music teacher.

Students of William B. McMichael in 1936
Ruth Glover Collection

How did William B. McMichael rate as a teacher-agent sales rep for Gibson? In 1935 he ordered 70 instruments including 10 banjos, 10 mandolins, 23 Spanish guitars, and 9 Hawaiian guitars. Eighteen of these were Kalamazoo brand, but six were Mastertone tenor banjos and another nine were Roy Smeck Stage Deluxe Hawaiian guitars. The total retail value of all these instruments and their cases exceeded $3,400. At the depth of the Great Depression, this was a considerable sum, and when multiplied over the 40 years that McMichael was a Gibson teacher-agent, it is easy to see that his value to the company was considerable.

Betty Reichenbach

Betty Reichenbach was born December 10, 1913 in East Orange, New Jersey, but her family moved to Lansdale, Pennsylvania during her childhood. Reichenbach attended a music college in Philadelphia and played piano, organ, accordion, tenor banjo, guitar, Hawaiian guitar, mandolin, lap steel, marimba, and xylophone. After graduation, her father Victor S. Reichenbach set her up in business with a music teaching studio at 128 South Broad Street in Lansdale. She married fellow musician and teacher John H. Richard in 1947, and together they covered the gamut of musical possibility. He specialized in brass and woodwind band instruments.

While Betty was also a very successful Gibson teacher-agent, her experience was slightly different because she came late to the system, only beginning with the company in about 1933. By that time, the mandolin craze was over, tenor banjo was tentatively holding its own, and the popularity of guitar was on the rise. There is no evidence that she ever joined the American Guild of Banjoists, Mandolinists and Guitarists. Her students did not attend national conventions like those of William B. McMichael. Teaching in Lansdale also meant that she had formidable competition in the form of long-time Gibson teacher-agent Forest K. Moyer.

So, being a student of Betty Reichenbach was something a little bit different from the normal experience. It was similar in that it meant marching in local parades and taking part in annual student recitals featuring elaborate costume changes. And to be sure there was also plenty of emphasis on tenor banjo music, but now Hawaiian melodies and western cowboy songs predominated as well, both of them featuring the new Gibson electric lap steel guitar. There were no fancy mandolin orchestras in the style of Forest K. Moyer. Women also played a more emphasized role in her world, with period photos showing several all-female student bands.

Betty Reichenbach (far right) and students, circa 1940
Joy Musselman Collection

Reichenbach's 1935 sales statistics are perhaps more typical of the average Gibson teacher-agent, with only 12 instruments shipped to her from Kalamazoo. Still, the retail value of the instruments and their cases was over $1,400. Like McMichael's 1935 orders, there are more guitars than banjos (eight to four), but unlike him, no mandolins or mandolin family instruments. Future orders from Betty would

be predominantly lap steels, flattop guitars, and even an RB-75 five-string banjo. She would still be a Gibson teacher-agent in the 1950's, perhaps one of the last such accounts. Betty Reichenbach Richard continued teaching music into the 1970's and died on March 9, 1980 in Bucks County, Pennsylvania.

The Fun of Playing With Others

THE greatest joy in music comes from playing with others—whether it is just an informal duet, a small family group, or a huge fretted instrument concert orchestra.

Music brings people together in a common understanding—sharing good times and knowledge—no wonder the greatest men in history hail music as the finest character builder.

When it comes to group playing, the fretted instruments claim the spotlight because no other instruments are so adaptable to orchestra combinations, large or small.

You may not be a natural congenial mixer, or perhaps you lack the ability to make those close friendships that add so much zest to life and living—yet music can help you overcome this handicap for it is a means of fellowship.

Group playing is the means to social advancement — travel — income — and education. Every year, fretted instrument orchestras gather at certain points throughout the United States for good times, concerts and contests—everyone has a part and a share.

Let fretted instruments open the gateway to happiness for you—whether you go into it as a serious career, or as a hobby, or as the most pleasant of pastimes—playing a fretted instrument is your answer.

BANJO, GUITAR AND MANDOLIN GROUPS ORGANIZED BY ALBERT BELLSON, ST. PAUL, MINNESOTA

The centerfold of a Gibson teacher-agent brochure, circa 1934, promoting the benefits of learning to play a fretted instrument.

Robert L. Hart Collection

Gibson Teacher-Agents: Individuals

Gibson had thousands of teacher-agents, and any attempt to identify and list them all would be difficult, if not impossible. The following table represents some of Gibson's most well-known and successful dealer-agents. It was reconstructed from Gibson shipping ledgers, catalogs, and other external sources. The location of the teacher-agent is shown if the data could be ascertained with reasonable certainty. The list is not intended to be comprehensive.

Last Name	First Name	Location	
Allen	Luella	Omaha	NE
Barr (Mr. & Mrs.)	William R.	Ft. Wayne	IN
Bellson	Albert	St. Paul	MN
Bellson	Julius	St. Paul	MN
Bellson	Louis	Rock Island	IL
Billek	John J.	Scranton	PA
Blakely (Mrs.)	Florence C.	Poughkeepsie	NY
Boehm	Walter A.	Boston	MA
Boote	Herbert	Hamilton	Ontario
Brinker	Wilman G.	Allentown	PA
Brockmeyer	Albert C.	St. Louis	MO
Brockmeyer	Dewey	St. Louis	MO
Bulla	Emmett	Bloomsburg	PA
Cady	Dale L.	Moline	IL
Cane	Bill	Spokane	WA
Caroselli	A.L.	Detroit	MI
Christensen	Howard	Lincoln	NE
Claycomb	Eugene E.	Collegeville	PA
Colonna	Frank	Apollo	PA
Cooke	Earle	Kansas City	MO
Crandall (Miss)	Sarah	Syracuse	NY
Dean	Warren N.	York	PA
Felton	Chester C.	Erie	PA
Fenimore	Francis	Vineland	NJ
Gill	Harry F.	Passaic	NJ
Hagen	Theodore R.	Muskegon	MI
Hartnett	Dennis E.	New York City	NY
Hetze (Mrs. Max)	Hulda	Eau Clair	WI
Hinchcliffe	Henry Garfield	Corona	NY
Kapua	Homer	Danville	IL
Landry	George Phillip	Lancaster	PA
Lopardo	Joseph	Utica	NY
Marchioni	S.	Connellsville	PA
McMichael	William B.	Newark	OH
Merrifield	Ada N.	Willimantic	CT
Merthe	Don	Elyria	OH
Midkiff	George Gilbert	Butte	MT
Miller	Lester K.	St. Joseph	MI
Moyer	Forest K.	Lansdale	PA
Moyer	Will D.	Harrisburg	PA

Gibson Teacher-Agents: Individuals (continued)

Last Name	First Name	Location	
Nicomede	Joseph	Altoona	PA
O'Callaghan (Miss)	Bessie	Staunton	VA
Ruhnow	Carl A.	LaCrosse	WI
Santos	Don	Rochester	NY
Scrivener	Austin	Hartford	CT
Secrest	George R.	Hardin	MT
Senay	Robert	Houston	TX
Shattuck	Carl C.	Kalamazoo	MI
Stacy	J.D.	Sturgis	MI
St. John	Stephen	Schenectady	NY
Templeman	C.A.	Sioux City	IA
Tolhurst	H. Blair	Jackson	MI
Trinkaus	Theodore P.	Stamford	CT
Truitt	Harry Russell	Pittsburgh	PA
Walker	C.C.	Rome	GA
Wells	Dee	Rockford	IL

Examples of *Mastertone Magazine*, one of Gibson's strongest marketing tools

Steve Huber Collection

Gibson Teacher-Agents: Schools and Studios

The following chart represents some of Gibson's more well-known and successful teacher-agents who worked in a studio or school. It was reconstructed from Gibson shipping ledgers, catalogs, and other external sources. The location of the school or studio is shown if the data could be ascertained with reasonable certainty. The list is not intended to be comprehensive.

Business Name	Location		Teacher-Agent
Bennage Music Studio	Milton	PA	C.A. Bennage
Bishop Studio			
Boston Academy			
Bush Music Studio			Frank Bush
Consentino School of Music	Lawrence	MA	Joe Consentino
Conservatory of Hawaiian Music	New York City	NY	
Cortland Conservatory of Music	Cortland	NY	
Custer Music Studio			
Dee Wells Music Studio	Louisville	KY	Dee Wells
Dixie Conservatory			
Dorrock School	Pasadena	CA	A. Thomas Wellesp
Edmonds Studio			J. Edmonds
Edwards Studio			
Elmira Conservatory of Music	Elmira	NY	
Falzone Music Company	Pittston	PA	Vincenzo Falzone
Gardners School of Music			
Gill School of Music	Passaic	NJ	Harry F. Gill
Griffith School of Music	Atlanta	GA	William B. Griffith
Guzzardo Studio	Rockford	IL	Joseph Guzzardo
Hagadorn School of Music	Hornell	NY	Lloyd E. Hagadorn
Halsted School of Music	Olcott	NY	Mrs. Althea L. Halsted
Harding Studio of Music			
Hartnett National Music Studio	New York City	NY	Dennis E. Hartnett
Hawaiian Guitar Studio			
Hess School of Music			Edwin Hess
Hissong School of Music		OH	Reefa G. Hissong
Honolulu Conservatory of Music	Honolulu	HA	
Joslin Music & Art Studio			
Kahakalau Studio	Lynn	MA	William Kahakalin
Kalauaina School of Music			
Kepples School of Music			
Knapp School of Music			
La Flamme Studio			F. La Flamme
La Flanner Studio			
Lamberton Studio			Charles H. Lamberton
Le Conservatoire de Musique			
Lehigh Institute of Music			
Lucas School of Music			
Malgeri Studio	San Diego	CA	Joseph S. Malgeri
Major Music Studio			

Gibson Teacher-Agents: Schools and Studios (continued)

Business Name	Location		Teacher-Agent
McNeil School of Music			
Modern School of Music			
Morrells School of Music			
Newton Music School Store			
Pauls Music Studio			
Pecks School of Music			
Peterson Banjo & Guitar Studio			A.J. Peterson
Pizzitola Music Studio	Holyoke	MA	Joseph F. Pizzitola
Reichenbach's Music Studio	Lansdale	PA	Betty Reichenbach
Robleys Music Rooms			
Ruhnow Music Studio	LaCrosse	WI	Carl Ruhnow
Sandberg's Music Studio			J.H. Sandberg
Sloan School of Music			
Smeck School of Music	New York City	NY	Roy Smeck
Stockaj Studio			R.A. Stockaj
United Artist Conservatory			
United Studio of Music			
Wack Sales Company	Milwaukee	WI	Adolph Waech
Warncastle Music Studio			L. Warncastle
Wells Music Studio	Louisville	KY	Dee Wells
Westbrook Conservatory of Music	Atlanta	GA	John Westbrook
White Music Studio			
Wirsing Music Studio	Flint	MI	Harry M. Wirsing

Chapter 8 - Artists and Endorsers

A phenomenal group of jazz guitarists, all Gibson endorsers, pose with general manager Guy Hart, western regional salesman George Post, and music store owner Hal Fife in Hollywood, California, circa 1936. Front row (left to right): Joe Ehrecke, Dick Roberts, Eddie Stockbridge, Henry Pendergraft, and Berdell Mathis, back row (left to right): Richard "Babe" Ehrecke, Guy Hart, George Smith, George Post, and Hal Fife.
John Post Collection

Overview

While hundreds of people endorsed Gibson instruments before World War II, the company had only two official artists during that period: Nick Lucas and Roy Smeck. Prominent musicians like Harry Reser, Alvino Rey, Carson J. Robison, and Andy Sannella came close, but neither they nor any other musicians ever got their names on a specific pre-war, Gibson-brand, production-model instrument. Lucas and Smeck are set apart from all other Gibson endorsers because of the "Nick Lucas Special" guitar and the "Roy Smeck Stage Deluxe" and "Radio Grande" Hawaiian guitars.

Today we assume that being a Gibson artist would mean receiving a free or reduced-cost instrument. However, it is unclear whether or not Lucas and Smeck ever got such a benefit. In an interview with Gibson historian Walter Carter, pre-war mandolinist Walter K. Bauer stated that Gibson never gave anything away. This statement is borne out by an incident which took place on April 25, 1927 in which general manager Guy Hart traveled to Cleveland, Ohio to present well-known banjoist and Gibson endorser Jack Rose with his custom-made TB-Florentine. The following week *Music Trade Review* magazine contained an article covering this event, pointedly stating in the text that Mr. Rose had purchased the banjo through the local Gibson dealer, Grossman Brothers. Nobody was getting anything for free from Gibson.

<u>**Nick Lucas (1897-1982)**</u>

Dominic Nicholas Anthony Lucanese, a.k.a. "Nick Lucas," was arguably the first American pop superstar vocalist-guitar virtuoso. Through a combination of talent, hard work, and good timing, he rose to national fame in the first half of the 20th century, relying on a "crooning" vocal style and hot flatpicking jazz guitar. He was born on August 22, 1897 in Newark, New Jersey to Italian immigrants Ottone and Carmalia Lucanese. The family was very musical, and as a young boy Nick played his first local gigs on mandolin with his older brother Frank on accordion. He began working in vaudeville about 1915 and by 1921 was recording as a sideman with the Vernon Country Club Orchestra. In 1922 Nick recorded two original songs on the Pathe label which would change his life. "Picking the Guitar" and "Teasing the Frets" would bring him national attention and still stand today as the first "hot" solo guitar records. He went on to appear on Broadway and in several early movies prior to World War II.

In a 1980 interview with *Guitar Player Magazine* editor Jas Obrecht, Lucas stated that the Gibson Company contacted him in 1924 and asked him to play one of their guitars. At the time he was performing in Chicago with Ted FioRito and the Oriole Terrace Orchestra (this popular musical group may have been the basis for Gibson's "Oriole" line of entry-level instruments which debuted in the mid-1920's). At the time he was approached, Lucas was using a Galliano guitar, which he had purchased in New York City. After switching to Gibson, he found several drawbacks to the stock guitars and asked the company build him a custom instrument. He wanted a wider fingerboard, allowing a little extra space between the first and second strings only. This was because when Lucas placed his index finger on the second string at the first fret it unintentionally also muted the first string. He also specified a slightly deeper body and a matte-black finish. The latter requirement was intended to reduce the reflective glare when he was in the spotlight. He had noticed that in such situations the members of his audience were sometimes temporarily blinded by the gloss finish on his Galliano.

We do not know the exact date when Lucas received his original custom Gibson guitar. A *Music Trade Review* magazine article dated March 30, 1925 describes him as "performing on Gibson instruments" but does not mention a custom guitar. In the same piece Gibson sales manager Frank B. Campbell stated that Gibson guitar sales were being noticeably assisted by Lucas's popularity. During the last week of June 1925, Lucas visited the Gibson factory at Kalamazoo, and *Music Trade Review* magazine dutifully reported on the event in an article dated July 11th. Lucas was quoted as attributing much of his success to his "wonderful Gibson instrument," without stating clearly which instrument he was referring to. Photographs from this period show him with various Gibson archtop models. It seems likely that his original custom Gibson flattop guitar might have been ordered during the factory tour of June 1925. This idea is supported by a 1981 newspaper interview in which Lucas himself stated that he took delivery of the guitar in 1925.

A Gibson dealer price list dated March 1928 contains the earliest known, official mention of a "Nick Lucas Special" production model guitar. Gibson catalog "Q" (also dated 1928) is the first catalog to mention the model. Yet, at least one guitar with Nick Lucas-type features and a factory order number dating to 1927 has been seen. In all likelihood, because of his popularity and constant exposure, Gibson probably made multiple copies of the original Nick Lucas guitar in 1926 and 1927. Then, in the face of a constant demand, they finally gave in and created a production model for 1928. This "self-perpetuating" market is what separated Nick Lucas from other endorsers and raised him to the level of a Gibson artist.

The production model seems to have been slightly different from the original in several aspects. The original Lucas guitar is believed to have had simple dot inlays in the fingerboard and used banjo-style tuners. The later production models had a fancier fingerboard inlay very similar to that in the Galliano guitar which Lucas had used prior to 1925. Strangely, this specific inlay was also used by Gibson in their style 2 tenor banjos beginning in 1925, predating the "Nick Lucas Special" production model guitars by three years. The banjo-type tuners used in the original were also eventually replaced with regular guitar tuners. Other specifications such as body size, bridge type, finish, etc., would change over the next decade as well. Gibson did not list the "Nick Lucas Special" in a catalog after 1937 but continued to ship new-old-stock up through 1941. Gibson probably manufactured about 300 of the production model instruments.

After World War II Nick Lucas continued to work but never again reached the kind of stardom he had previously achieved. He was a successful night club entertainer and became one of the early stars of the Las Vegas showrooms. He died on July 28, 1982 at Colorado Springs, Colorado.

Roy Smeck

LeRoy G.A. Schmeck, a.k.a. "Roy Smeck," was born February 6, 1900 in Reading, Pennsylvania, the son of working-class parents Harry A. and Rosa E. Ginader Schmeck. The family was living in Binghamton, New York by 1917 where Roy found work as a clerk in a piano store. Smeck would later claim that he did not start playing music until he was 20 years old and then learned everything he knew by listening to phonograph records, perhaps being one of the first to do so. Smeck was no singer and so he concentrated on becoming a multi-instrumentalist, playing tenor banjo, regular banjo, mandolin, Spanish guitar, Hawaiian guitar, harp-guitar, and ukulele. He also performed on a guitar-type instrument known as the "octa-chorda" which was an invention of Harry Skinner at Lyon & Healy in Chicago. He found his first show business break in 1923 working as an accompanist to singer Olga Myra (whom he married in 1927) on the Keith and Orpheum vaudeville circuit. He joined Paul Specht and the Alamac Orchestra in June 1924 as an instrumental soloist.

His ability on each of the instruments he played was nothing short of astounding. In addition to a solid understanding of jazz, Smeck had a repertoire of "tricks" which he used to set himself apart from similar vaudeville acts. One of these was a two-handed, string-tapping technique which rocker Eddie Van Halen would use to good effect on electric guitar in the 1980's. In a typical ukulele performance, Smeck would blow across the soundhole (producing a note), tap out a rhythm on the back of the instrument, twirl it on its axis, swing it out from his body, and somehow never stop playing the song. He became nationally known in 1926 as the result of appearing in a Warner Brothers short called "His Pastimes." This film used the new Vitaphone "sound-on-disc" system and allowed Smeck to show off the full range of his trick playing. As a result, Smeck became an overnight sensation known as "The Wizard of the Strings."

Roy Smeck's first instrument endorsement was not for Gibson. Not even close. In fact, Smeck might be considered the most prolific instrument endorser in history. In 1924 he heartily promoted the Washburn brand products of Chicago manufacturer Lyon & Healy, claiming "I always have the pleasant feeling that they will respond to everything I ask of them." Evidently at some point he asked too much and they didn't respond because by 1927 he was working with the Harmony Company of Chicago, endorsing their "Vita-Uke." While on tour, he would make a personal appearance at a local music store during the day, giving a brief performance and helping the store owner to promote Harmony products. By 1928 he was simultaneously promoting the "Vita-Uke" and "Vita-Guitar" for Harmony *and* the "Roy Smeck Silver Bell" banjo line for Fred Bacon and David L. Day. The Harmony Company added the "Roy Smeck Grand Concert" guitar and "Roy Smeck Hawaiian Grand Concert" guitar to their line in 1930.

Late in 1933 Gibson was looking for a way to get out of the toy-making business and back into the musical instrument market. Two flashy, new Hawaiian guitar models with the endorsement of a top artist seemed like the way. It wasn't a great leap of imagination for somebody on the Gibson staff to think of Roy Smeck as the artist. The details of the offer are lost to history, but Smeck accepted (not a surprise) and in the 1934 catalog the "Roy Smeck Stage Deluxe" and "Roy Smeck Radio Grande" Hawaiian guitar models appeared.

But there were two problems. First of all, the market for acoustic Hawaiian guitars was about to be instantly obliterated by the Rickenbacker Company and their electric lap steel guitar. Gibson would respond to this threat quickly, producing their own lap steel guitars by late in 1935, without a Smeck endorsement. Secondly, unlike the organic growth of the Nick Lucas phenomenon, the Smeck models were the artificial product of the Gibson marketing department. Consequently, neither of the Smeck models lasted very long. The "Radio Grande" made its last appearance in the 1936 Gibson catalog, with the last batch produced in 1937. The "Stage Deluxe" held on through 1942, with a single batch produced that year. No other production model Gibson brand instrument would be made with a Roy Smeck endorsement. After World War II, Smeck returned to the Harmony Company as an artist/endorser.

Because Roy Smeck was not a vocalist, he has perhaps been unfairly branded as more of a novelty act than a full-fledged entertainer. Throughout his life he was deeply interested in teaching music, and in his final decades he concentrated his efforts in this area. A legion of students made the trek to his apartment on West End Avenue in the Upper West Side of New York City to study with "The Wizard of the Strings." Roy Smeck died peacefully in his sleep on April 5, 1994 at the advanced age of 94.

Gibson Endorsers: 1917-1942

As far as can be determined, there were no particular criteria for being a Gibson endorser. Anyone who sent a photograph to the company appears to have been eligible, and many such submissions were subsequently selected to appear in Gibson's catalogs, brochures, and magazines. The names on the following list are taken from these sources and are shown as of their earliest known listing, playing the instrument they endorsed at that time. Many of them were multi-instrumentalists and later endorsed other types of Gibson instruments as well. Some endorsers were also teacher-agents or ran retail music stores. The location and instrument type of each endorser are given if they could be determined. Many endorsers traveled in touring orchestras or as part of a vaudeville show and therefore had no permanent residence. No list of this type could ever be complete and such is not intended here.

Although the names of most Gibson endorsers have long been forgotten, some of them remain familiar to modern musicians. Among these are: Dave Apollon ("The World's Greatest Mandolin Virtuoso"), Gene Autry ("The Singing Cowboy"), Perry Bechtel ("The Man With 10,000 Fingers"), Uncle Dave Macon ("The Dixie Dewdrop"), Bill Monroe ("The Father of Bluegrass Music"), Les Paul ("Rhubarb Red"), Eddie Peabody ("King of the Banjo"), and Tex Ritter ("America's Most Beloved Cowboy").

Last Name	First Name	Location		Instrument	Year
Aarons	Herbert	Chicago	IL	Banjo (tenor)	1925
Alaimo	John	Boston	MA	Guitar	1937
Alkire	Eddie	Easton	PA	Lap steel guitar	1936
Allen	Lee	Los Angeles	CA	Guitar	1937
Allen	Luella	Omaha	NE		1924
Amberger	Charles	New York City	NY	Guitar	1937
Anderson	David	Norfolk	VA	Hawaiian guitar	1932
Anderson	Tom	San Diego	CA	Guitar	1937
Andrews	Orville A.	St. Louis	MO	Banjo (plectrum)	1930
Andrus	Frank			Banjo (tenor)	1924
Apollon	Dave	Queens	NY	Mandolin	1930
Ardi	Ernie			Console Grande	1942
Aten	Maurice E.	New York City	NY	Guitar	1928
Atkinson	Hal			Guitar	1939
Autry	Gene	Hollywood	CA	Guitar	1939
Avalloni	James	Boston	MA	Hawaiian guitar	1932
Avola	Al			Guitar	1937
Backus	Earl	Kansas City	MO	Guitar	1936
Bankey	Jack	Pittsburgh	PA	Guitar	1929
Barbour	Dave	Los Angeles	CA	Guitar	1939
Barnes	George	Chicago	IL	Guitar	1942
Barnitz	Al	Chicago	IL	Guitar	1936
Barr	W.R. "Ted"	Ft. Wayne	IN	Guitar	1924
Battist	Don	Pittsburgh	PA	Guitar	1937
Bauer	Walter Kaye	Hartford	CT	Mandolin	1922
Baum	W.F.	Lemoore	CA	Banjo (tenor)	1925
Becker	Leroy	Milwaukee	WI	Guitar	1937
Berman	Walt	Los Angeles	CA	Banjo (tenor)	1932

Last Name	First Name	Location		Instrument	Year
Bechtel	Perry	Cleveland	OH	Guitar	1928
Bevis	A.L.			Mandolin	1917
Binford	Ken	New York City	NY	Guitar	1942
Biondi	Remo	Chicago	IL	Guitar	1939
Birch	Gorde	Chicago	IL	Guitar	1936
Bjurmark	Bill	New York City	NY	Lap steel guitar	1939
Blanchette	Jack			Guitar	1935
Bonnie	Lou			Guitar	1934
Boote	Herbert	Hamilton	Canada	Hawaiian guitar	1929
Botkin	Perry			Guitar	1939
Brock	C.L. (Mrs.)	Houston	TX	Mandolin	1924
Brooks	Ted	Birmingham	AL	Guitar	1936
Brown	Earl	Salt Lake City	UT	Guitar	1939
Brown	Royal	San Antonio	TX	Banjo (tenor)	1937
Bruce	Kenneth	Duluth	MN	Guitar	1936
Brugge	Charles J.	New York City	NY	Mandolin	1930
Bruno	Benny			Guitar	1939
Bryant	Slim			Guitar	1934
Burns	Bill	Chicago	IL	Lap steel guitar	1936
Byram	Mildred	Dover	NJ	Mandolin	1930
Cain	Bob			Banjo (tenor)	1925
Calderello	Joe	Kansas City	MO	Guitar	1936
Caldwell	D.A.			Banjo (tenor)	1920
Cali	John	New York City	NY	Guitar	1930
Camp	Eleanor			Mando-Bass	1924
Campbell	Floyd	New York City	NY	Guitar	1928
Cane	Bill	Spokane	WA	Banjo (plectrum)	1930
Canfield	Ray			Ukulele	1928
Canzoneri	Joe	New York City	NY	Guitar	1934
Caprano	Joe	New Orleans	LA	Guitar	1930
Carlos	Jack	Jackson	MI		1925
Caroselli	A.L.	Detroit	MI	Banjo (tenor)	1929
Carpenter	Vic	Los Angeles	CA	Banjo (tenor)	1930
Castle	C.C.			Mandolin	1917
Catanese	Vincent	New York City	NY	Banjo (tenor)	1930
Catania	A.N.			Mandolin	1924
Chalfie	Eli			Guitar	1942
Chan	Peter			Banjo (tenor)	1925
Chester	Charles			Guitar	1937
Choi	Richard P.	Chicago	IL		1930
Christensen	Howard	Lincoln	NE	Banjo (tenor)	1930
Christman	Violet	Philadelphia	PA	Mandolin	1932
Clark	Watts	Allentown	PA	Guitar	1937
Clarke	Franklin W.	Madison		Banjo (tenor)	1930

Gibson Endorsers: 1917-1942 (continued)

Last Name	First Name	Location		Instrument	Year
Cola	Ned			Guitar	1939
Colicchio	Tony	New York City	NY	Guitar	1939
Collins	Eddie	Detroit	MI	Guitar	1936
Cooke	Earl	Kansas City	MO	Banjo (tenor)	1925
Cookson	Franklin W.	Salt Lake City	UT	Banjo (tenor)	1929
Copelin	Harold	Cleveland	OH		1939
Cordora	Ben	Passaic	NJ	Guitar	1934
Corrigan	Glenn	Seattle	WA	Guitar	1937
Corrigan	Ray	Hollywood	CA	Guitar	1939
Covey	Arnold			Guitar	1939
Cox	Al	Detroit	MI	Guitar	1936
Cox	Ed	Pocatello	WA		1924
Crabtree	A.D.	Charleston	SC	Guitar	1932
Crandall	Sarah (Miss)	Syracuse	NY	Banjo (tenor)	1925
Crookes	A.W. "Bill"	Hartford	CT	Banjo (tenor)	1919
Crosley	W.J.	Bridgeport	CT	Banjo (tenor)	1924
Culp	Cyril			Banjo (tenor)	1924
Cummins	Walter			Guitar (tenor)	1939
Cunningham	M. Clayton	Chicago	IL		1930
D'Abate	Jimmy	Montreal	Canada	Mandolin	1936
Davidson	Julian			Guitar	1932
Davidson	William Z.	Los Angeles	CA	Mandolin	1930
Davis	Ira	Los Angeles	CA	Banjo (plectrum)	1930
Davis	Tommy	Kansas City	MO	Guitar	1936
De Armond	Harry	Toledo	OH	Guitar	1936
De Vekey	Aladar		England	Mandolin	1917
Dean	Warren N	York	PA	Mandolin	1924
Dean	W.C.	Des Moines	IA	Banjo (tenor)	1924
Deets	R.W.	Hershey	PA		1925
Derwin	Hal			Guitar	1939
Deus	Eddie			Lap steel guitar	1936
Dexter	Ralph	New York City	NY	Banjo (tenor)	1919
Dishman	Wallie	Los Angeles	CA	Banjo (plectrum)	1930
Domenick	Robert			Guitar	1936
Dorson	Sunny			Guitar	1939
Downer	John	Philadelphia	PA	Banjo (tenor)	1920
Dring	Perry			Banjo (tenor)	1930
Drugan	Seymore	Chicago	IL	Guitar	1936
Dunigan	Jack			Guitar	1934
Durnell	Harold	Akron	OH	Guitar	1934
Duron	F.J.	Baton Rouge	LA	Harp guitar	1928
Efner	L. DeWitt	Schenectady	NY		1917
Ehrecke	Richard "Babe"	Los Angeles	CA	Guitar	1934
Esterdahl	Len	Chicago	IL	Guitar	1939

Last Name	First Name	Location		Instrument	Year
Fattaruso	Tom	Newark	NJ	Hawaiian guitar	1932
Fava	Joe	Detroit	MI	Guitar	1936
Fenimore	Francis	Vineland	NJ	Mandolin	1936
Filiberto	Roger	New Orleans	LA	Guitar	1934
Fillis	Len	London	England	Guitar	1929
Fisher	Charles L.	Kalamazoo	MI		1925
Florestano	Frank	Duluth	MN	Guitar	1936
Fluette	Henry	Toledo	OH	Guitar	1936
Foy	Jerry	Pittsburgh	PA	Guitar	1932
Freeman	Andrew			Banjo (plectrum)	1930
French	Jimmy	Minneapolis	MN	Guitar	1937
Gagnon	Cecille	Nashua	NH	Guitar	1936
Galvan	Don			Guitar	1939
Gange	Marion	New York City	NY	Guitar	1936
Garcelon	George P.	Joplin	MO	Mandolin	1917
Gatwood	Chic	Cincinnati	OH	Guitar	1937
Gebelein	Conrad	Baltimore	MD	Banjo (tenor)	1920
Gerarden	Mae	Denver	CO	Mandolin	1924
Gerstein	Hime	Omaha	NE	Mandolin	1928
Gibson	Bill	Washington	DC	Lap steel guitar	1942
Gillmore	Ted	Chicago	IL	Guitar	1930
Giradi	Tony			Guitar	1936
Glass	Mona			Guitar	1942
Graham	Floyd	Kansas City	MO	Guitar	1936
Grauenhorst	Mort	San Francisco	CA	Banjo (plectrum)	1930
Green	Katheryn	Seattle	WA	Guitar	1936
Griffith	William B.	Atlanta	GA	Mandolin	1924
Grinnell	Francis Allan	Detroit	MI	Banjo (tenor)	1932
Guillot	Nelson	New Orleans	LA	Guitar	1939
Gunn	Malon			Guitar	1937
Hackler	Lou	Kansas City	MO	Guitar	1936
Hackman	Chuck	Peoria	IL	Guitar	1939
Haid	Bill	Chicago	IL	Mandolin	1924
Hall	Herman	Indianapolis	IN	Guitar	1936
Hall	Nelson			Guitar	1932
Hammill	G.D.	New York City	NY	Banjo (tenor)	1932
Harper	George B.	Memphis	TN	Mando-Bass	1928
Harvey	Ellison	New York City	NY	Lap steel guitar	1939
Harvey	Ken	London	England	Banjo (plectrum)	1939
Hayes	Grace	New York City	NY	Banjo	1929
Hendley	Fisher	Albemarle	NC	Banjo (regular)	1929
Henneberry	Percy	Milwaukee	WI		1924
Henry	Francis		Canada	Banjo (tenor)	1930
Hewitt	Glenn	Ft. Worth	TX	Banjo (regular)	1929

Gibson Endorsers 1917-1942 (continued)

Last Name	First Name	Location		Instrument	Year
Hill	Jack	Detroit	MI	Guitar	1936
Hilpot	Billy			Guitar (tenor)	1930
Hokans	Henry L.	Worcester	MA	Mandolin	1924
Holt	Walter	Washington	DC		1924
Hughes	Lena	San Antonio	TX	Mandolin	1928
Huston	Don			Guitar	1939
Ireland	Virgil J.	Anderson	IN		1930
Jackson	Giff	Buffalo	NY	Guitar	1937
Jarrett	Arthur			Guitar	1932
Johnson	Ray			Guitar	1934
Johnston	James H.	Kalamazoo	MI	Mandolin	1917
Kammer	Fred	Kansas City	MO	Guitar	1929
Kaplan	Kappy	Chicago	IL	Guitar	1936
Kapua	Homer	Danville	IL	Guitar	1929
Kay	Tommy			Guitar	1942
Kelley	Vincent	LaSalle	IL	Banjo (tenor)	1925
Kettering	Frank	Chicago	IL	Guitar (tenor)	1939
Kincaid	Bradley	Nashville	TN	Guitar	1934
Kinder	Danny	McCordsville	IN	Banjo (tenor)	1937
Kingsland	Fritz	Detroit	MI	Guitar	1936
Klinger	Frank			Guitar	1932
Kola	Walter	Lyndhurst	OH	Mandolin	1924
Kratoska	Herb	Kansas City	MO	Guitar	1934
Kress	Carl	New York City	NY	Guitar	1934
Krick	George C.	Philadelphia	PA		1924
Labato	Patty	Youngstown	PA	Guitar	1930
Ladas	Andrew	Detroit	MI		1925
Ladas	William	Detroit	MI	Mandolin	1924
Lang	Eddie	New York City	NY	Guitar	1928
Lauber	Sigmund A.	New Haven	CT		1924
Lavery	Marguerite B.	Detroit	MI	Mandolin	1928
Lawton	Nate	Toledo	OH	Guitar	1936
Lee	Bud	San Diego	CA	Guitar	1937
Lee	Lorry			Lap steel guitar	1939
Lehrmann	Robert	St. Louis	MO	Mandolin	1924
Lehritter	George	Asbury Park	NJ	Mandolin	1917
LeMaire	Jack			Guitar	1939
LeMieux	R.J.	Green Bay	WI	Mandolin	1928
Lenard	Jack	Portland	OR	Guitar	1937
Lichtenstein	Percy V.	Pitcairn	PA	Mandolin	1928
Loar	Lloyd A.	Kalamazoo	MI	Mandolin	1920
Lung	Wilma	Syracuse	NY	Guitar	1936
Mack	Gene			Lap steel guitar	1937
Macon	Dave	Readyville	TN	Banjo (regular)	1930

Last Name	First Name	Location		Instrument	Year
Macrow	Charlie	Johannesburg	S. Africa	Banjo (plectrum)	1936
Magann	Ernie	Toronto	Canada	Lap steel guitar	1936
Magee	Alex	New Rochelle	NY	Banjo (regular)	1930
Mallet	Nardi	Richmond	VA	Guitar	1936
Mancuso	Emile	New Orleans	LA	Lap steel guitar	1942
Mano	Carl	Rochester	NY	Guitar	1936
Manuel	Russell C.	Wichita	TX	Banjo (tenor)	1920
Marcellino	Muzzy	San Francisco	CA	Guitar	1934
Mareno	Buddy			Guitar	1937
Marshall	Charles	San Francisco	CA	Harp guitar	1929
Martin	Paul	San Francisco	CA	Guitar	1934
Martori	Joseph	Boston	MA	Guitar	1937
Marzluff	John	Toledo	OH	Guitar	1936
Mathis	Berdell	Hollywood	CA	Guitar	1934
Mazza	Ralph	Chicago	IL	Guitar	1936
McBurney	Alvin	New York City	NY	Guitar	1929
McDonough	Dick			Guitar	1937
McDougal	Don	Miami Beach	FL	Guitar	1939
McMichael	William B.	Newark	OH	Banjo (plectrum)	1936
McNeil	Charles			Banjo (tenor)	1919
Melia	Nick	New York City	NY	Guitar	1936
Merrifield	Ada N.	Willimantic	CT	Mandolin	1928
Midkiff	George Gilbert	Butte	MT	Banjo (tenor)	1930
Milhollan	J.B.	Oklahoma City	OK		1924
Militello	Tony	Buffalo	NY	Guitar	1942
Miller	Paul	Salt Lake City	UT	Guitar	1939
Mitchell	John T.	New York City	NY	Banjo (plectrum)	1928
Mitchell	William M.	New York City	NY	Banjo (plectrum)	1928
Moldthan	Edward	Ft. Wayne	IN	Electraharp	1942
Monroe	Bill			Mandolin	1936
Monroe	Charlie			Guitar	1936
Moos	Melvie	Pittsburgh	PA		1925
Morgan	Dick			Guitar	1936
Mottola	Tony	Kearny	NJ	Guitar	1942
Moyer	William D.	Harrisburg	PA	Banjo (tenor)	1920
Murr	Emma	White Plains	NY	Mandolin	1929
Myers	Fred, Jr.	St. Louis	MO	Lap steel guitar	1939
Nason	J. Clifford	Kasota	MN		1925
Natale	Frank	Pittsburgh	PA	Guitar	1939
Newman	Grace	Regina	Canada	Mandolin	1924
Nickle	Frank	Baltimore	MD	Guitar	1934
Nicomede	Joe	Altoona	PA	Banjo (tenor)	1920
Noble	Eddie			Banjo (tenor)	1924
North	Bill			Guitar	1939

Gibson Endorsers: 1917-1942 (continued)

Last Name	First Name	Location		Instrument	Year
Oehler	Carl W.	Sacramento	CA	Banjo (plectrum)	1925
Ogle	Cecil	Toledo	OH	Guitar	1936
Oliver	Tony			Guitar	1936
Pantzer	Charles	New York City	NY	Mandolin	1932
Pariso	John			Guitar	1939
Patrick	George	Milwaukee	WI	Guitar	1934
Patton	A.E.	Elgin	IL	Mandolin	1939
Paul	Les	Chicago	IL	Guitar	1936
Payne	Goody	Butte	MT	Banjo (plectrum)	1929
Peabody	Eddie			Banjo (tenor)	1919
Pendergraft	Hugh	Hollywood	CA	Guitar	1937
Perri	Dan	London	England	Guitar	1937
Perry	Gene	Los Angeles	CA	Ukulele	1930
Perry	Ruth	Knoxville	TN	Mandolin	1932
Pesci	Orey			Guitar	1942
Pet	Jac	Rotterdam	Holland	Guitar	1930
Peters	Frye	Chicago	IL	Guitar	1934
Peterson	Charles			Banjo (tenor)	1930
Petroni	Joe			Guitar	1942
Pierce	Charley	Los Angeles	CA	Banjo (tenor)	1930
Place	William (Jr.)	Providence	RI	Mandolin	1924
Planque	F. Monroe	Vancouver	WA	Mandolin	1924
Powell	Ted			Guitar	1932
Price	Leslie H.	Reading	PA	Banjo (tenor)	1930
Priest	Glen	Butte	MT	Guitar	1934
Principato	Guy	Boston	MA	Lap steel guitar	1937
Quigley	Frank	York	PA	Guitar	1939
Quinn	Eddie	Shreveport	LA	Guitar	1932
Rathert	Norman	St. Louis	MO	Banjo (tenor)	1924
Reeves	Gobel	Dallas	TX	Guitar	1930
Remley	Frank			Guitar	1939
Reser	Harry	New York City	NY	Banjo (tenor)	1930
Reuss	Allan	New York City	NY	Guitar	1939
Rey	Alvino	San Francisco	CA	Guitar	1932
Richards	Lawrence			Ukulele	1930
Richie	Jack			Guitar	1939
Ritter	Tex	Hollywood	CA	Guitar	1939
Rizzo	Joe	New York City	NY	Lap steel guitar	1942
Robb	Jimmy	Minneapolis	MN	Guitar	1937
Roberts	Dick	Hollywood	CA	Guitar	1936
Roberts	Earl	Chicago	IL	Banjo (tenor)	1919
Roberts	Hal	San Francisco	CA	Guitar	1937
Roberts	Wendell	Commerce	GA	Banjo (tenor)	1925
Robison	Carson	New York City	NY	Guitar	1928

Last Name	First Name	Location		Instrument	Year
Rohrer	Wesley	Johnstown	PA		1924
Romano	Tony	Hollywood	CA	Guitar	1939
Rose	B.A.	Minneapolis	MN	Mandolin	1917
Rose	George	Detroit	MI	Guitar	1937
Rose	Jack	Cleveland	OH	Banjo (tenor)	1924
Roth	Bart			Guitar	1942
Rowden	C.C.	Chicago	IL		1924
Ryerson	Art	New York City	NY	Guitar	1939
Salamack	Anthony			Banjo (tenor)	1924
Sampietro	Harry	Portland	OR	Guitar	1937
Santella	Andy	New York City	NY	Hawaiian guitar	1929
Santos	Don	Rochester	NY	Mandolin	1928
Santos	Veda	Rochester	NY	Mandolin	1928
Sanvito	Charles	West Hoboken	NJ		1924
Saputo	Frank			Guitar	1937
Savale	F.E.	Orange			1924
Schelp	Walter	Seattle	WA	Guitar	1934
Scher	Harry	St. Louis	MO	Banjo (tenor)	1925
Schneider	Wesley			Banjo (tenor)	1925
Scott	Percy		Canada	Mandolin	1932
Seckler	Bill	Los Angeles	CA	Guitar	1930
Senay	Robert	Houston	TX	Banjo (tenor)	1930
Sharp	Ames	Memphis	TN	Banjo (tenor)	1925
Sharp	Robert L.	Memphis	TN	Guitar	1928
Sherwood	Bobby	Hollywood	CA	Guitar	1936
Skrivanek	Eddie	Hollywood	CA	Guitar	1936
Smedley	Roy M.	Sydney	Australia	Mandolin	1936
Smith	Duane	Grand Rapids	MI	Guitar	1937
Smith	George	Hollywood	CA	Guitar	1934
Smith	Herbert J.	Syracuse	NY	Lap steel guitar	1936
Smith	Jimmie	New York City	NY	Banjo (tenor)	1930
Smith	Roland	Toledo	OH	Guitar	1936
Smith	Russ	New York City	NY	Guitar	1936
Smith	Russell	Pittsburgh	PA	Guitar	1930
Smyser	Carl Alex	York	PA	Banjo (tenor)	1936
Socci	Charles			Guitar	1936
Sodja	Joe	Cleveland	OH	Guitar	1939
Soldano	Pat	Utica	NY	Guitar	1937
Spears	Ken	Minneapolis	MN	Guitar	1937
Spergel	Sam			Banjo (tenor)	1930
Staffa	Frank			Guitar	1934
Stanistreet	Edgar	Philadelphia	PA	Mandolin	1936
Steiner	Rudolph	Indianapolis	IN	Banjo (tenor)	1932
Stephens	M.H.	Livingston	MT	Banjo (tenor)	1925

Gibson Endorsers: 1917-1942 (continued)

Last Name	First Name	Location		Instrument	Year
Stockbridge	Eddie	Hollywood	CA	Guitar	1936
Stoker	J.E.			Banjo (guitar)	1924
Stornman	Eddie	St. Louis	MO	Guitar	1924
Stout	Russ	Milwaukee	WI	Banjo (tenor)	1930
Stover	William	Los Angeles	CA	Guitar (tenor)	1930
Strafino	Vincent	New York City	NY	Banjo (guitar)	1924
Sunseri	Tony			Guitar	1939
Sweeney	W.H.	Pittsburgh	PA		1924
Szot	Joe	Milwaukee	WI	Guitar	1936
Tabaka	Lovetta	Chicago	IL	Mandolin	1924
Taddeo	Lucille	Seattle	WA	Guitar	1936
Tamberg	White	San Francisco	CA	Guitar	1939
Tanquary	E.H.	Memphis	TN	Mandolin	1928
Tatham	Val	Kansas City	MO	Guitar	1936
Toby	Louise	New York City	NY	Guitar	1936
Tolhurst	H. Blair	Jackson	MI	Banjo (tenor)	1930
Towle	F.W.	Pasadena	CA	Mandolin	1917
Tremaine	Bert M.	Los Angeles	CA	Banjo (tenor)	1930
Trietsch	Ken	Chicago	IL	Guitar (tenor)	1939
Tringham	W.D.		England	Guitar	1932
Truitt	H. Russell	Pittsburgh	PA	Mandolin	1924
Valero	Louis			Guitar	1942
Van	Billy	New York City	NY	Guitar	1937
Van Horn	George	Harrisburg	PA	Guitar	1942
Victor	Frank	New York City	NY	Guitar	1934
Volpe	Harry	New York City	NY	Guitar	1934
Voornas	Peter	Chicago	IL	Mandolin	1928
Wakely	Jimmy	Hollywood	CA	Guitar	1942
Wampler	Bill	Kansas City	MO	Guitar	1936
Warren	C.C.	Binghamton	NY		1924
Warren	Kenneth	Binghamton	NY	Banjo (tenor)	1932
Wartner	George			Guitar	1936
Weber	Robert	Tacoma	WA	Banjo (tenor)	1930
Weber	Tommy	Los Angeles	CA	Banjo (tenor)	1929
Webster	Bud	Detroit	MI	Guitar	1936
Welch	Gordon	Detroit	MI	Guitar	1936
Wellesp	A. Thomas	Pasadena	CA		1925
Wernert	Buzz	Toledo	OH	Guitar	1936
Wesnitzer	Mary	St. Louis	MO	Guitar	1939
Weston	Don	Lexington	KY	Guitar	1937
White	Evan	Niagara Falls	NY	Lap steel guitar	1936
White	Hy			Guitar	1939
Whitley	Ray	Hollywood	CA	Guitar	1939
Wickner	Eddie	Minneapolis	MN	Guitar	1937

Last Name	First Name	Location		Instrument	Year
Widmer	Mike	New York City	NY	Guitar	1937
Wingert	Ralph	Harrisburg	PA		1932
Wolfe	J.M.	Chicago	IL	Banjo (tenor)	1924
Wolverton	Joe			Guitar	1939
Wolverton	Ralph	Chicago	IL	Banjo (tenor)	1932
Woodworth	Ami	Benton Harbor	MI	Banjo (tenor)	1920
Woolsey	Tom	New York City	NY	Guitar	1930
Worrell	Frank	New York City	NY	Guitar	1936
Wright	James D.	Boston	MA	Banjo (tenor)	1920
Yeaton	I.D.	Tacoma	WA	Banjo (tenor)	1925
Yeomans	Jerry			Lap steel guitar	1937
Yocum	Clark			Guitar	1937
Zeller	Walla	Cleveland	OH		1924

Metronome Gibson Advertisement of Carson Robison, June 1930 (partial)

Centerstream Archives

This ad appeared in the August 1928 issue of Mastertone Magazine and is the earliest known documentation of the style 6 banjo.
Steve Huber Collection

Chapter 9 - The Instruments

Overview

Presenting a comprehensive list of Gibson pre-World War II, production-model instruments is a difficult task. Instrument specifications were subject to change at any time, rendering any list of standard features open to debate. The best method for identification of any Gibson instrument is by examining its physical features and consulting the factory order number lists and serial number indexes in this book.

Lloyd Loar's Master Models

The addition of acoustical engineer Lloyd A. Loar to the Gibson staff in 1919 was a catalyst that produced an explosion of innovative new designs, the majority of which would later become iconic archetypes. Orville H. Gibson brought the concept of "violin-type" construction to his mandolins and guitars, but Loar took this thought to a whole new level. He advocated tap tuning each part of an instrument so that after being assembled the separate pieces worked together in a way that gave a desired, reproducible result. He experimented with body size, increasing and reducing the volume of the air chamber, as well as the placement and size of soundholes. Loar also changed the scale length on fingerboards, moving the bridge location to what he considered optimal.

In 1922 the Gibson "Master Model" product line debuted, combining the best of their traditional designs with Loar's work. These instruments included the F-5 mandolin, H-5 mandola, K-5 mando-cello, and L-5 guitar. Loar also contributed some innovations to the existing style 5 banjo, which now became known as a "Mastertone." All of these models (except the banjos) contained a signed and dated paper label on the interior stating that the various components had been tuned prior to assembly and that Loar himself had personally inspected the completed instrument. They were priced high and initially did not sell in large quantities. Loar left Gibson in 1924, but external evidence shows that the company was still shipping unsold F-5 Loar-signed mandolins as late as 1928.

As a group, the "Master Models" received a mixed review. The H-5 mandola and K-5 mando-cello were never produced in large numbers simply because they were intended for use in mandolin orchestras, a type of musical group which had been largely passé for about five years. The instruments quickly faded from view. The L-5 guitar fared much better, finding existing markets in both dance bands and the embryonic world of jazz. It was loud and had the all-important "cutting power" for radio work. It continued to sell well, even after the departure of Loar in 1924. It underwent a number of redesigns, adapting it further for the jazz market, and within ten years became the professional guitar of choice. The F-5 mandolin would not find a home until bluegrass music became popular in the 1960's. In an ironic twist, Loar's classical creation was perfectly adapted to playing the complex variant of country music created by mandolinist Bill Monroe. Today, original F-5 examples from Loar's hands are sold for six figures, and his design is probably the most copied mandolin form.

Mastertone Banjos 1925-1941

The "Mastertone" banjo had its debut in 1922 as one of Lloyd Loar's "Master Models." It was initially a complicated design, featuring a "floating tone tube" that rested on ball bearings. The original Mastertone banjos did not contain a signed and dated paper label from Loar, probably because there was very little about a banjo that could be "tuned" in the manufacturing sense. However, it is generally believed that Loar did specify the exact measurements of Mastertone banjo rims, dimensions which persist to this day. Unfortunately, the initial 1922 offering of the "Mastertone" banjo was largely met with indifference. Most professional players of the time preferred a Paramount or Bacon banjo. Loar's original Mastertone banjo design was quickly deemed too complex, and it was replaced in April of 1925 with a slightly different product, but still marketed under the Mastertone designation. In fact, the Gibson Mastertone banjo did not reach its commercial zenith until after additional redesign work in 1926 and 1928.

It has been noted by many Gibson scholars that the 1925 banjos borrowed heavily from existing Paramount banjo features. These included a "violin-shaped" peghead, a "bowl-type" convex resonator, and a perforated metal flange plate known as a "tone band" at Paramount, and then as a "resonator band" at Gibson. All of these design elements were available on Paramount banjos as early as 1921. Gibson's blatant "adoption" of them in 1925 is probably proof of their popularity on Paramount instruments. It may also be partially explained by the fact that while Paramount banjos had these features in 1921, company owner William L. Lange was not able to receive a patent for them until August 25th, 1925.

Lange did not take this infringement lightly and moved quickly to protect his rights. In the September 5th, 1925 issue of *Music Trade Review*, Lange made the following statement concerning his patent:

> "It covers the salient features of the Paramount banjo to the extent of the allowance of thirty-two claims, all of which are directed to those obviously novel features *which have been copied by other manufacturers*. This has, of course, been a tacit acknowledgement of the superiority of the structural features of the Paramount by imitators. I desire to call the attention of the trade to my purpose actively and aggressively to protect all my rights under this patent and *if necessary to take steps to compel imitators to desist from further imitation*."

Whether or not Lange pursued legal proceedings against Gibson remains unknown. Gibson ordered their own pre-World War II legal records destroyed in the 1960s. However, some significance may be found in the actions of the company. In 1928 they initiated another major overhaul of their banjo line. Among other things, the renovations included two new peghead shapes, one which they called the "scroll" peghead (now more commonly known as the "double-cut" peghead) and a second, simplified version of their existing "violin" peghead. The resonator band (flange) was also changed, with the new version being cast in one piece from pot metal rather than featuring a tube and plate. The Paramount-style resonator was retained, possibly signifying that Gibson was still willing to take a chance on litigation. The redesigned banjos were placed in production during the second quarter of 1929. In retrospect it would seem that the overhaul of the banjo line served two purposes. First, the simpler pegheads and the one-piece flange both streamlined banjo production, thereby lowering labor costs. Secondly, it moved the company away from possible litigation by William L. Lange.

Failures and Flops

With so many models and such a strong commitment to experimentation, Gibson was certain to have produced a few "stinkers." Some of these instruments were stifled before getting to market, while others made their debut and then faded quickly from the public eye.

Gibson's pre-war management was notoriously slow to react to changing markets, prolonging production of some types after demand had died and not bringing new instrument types to market in a timely manner. The mass market for mandolins died with the entry of America into World War I in 1917. Yet, Gibson continued producing large numbers of mandolins up through 1925. In the reverse case, the market for "tango" banjos (now known as tenor banjos) was on the rise from about 1910. Yet, Gibson made no attempt to enter the banjo market until 1919.

Gibson made attempts at various times to revive "dead" markets, without success. They introduced the ultimate "Master-Model" F-5 mandolin in 1922 at a time when the tenor banjo was reaching new heights of popularity. Predictably, the F-5 did not sell well. Their line of top-tension banjos (style 7, style 12, and style 18) were introduced in 1937 at a time when playing the guitar was the trend of the day. With art-deco styling, radiused fingerboards, guitar style inlays and a head that could be tightened without removing the resonator, these banjos were clearly aimed at the professional musician (the entry-level banjos did not receive any of the new features). Even with a specific target audience in mind, the top-tension banjos did not sell in large numbers, and Gibson had to re-learn the painful lesson that a "dead" market could not be easily brought back to life.

What could be termed "over enthusiasm" was also a problem from time to time. The cello-banjo, mando-bass, and banjo-bass are examples of instruments which Gibson created for negligible markets. Their little-known tenor lute of 1924-25 is another prime example of this phenomenon. In some cases it took decades to clear out the back inventory of these obscure models. The style 6 banjo was created in 1928 to fill a niche that did not exist. Gibson already offered several gold-plated, engraved, curly maple banjos at that time. To make things worse, the style 6 featured a unique green-orange finish called "Argentine Grey" and was priced very high at $300. It was not well accepted by the buying public and the shipping ledgers reveal that Gibson was still trying to clear out some 1928-1929 production-year inventories on this model at the start of World War II.

The company sometimes over diversified their model offerings in an attempt to have instruments available at every possible price point. This poor idea failed repeatedly. Statistics show that the most consistently purchased Gibson instruments of any type were the entry-level model and the lowest-priced, professional-grade model. But this did not stop Gibson from doing inexplicable things like introducing three new mandolin models, the F-7 ($125), the F-10 ($150) and the F-12 ($175) at the worst point of the Great Depression in 1934. The three instruments were basically of identical construction with slightly different appointments. Predictably, all three models did not sell well. Too many choices confused the buyers, absorbed production capacity, and tied up raw materials in models that did not sell.

In 1939 Gibson decided to break into the violin market, a move that must have stunned industry insiders for its quixotic qualities. At that time, the center of the violin manufacturing universe was located in Europe, specifically in the countries of Germany, France, Italy, and Czechoslovakia. The majority of high-quality, hand-made instruments and even the cheaper "catalog fiddles" originated there. Perhaps the political unrest in those areas led Gibson to predict an opening in the market, as instruments from those countries became unavailable. They barreled ahead with a full line of violins, violas, cellos and basses, along with bows and accessories. The violin line never sold in great numbers and was quietly dropped at the end of World War II.

Unauthorized Copies

In four decades of pre-World War II operation, Gibson designed and produced instruments that continue to be regarded as the epitome of their type. Many modern-day instrument builders look to these models as blueprints for their own work, with the result that Gibson has been forced to bring legal action from time to time when the replicas become too imitative. Nor is this adoration limited to the post-World War II era. Guitars and mandolins built by the Dayton String Instrument Company of Dayton, Ohio in the 1920's are extremely close to Gibson designs. Company founder Charles B. Rauch had been a Gibson endorser in 1910 and even went so far as to have "The Dayton" silk-screened on the peghead of his instruments, in imitation of "The Gibson." It is not known if Gibson ever took punitive action against Rauch.

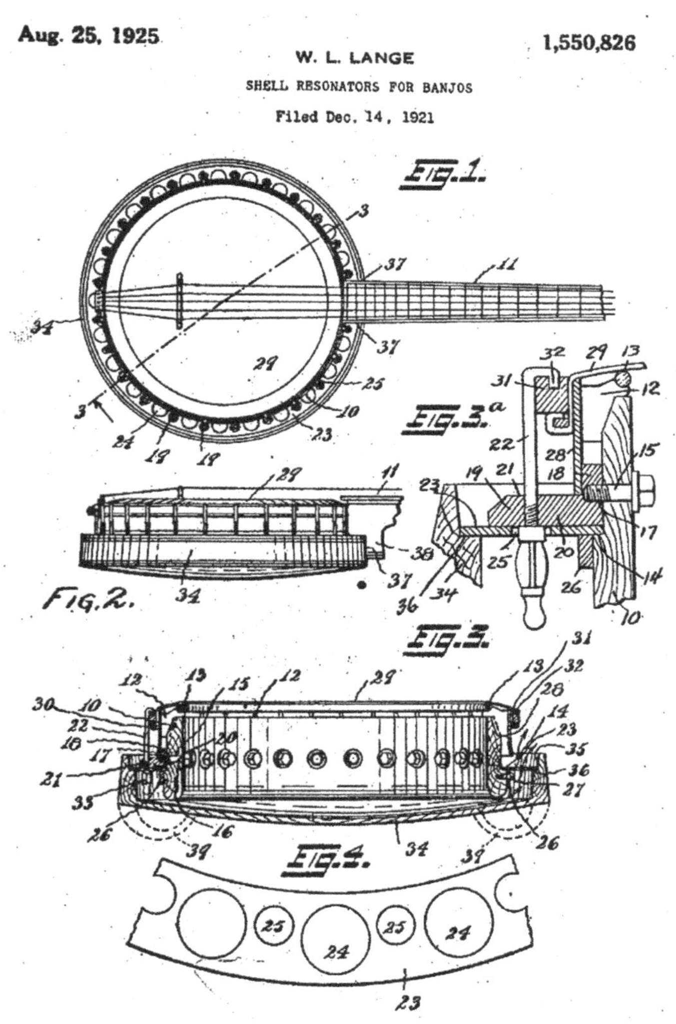

William Lange's patent for the "shell resonator" and "tone band". Gibson copied these features in their 1925 overhaul of the banjo line.
Collection of the author

Gibson Brand Instrument Models: 1903-1941

The data contained in this table are for Gibson-brand instruments only. Standard Gibson model abbreviations are used. The production dates given are based on observed instruments which have been dated by the author using the corrected serial number chronology and FON data extracted from Gibson's shipping ledgers. For a more detailed structural description of Gibson-brand guitars and mandolins, the reader is referred to *Gruhn's Guide to Vintage Instruments.* For details of banjo construction, please see Appendix A in this volume.

Model	Type	Description	Years Produced
A	Mandolin	Teardrop body	1903-33
A-0	Mandolin	Teardrop body	1927, 1930-34
A-00	Mandolin	Teardrop body	1933-41
A-1	Mandolin	Teardrop body	1904-27, 1929-30, 1933-41
A-2	Mandolin	Teardrop body	1905-09, 1911, 1913-14, 1916-27
A-2z	Mandolin	Teardrop body	1923-26
A-3	Mandolin	Teardrop body	1904-23
A-4	Mandolin	Teardrop body	1904-06, 1908-31, 1933
A-50	Mandolin	Teardrop body	1933-41
A-75	Mandolin	Teardrop body	1935-37
A-C	Mandolin	Teardrop body	1933-34, 1936-37
Advanced Jumbo	Guitar	Jumbo Flattop	1936-39
A-Jr	Mandolin	Teardrop body	1921-30
Banjo-Bass	Banjo-Bass	none	1929
Black Special	Guitar	Archtop	1934-39
Black Special 2	Guitar	Archtop	1937-40
Black Special 3	Guitar	Archtop	1938-41
Black Special 4	Guitar	Archtop	1936-37, 1939, 1941
Black Special 5	Guitar	Archtop	1939-41
Black Special 7	Guitar	Archtop	1941
C-1	Mandolin	Teardrop body	1931, 1933
CB	Cello-Banjo	none	1919-20
CB-3	Cello-Banjo	Style 3	1934-35
CB-4	Cello-Banjo	Style 4	1920-22
Console Grande	Electric Hawaiian Guitar	Solid wooden body	1938-40
Custom Uke	Ukulele	Painted body	1927-29
DY	Mandolin	Teardrop body	1917-18, 1920
EB-150	Electric Bass	Electric	1938
EH	Electric Hawaiian Guitar	Aluminum body	1935
EH-100	Electric Hawaiian Guitar	Solid wooden body	1937-40
EH-150	Electric Hawaiian Guitar	Solid wooden body	1937-40
EH-185	Electric Hawaiian Guitar	Solid wooden body	1939-40
EH-275	Electric Hawaiian Guitar	Solid wooden body	1940
EH-Dbl	Electric Hawaiian Guitar	Solid wooden body	1937-39
Electraharp	Similar to pedal steel	Solid wooden body	1937-39
EM-100	Electric Mandolin	Teardrop body	1937-41
EM-125	Electric Mandolin	Teardrop body	1940-41
EM-150	Electric Mandolin	Teardrop body	1937-41
EPB-150	Electric Plectrum Banjo	Solid wooden body	1937-40
ERB-150	Electric Regular Banjo	Solid wooden body	1938

Gibson Brand Instrument Models: 1903-1941 (continued)

Model	Type	Description	Years Produced
ES-100	Electric Guitar	Archtop	1938-41
ES-125	Electric Guitar	Archtop	1940-41
ES-150	Electric Guitar	Archtop	1937-41
ES-250	Electric Guitar	Archtop	1939-40
ES-300	Electric Guitar	Archtop	1939-41
ETB-150	Electric Tenor Banjo	Solid wooden body	1937-40
ETG-100	Electric Tenor Guitar	Archtop	1938-39
ETG-150	Electric Tenor Guitar	Archtop	1937-41
F	Mandolin	Points & scroll body	1904-06
F-2	Mandolin	Points & scroll body	1904-34
F-3	Mandolin	Points & scroll body	1904-05
F-4	Mandolin	Points & scroll body	1905-06, 1909-41
F-5	Mandolin	Points & scroll body	1922-24, 1926-39, 1941
F-7	Mandolin	Points & scroll body	1934-39
F-10	Mandolin	Points & scroll body	1934-36
F-12	Mandolin	Points & scroll body	1934-37, 1940-41
GB	Guitar-Banjo	none	1919-20
GB-1	Guitar-Banjo	Style 1	1926-31, 1934, 1937, 1939
GB-3	Guitar-Banjo	Style 3	1920, 1922, 1925-30
GB-4	Guitar-Banjo	Style 4	1919-24
GB-BV	Guitar-Banjo	Style Bella Voce	1927
GB-G	Guitar-Banjo	Style Granada	1927-28
GS-35	Gut-String Guitar	Classical	1938-40
GS-85	Gut-String Guitar	Classical	1938-41
H	Mandola	Teardrop body	1903?
H-0	Mandola	Teardrop body	1935, 1937-41
H-1	Mandola	Teardrop body	1905-06, 1909-31, 1933-35, 1941
H-2	Mandola	Teardrop body	1906, 1909-23, 1934
H-4	Mandola	Points & scroll body	1910, 1912-24, 1927, 1929-31, 1935-37
H-5	Mandola	Points & scroll body	1923-24, 1928, 1930-31, 1937, 1939
HG-0	Hawaiian Guitar	Flattop	1937-40
HG-00	Hawaiian Guitar	Flattop	1936-41
HG-20	Hawaiian Guitar	Flattop	1932
HG-22	Hawaiian Guitar	Flattop	1932
HG-24	Hawaiian Guitar	Flattop	1932-33
J	Mando-Bass	Teardrop body	1906, 1912-14, 1917, 1921-22, 1928-31
J-35	Guitar	Jumbo Flattop	1936-41
J-45	Guitar	Jumbo Flattop	1941
J-50	Guitar	Jumbo Flattop	1941
J-55	Guitar	Jumbo Flattop	1939-41
Jumbo	Guitar	Jumbo Flattop	1934-37
K	Mando-Cello	Teardrop body	1903?
K-1	Mando-Cello	Teardrop body	1906, 1909-22, 1924-25, 1930, 1932, 1935, 1937-39, 1941
K-2	Mando-Cello	Teardrop body	1908, 1910-22

Model	Type	Description	Years Produced
K-4	Mando-Cello	Points & scroll body	1906, 1911-15, 1917, 1919-23, 1924, 1927-28, 1931
K-5	Mando-Cello	Guitar-type body	1924, 1928, 1934
L	Guitar	Archtop	1903?
L-0	Guitar	Archtop or Flattop	1926-34, 1936-41
L-0 3/4	Guitar	Flattop	1931, 1937
L-00	Guitar	Flattop	1931-41
L-1	Guitar	Archtop or Flattop	1904-24, 1926-36
L-2	Guitar	Archtop or Flattop	1923-25, 1927, 1929-33, 1935
L-3	Guitar	Archtop	1906, 1908, 1911-32
L-4	Guitar	Archtop	1908-10, 1912-41
L-5	Guitar	Archtop	1922-41
L-7	Guitar	Archtop	1933-41
L-10	Guitar	Archtop	1931-39
L-12	Guitar	Archtop	1932-41
L-30	Guitar	Archtop	1935-41
L-37	Guitar	Archtop	1935-41
L-47	Guitar	Archtop	1937, 1940-41
L-50	Guitar	Archtop	1933-41
L-75	Guitar	Archtop	1933-39, 1941
L-C	Guitar	Flattop	1933-39
L-Jr	Guitar	Archtop	1921-25, 1927
MB	Mandolin Banjo	none	1919-20
MB-0	Mandolin Banjo	Style 0	1921-22, 1925-28
MB-00	Mandolin Banjo	Style 00	1938-41
MB-1	Mandolin Banjo	Style 1	1920-37
MB-2	Mandolin Banjo	Style 2	1922-23, 1925-27, 1931-32, 1935-36
MB-3	Mandolin Banjo	Style 3	1920, 1923-29, 1931-32, 1935-37
MB-4	Mandolin Banjo	Style 4	1919-24, 1928
MB-5	Mandolin Banjo	Style 5	1928
MB-11	Mandolin Banjo	Style 11	1936-41
MB-BV	Mandolin Banjo	Style Bella Voce	1927
MB-G	Mandolin Banjo	Style Granada	1927-28
MB-Jr	Mandolin Banjo	Style Junior	1920, 1922-25
NL	Guitar	Nick Lucas Special	1927-41
O	Guitar	Archtop	1903-07, 1909-28
O-1	Guitar	Archtop	1903?
O-2	Guitar	Archtop	1906
O-3	Guitar	Archtop	1903?
PB-"12"	Plectrum Banjo	Style "12"	1933
PB-00	Plectrum Banjo	Style 00	1935-40
PB-1	Plectrum Banjo	Style 1	1925-30, 1934-37
PB-2	Plectrum Banjo	Style 2	1930
PB-3	Plectrum Banjo	Style 3	1925-32, 1935-37
PB-4	Plectrum Banjo	Style 4	1925-30, 1935

Gibson Brand Instrument Models: 1903-1941 (continued)

Model	Type	Description	Years Produced
PB-5	Plectrum Banjo	Style 5	1925-27
PB-6	Plectrum Banjo	Style 6	1928-30, 1934
PB-7	Plectrum Banjo	Style 7	1938-39
PB-11	Plectrum Banjo	Style 11	1931, 1938-39
PB-12	Plectrum Banjo	Style 12	1938, 1940
PB-18	Plectrum Banjo	Style 18	1937, 1939
PB-75	Plectrum Banjo	Style 75	1937-39
PB-BV	Plectrum Banjo	Style Bella Voce	1927-29
PB-F	Plectrum Banjo	Style Florentine	1927-29
PB-G	Plectrum Banjo	Style Granada	1925-30, 1936
PB-Jr	Plectrum Banjo	Style Junior	1924
PB-Oriole	Plectrum Banjo	Style Oriole	1927
PG-0	Plectrum Guitar	Flattop	1931
PG-00	Plectrum Guitar	Flattop	1931, 1940
PG-1	Plectrum Guitar	Archtop or Flattop	1927, 1930-31, 1933-34
PG-4	Plectrum Guitar	Archtop	1927, 1930-31, 1933-34, 1937
PG-7	Plectrum Guitar	Archtop	1939
PG-30	Plectrum Guitar	Archtop	1939
PG-37	Plectrum Guitar	Archtop	1937
PG-50	Plectrum Guitar	Archtop	1934
PG-75	Plectrum Guitar	Archtop	1939
R	Harp Guitar	Archtop Harp Guitar	1905-06
R-1	Harp Guitar	Archtop Harp Guitar	1903?
RB-"12"	Regular Banjo	Style "12"	1933
RB-00	Regular Banjo	Style 00	1935-41
RB-1	Regular Banjo	Style 1	1925-40
RB-2	Regular Banjo	Style 2	1929-30, 1932, 1937-38
RB-3	Regular Banjo	Style 3	1924-32, 1936-37
RB-4	Regular Banjo	Style 4	1924-25, 1927-30, 1932
RB-6	Regular Banjo	Style 6	1929
RB-7	Regular Banjo	Style 7	1938-40
RB-11	Regular Banjo	Style 11	1931-41
RB-12	Regular Banjo	Style 12	1938
RB-18	Regular Banjo	Style 18	1937-40
RB-75	Regular Banjo	Style 75	1937-41
RB-BV	Regular Banjo	Style Bella Voce	1927-28
RB-F	Regular Banjo	Style Florentine	1927
RB-G	Regular Banjo	Style Granada	1927-30
RB-Jr	Regular Banjo	Style Junior	1924
Royal PT	Plectrum-Tenor Banjo	Style Royal	1929
S-1	Hawaiian Guitar	Smeck Stage Deluxe	1934-40
S-2	Hawaiian Guitar	Smeck Radio Grande	1934-37
SJ-100	Guitar	Jumbo Flattop	1939-41
SJ-200	Guitar	Jumbo Flattop	1938-41

Model	Type	Description	Years Produced
Southerner Jumbo	Guitar	Jumbo Flattop	1941
Super 400	Guitar	Archtop	1935-41
TB	Tenor Banjo	none	1919-20
TB-"12"	Tenor Banjo	Style "12"	1933
TB-0	Tenor Banjo	Style 0	1921-22, 1925-28
TB-00	Tenor Banjo	Style 00	1935-41
TB-1	Tenor Banjo	Style 1	1920, 1922-32, 1934-40
TB-2	Tenor Banjo	Style 2	1925-31, 1934-35
TB-3	Tenor Banjo	Style 3	1920, 1922, 1924-30, 1932, 1934-37
TB-4	Tenor Banjo	Style 4	1919-30, 1932, 1934-37
TB-5	Tenor Banjo	Style 5	1923-28
TB-6	Tenor Banjo	Style 6	1928-30
TB-7	Tenor Banjo	Style 7	1937, 1939-41
TB-11	Tenor Banjo	Style 11	1931-41
TB-12	Tenor Banjo	Style 12	1937, 1939-40
TB-18	Tenor Banjo	Style 18	1937-39
TB-75	Tenor Banjo	Style 75	1937-41
TB-AA	Tenor Banjo	Style All-American	1930-31
TB-BV	Tenor Banjo	Style Bella Voce	1927-28
TB-F	Tenor Banjo	Style Florentine	1927-30, 1937
TB-G	Tenor Banjo	Style Granada	1925-30, 1935-36
TB-Jr	Tenor Banjo	Style Junior	1920-25
TB-Oriole	Tenor Banjo	Style Oriole	1927
TB-X	Tenor Banjo	Style X	1935-36
TG-0	Tenor Guitar	Flattop	1927-32, 1935, 1938
TG-0 3/4	Tenor Guitar	Flattop	1927-31
TG-00	Tenor Guitar	Flattop	1931-35, 1937-41
TG-1	Tenor Guitar	Archtop or Flattop	1927-31, 1933, 1935-36
TG-2	Tenor Guitar	Archtop or Flattop	1927-30, 1933, 1937
TG-3	Tenor Guitar	Archtop	1930, 1932
TG-4	Tenor Guitar	Archtop	1930, 1932, 1934-37, 1939, 1941
TG-5	Tenor Guitar	Archtop	1930-31, 1935
TG-7	Tenor Guitar	Archtop	1934-40
TG-10	Tenor Guitar	Archtop	1936
TG-12	Tenor Guitar	Archtop	1936-39
TG-30	Tenor Guitar	Archtop	1935-38
TG-37	Tenor Guitar	Archtop	1935-38
TG-50	Tenor Guitar	Archtop	1934-41
TG-75	Tenor Guitar	Archtop	1935, 1937
TG-Jumbo	Tenor Guitar	Jumbo Flattop	1938
TG-NL	Tenor Guitar (Lucas)	Flattop (Nick Lucas)	1938
TL-1	Tenor Lute	Teardrop body	1924-25
TL-4	Tenor Lute	Teardrop body	1924-25
TU	Tenor Ukulele		1927-40

Gibson Brand Instrument Models: 1903-1941 (continued)

Model	Type	Description	Years Produced
U	Harp-Guitar	Archtop Harp Guitar	1904-07, 1909-21, 1923, 1925-26, 1930-31
U-1	Harp-Guitar	Archtop Harp Guitar	1903?
UB	Ukulele Banjo		1924-25
UB-1	Ukulele Banjo		1926-40
UB-2	Ukulele Banjo		1926-40
UB-3	Ukulele Banjo		1926-39
UB-4	Ukulele Banjo		1927-35, 1938
UB-5	Ukulele Banjo		1927-28
Uke-1	Ukulele		1925-40
Uke-2	Ukulele		1925-36, 1938
Uke-3	Ukulele		1925-36
V-15	Violin		1939-41
V-15 3/4	Violin	3/4 size violin	1939-41
V-25	Violin		1939-41
V-30	Violin		1940-41
V-50	Violin		1939-41
V-100	Violin		1940-41
V-250	Violin		1939-41
VA-25	Viola		1941
VA-42	Viola		1940-41
VC-110	Cello		1939-41
B-300	Bass Viola		1939-41

A rare 1939 illustration showing Gibson's violin family instruments

Collection of the author

Kalamazoo Brand Instrument Models: 1933-1941

The data contained in this table are for Kalamazoo-brand instruments only. Standard Gibson model abbreviations are used. The production dates given are based on data extracted from Gibson's shipping ledgers. For a more detailed description of Kalamazoo-brand guitars and mandolins, along with a chronology of structural changes, the reader is referred to *Gruhn's Guide to Vintage Instruments*.

Model	Description	Years Produced
KEH	Electric Hawaiian Guitar	1940-41
KES	Electric Spanish Guitar	1940-41
KG	Flattop Guitar	1933-34
KG "3/4"	Flattop Guitar	1937
KG "Sport"	Flattop Guitar	1940-41
KG-Sr	Flattop Guitar	1933-34
KG-11	Flattop Guitar	1933-37
KG-12	Flattop Guitar	1939-41
KG-14	Flattop Guitar	1936-37
KG-21	Archtop Guitar	1934-39
KG-22	Archtop Guitar	1939-41
KG-31	Archtop Guitar	1933-37, 1939
KG-32	Archtop Guitar	1940-41
KGN-12	Flattop Guitar	1938, 1940-41
KGN-32	Archtop Guitar	1940-41
KG-Sr	Flattop Guitar	1933-34
KHG-11	Hawaiian Guitar	1933-38
KHG-12	Hawaiian Guitar	1941
KHG-14	Hawaiian Guitar	1936-38
KHG-21	Hawaiian Guitar	1935-37
KHG-31	Hawaiian Guitar	1936
KJ	Mando-Bass	1933, 1935-37
KK-31	Mando-Cello	1935-38
KM-11	Mandolin	1933-37
KM-12	Mandolin	1940-41
KM-21	Mandolin	1935-38
KM-22	Mandolin	1940-41
KMB	Mandolin Banjo	1936-40
KMN-12	Mandolin	1940-41
KPB	Plectrum Banjo	1936-40
KRB	Regular Banjo	1936-40
KTB	Tenor Banjo	1936-40
KTG-11	Tenor Guitar	1933-38
KTG-14	Tenor Guitar	1936, 1938
KTG-21	Tenor Guitar	1935-38
KTG-31	Tenor Guitar	1935-38
KV-44	Violin	1939-40

Recording King (Montgomery Ward) Brand Instrument Models: 1929-1940

The data contained in this table are for Recording King-brand instruments only. Model numbers from the Montgomery Ward catalogs are used. The production dates given are based on data extracted from the Gibson shipping ledgers, and the Montgomery Ward catalogs. For a more detailed description of Recording King-brand instruments, along with a chronology of structural changes, the reader is referred to *Gruhn's Guide to Vintage Instruments.*

Model	Instrument	Description	Production Years
# 505	Tenor Banjo	chrome-plated metal, curly maple neck & resonator	1929
# 506	Tenor Banjo	chrome-plated metal, curly maple neck & resonator	1930
# 507	Tenor Banjo	gold-plated metal, curly maple neck & resonator	1930
# 641	Plectrum Banjo	nickle-plated metal, mahogany neck & resonator	1930
# 645	Tenor Banjo	nickle-plated metal, mahogany neck & resonator	1929-30
# 681	Flattop Guitar	maple B&S, 14-fret, small body, ladder braced, tailpiece	1934
# 682	Hawaiian Guitar	mahogany B&S, Jumbo body, 12-fret, "Andy Sannella" model	1934
# 701	Tenor Banjo	nickle-plated, pearloid resonator & fingerboard	1930
# 731	Tenor Banjo	single-bound maple resonator, mahogany neck, red finish	1934
# 732	Tenor Banjo	double-bound curly maple resonator, maple neck, brown finish	1934-35
# 774	Tenor Banjo	same as #645	1932
# 803	Tenor Banjo	figured walnut reso, walnut neck, tone ring	1933
# 807	Flattop Guitar	extra-deep body, mahogany B&S, 12-fret, black finish, X-braced	1930-31
# 807	Mandolin	mahogany B&S, round hole, sunburst top, flat-topped peghead	1933-35
# 811	Flattop Guitar	extra-deep body, curly maple B&S, 12-fret, sunburst top, X-braced	1931-32
# 853	Archtop Guitar	curly maple B&S, 14-fret, F-holes	1934
# 926	Flattop Guitar	mahogany B&S, 14-fret, "Carson Robison"	1933-36
# 952	Banjo		1939-40
# 953	Banjo		1939-40
# 954	Banjo		1939-40
# 955	Banjo		1939-40
# 956	Banjo		1939-40
# 957	Banjo		1939-40
# 969	Mandolin	curly maple B&S, natural finish, dark celluloid body binding	1939-40
# 1005	Electric Hawaiian Gtr	6-string, mahogany B&S, maple top, "Model D"	1938-39
# 1007	Archtop Guitar	electric pickup	1938
# 1008	Amplifier		1938
# 1009	Guitar Outfit	#1010 spanish gtr with amplifier	1938-39
# 1010	Archtop Guitar	F-holes, Super Auditorium body, mahogany B&S, electric pickup	1939
# 1011	Guitar	electric pickup	1938
# 1012	Guitar Outfit	#1127 guitar with amplifier, "Roy Smeck" model	1938-40
# 1013	Amplifier	12" speaker, 12-15 watt output, aeroplane cloth covered	1939-40
# 1015	Guitar		1939-40
# 1020	Guitar Outfit	#1021 lap steel gtr with amplifier	1938-39
# 1021	Electric Hawaiian Gtr	6-string, maple body, "Model A"	1939
# 1022	Guitar Outfit	#1023 lap steel gtr with amplifier	1939
# 1023	Electric Hawaiian Gtr	6-string, curly maple body, "Roy Smeck" model	1939
# 1024	Guitar Outfit	#1025 console steel gtr with amplifier	1939
# 1025	Electric Hawaiian Gtr	8-string, console model, curly maple, "Roy Smeck" model	1939
# 1027	Flattop Guitar	jumbo body, rosewood B&S, X-braced, "Ray Whitley" model	1938-39
# 1028	Flattop Guitar	jumbo body, mahogany B&S, X-braced, "Ray Whitley" model	1939-40
# 1052	Flattop Guitar	Grand Auditorium body, mahogany B&S, 14-fret, ladder braced	1939-40
# 1101	Archtop Guitar	curly maple B&S, natural finish	1939-40

Recording King (Montgomery Ward) Brand Instrument Models: 1929-1940 (continued)

Model	Instrument	Description	Production Years
# 1103	Archtop Guitar	16 1/4" lower bout, blond, curly maple B&S, carved top, 5-ply neck	1939-40
# 1105	Guitar	electric pickup	1938
# 1108	Guitar Outfit	#1109 Hawaiian guitar with amplifier	1939-40
# 1109	Electric Hawaiian Gtr	6-string, maple body, dark mahogany finish, rosewood fngrbd	1939-40
# 1110	Guitar Outfit	#1111 with amplifier	1939
# 1111	Archtop Guitar	mahogany B & S, spruce top, rosewood fngrbd, electric pickup	1939
# 1113	Guitar Outfit	#1114 guitar with amplifier	1939-40
# 1114	Archtop Guitar	maple B&S, spruce top, rosewood fngrbd, electric pickup	1939-40
# 1115	Flattop Guitar	Grand Concert body, mahogany B&S, sunburst, "Model K"	1937-39
# 1121	Archtop Guitar	17" lower bout, curly maple B&S, brown finish, 5-ply maple neck	1939-40
# 1122	Archtop Guitar	same as #1121 with carved back and gold-plated metal	1939-40
# 1123	Archtop Guitar	curly maply B&S, spruce top, sunburst, bound pghd, "Model M-4"	1937-39
# 1124	Archtop Guitar	curly maple B&S, deep body, checkerboard binding, "Model M-5"	1937-39
# 1127	Archtop Guitar	maple B&S, spruce top, electric pickup, "Roy Smeck" model	1938-40
# 1128	Guitar		1937-38
# 1129	Guitar		1937-38
# 1134	Hawaiian Guitar	# 1115 (1939) or #1052 (1940) set up for Hawaiian style	1938-40
# 1135	Tenor Hawaiian Gtr	Same as #1115, but tenor neck	1938-39
# 1136	Archtop Guitar	16 3/4" lower bout, maple B&S, sunburst, carved top, "Model M-2"	1938-40
# 1137	Archtop Guitar	like #1103, curly maple, red finish, sunburst, "Model M-3"	1938-40
# 1150	Archtop Guitar	mahogany B&S, spruce top, sunburst finish	1939-40
# 1151	Archtop Guitar	#1150 with a flannel case	1939-40
# 1152	Archtop Guitar	birch body, "ebonized" fngrbd	1939-40
# 1171	Archtop Guitar	like #1124, hand carved back and top, gold-plated, "Model M-5"	1939
# 1201	Flattop Guitar	same as # 926, mahogany B&S, "Carson Robison" model	1935-37
# 1202	Guitar		1936
# 1203	Guitar	Tenor guitar?	1935
# 1204	Tenor Guitar	same specs as #1201	1935-36
# 1205	Guitar	Archtop guitar?	1935
# 1206	Guitar	Plectrum guitar?	1935
# 1207	Guitar		1935
# 1228	Archtop Guitar	curly maple B&S, 14-fret, F-holes, natural finish	1936-37
# 1241	Guitar	Archtop guitar?	1935-36
# 1242	Archtop Guitar	mahogany B&S, F-holes, carved top & back	1935-36
# 1254	Archtop Guitar	maple B&S, 14-fret, F-holes, sunburst finish	1936-37
# 1270	Archtop Guitar	maple B&S, F-holes, electric pickup	1936-37
# 1271	Electric Hawaiian Gtr	6-strings, mahogany body	1936-37
# 1281	Flattop Guitar	mahogany B&S, 14-fret, Grand Concert body, "Carson Robison"	1936-37
# 1282	Guitar	"Tone-Crest" brand	1936
# 1283	Guitar	"Tone-Crest" brand	1935-36
# 1284	Guitar		1936
# 1285	Archtop Guitar	curly maple B&S, 14-fret, F-holes, sunburst finish	1936-37
# 1584	Regular Banjo	deep resonator	1937-39
# 1586	Tenor Banjo		1935-36
# 1593	Tenor Banjo	deep resonator	1936-39
# 1594	Regular Banjo	deep resonator, "Model M-6"	1938
# 1607	Mandolin	mahogany B&S, F-holes, "Arco-Arch" top, flat-topped pghd	1935-36
# 1610	Mandolin		1935-36
# 1642	Mandolin		1936-37

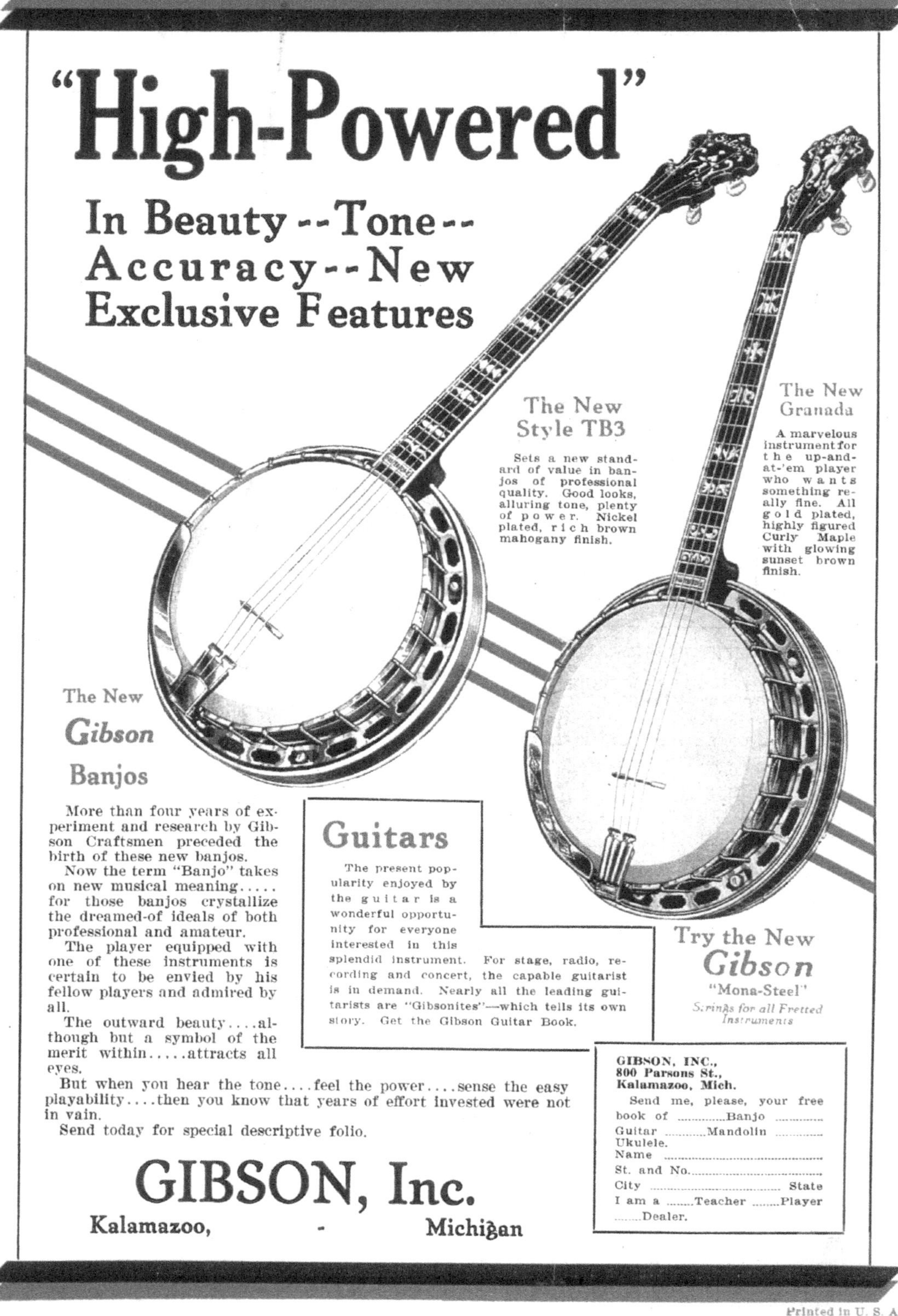

This ad appeared in the October 1929 issue of *Mastertone Magazine* and is one of the earliest company documents showing the new "one-piece flange" banjos.
Steve Huber Collection

Appendix A – Gibson Banjo Model Descriptions (1919 – 1941)

Overview

The descriptions given in the following text reflect the construction features of the majority of observed instruments. With Gibson there are *always* exceptions to the standard model specifications as given in the catalog. Production totals are given as a best estimate, based on data from shipping ledgers, compiled factory order number lists, and compiled serial number lists. Allowance has been made for spoilage and factory sales.

Banjo: Style "none"
Production Dates: 1919-1920
Total Estimated Production: Cello neck (CB): *data insufficient*
Guitar neck (GB): *data insufficient*
Mandolin neck (MB): *data insufficient*
Tenor neck (TB): *data insufficient*
Pot: Multi-ply or block-type maple rim of 10.5″ outside diameter, shoe and bracket hardware, wooden dowel stick, stretcher band is of the simple hoop type, metal parts nickel-plated, no flange
Neck: Straight-grain maple, rosewood fingerboard, no binding
Resonator: None
Serial Number: Serial number appears on a small metal plate attached to the dowel rod
Factory Order Number: No factory order numbers appear on these instruments
Note: These are the first Gibson banjo models. They do not appear in any catalog, but are listed in the price lists dated September 1, 1919 and May 1920.

Banjo: Style "Junior"
Production Dates: 1920 - 1925
Total Estimated Production: Mandolin neck (MB): *data insufficient*
Five-string neck (RB): *data insufficient*
Tenor neck (TB): *data insufficient*
Pot: Multi-ply or block-type maple rim of 10.5″ outside diameter, shoe and bracket hardware, wooden dowel stick or single coordinator rod, stretcher band is of the simple hoop type, metal parts nickel-plated, no flange
Neck: Straight-grain maple, rosewood fingerboard, no binding, has truss rod
Resonator: None
Serial Number: Serial number die stamped on wooden dowel rod (1920 production *only*). 1921-1925 units have no serial number
Factory Order Number: Die-stamped on the interior rim wall or on wooden dowel stick (1921-1925 production *only*). 1920 units have no factory order number

Banjo: Style 0
Production Dates: 1925 - 1928
Total Estimated Production: Mandolin neck (MB): 240 units
Tenor neck (TB): 700 units
Pot: Multi-ply or block-type maple rim (.75" thick below the flange), catalog specified rims of 11" outside diameter, but many examples have been seen with 10.5" outside diameter, shoe and bracket hardware, single coordinator rod, stretcher band is of the simple hoop type, all metal parts nickel-plated
Neck: Straight-grain maple, rosewood fingerboard, catalog specified dot fingerboard inlays, but many examples have been seen with "Nick Lucas" style inlay, stenciled "The Gibson" script logo on peghead, has truss rod, friction-type tuners, cream-colored ivoroid binding
Resonator: None
Finish: Nitro-cellulose lacquer over Sheraton brown stain
Serial Number: No serial numbers used on this model
Factory Order Number: Die-stamped on the interior rim wall

Banjo: Style 00
Production Dates: 1935 – in production at the start of World War II (last shipped 1944)
Total Estimated Production: Mandolin neck (MB): 300 units
Plectrum neck (PB): 60 units
Five-string neck (RB): 500 units
Tenor neck (TB): 1,200 units
Pot: Multi-ply, maple rim of 11" outside diameter, early rims are .580" thick below the flange but later rims are .5" or thinner, one-piece die-cast flange, single coordinator rod, stretcher band is of simple hoop type, all metal parts nickel-plated
Neck: Straight-grain maple with no volute (handstop), rosewood fingerboard, catalog specified dot fingerboard inlays, but many inlay variants have been observed, no fingerboard binding, stenciled "Gibson" script logo on peghead, has truss rod, earlier models usually have Grover brand "two-tab" tuners and later models have Kluson brand "tulip-button" tuners
Resonator: Removable "convex-back" or "flat back" type, straight-grain maple veneer over a laminated poplar core, mounted with three thumbscrews, cream-colored ivoroid binding on bottom only.
Finish: Nitro-cellulose lacquer with no stain and black sunburst on neck and resonator.
Serial Number: Die-stamped, two-letter prefix type serial number located on back of peghead (1938-1940 ONLY), no serial number (1935-1937, 1941)
Factory Order Number: Usually none, but sometimes found written in pencil on neck heel

Banjo: Style 1 (First Model)
Production Dates: 1919-1920
Total Estimated Production: Tenor neck (TB): *data insufficient*
Pot: Multi-ply ash rim with a maple veneer of 10.5" outside diameter (.75" thick below the flange), shoe and bracket hardware, metal "tone tube"-type tone ring, simple tube flange, grooved stretcher band
Neck: Straight-grain maple, rosewood fingerboard, tuners are plate-mounted (two per plate), Mother-of-pearl "The Gibson" logo in peghead, dot fingerboard inlays, no binding, has truss rod
Resonator: None

Banjo: Style 1 (First Model - continued)
Finish: Varnish over Sheraton brown stain
Serial Number: Die-stamped on wooden dowel rod
Factory Order Number: No factory order numbers used on this model

Banjo: Style 1 (Second Model)
Production Dates: 1921 - 1924
Total Estimated Production: Mandolin neck (MB): *data insufficient*
Five-string neck (RB): *data insufficient*
Tenor neck (TB): *data insufficient*
Pot: Multi-ply ash rim with a maple veneer of 10.5" outside diameter (.75" thick below the flange), shoe and bracket hardware, metal "tone tube"-type tone ring, simple tube flange, grooved stretcher band, all metal parts nickel-plated
Neck: Straight-grain maple, rosewood fingerboard, tuners are plate-mounted (two per plate), Mother-of-pearl "The Gibson" logo in peghead, dot fingerboard inlays, no binding, has truss rod
Resonator: Tone projector "trap-door" type
Finish: Varnish or nitro-cellulose lacquer over brown mahogany stain
Serial Number: No serial numbers used on this model
Factory Order Number: Die-stamped on the interior rim wall or wooden dowel rod.

Banjo: Style 1 (Third Model)
Production Dates: 1925 - 1929 (except MB-1 model in production through 1937)
Total Estimated Production: Guitar neck (GB): 90 units
Mandolin neck (MB): 500 units
Plectrum neck (PB): 125 units
Five-string neck (RB): 60 units
Tenor neck (TB): 3,000 units
Pot: Multi-ply maple rim with 11" outside diameter (except MB models, 10.5" outside diameter) and .75" thick below the flange, shoe and bracket hardware, solid brass tube type tone ring, plate flange (diamond or hexagon pattern), grooved stretcher band, all metal parts nickel-plated
Neck: Straight-grain maple, rosewood fingerboard, friction-type tuners (except MB models), silk-screened "The Gibson" logo on peghead, dot fingerboard inlays, cream-colored ivoroid binding, has truss rod
Resonator: Removable "convex-back" type, straight-grain maple veneer over a laminated poplar core, mounted with four thumbscrews (or hex-head screws 1925-26 only), cream-colored ivoroid binding (bottom only)
Finish: Nitro-cellulose lacquer over Sheraton brown stain
Serial Numbers: No serial numbers used on this model
Factory Order Number: Die-stamped on the interior rim wall, also copied in chalk at the center of resonator interior, and repeated in red paint to the right of the neck notch

Banjo: Style 1 (Fourth Model)
Production Dates: 1929 - 1940
Total Estimated Production: Guitar neck (GB): 33 units
Plectrum neck (PB): 180 units
Five-string neck (RB): 200 units
Tenor neck (TB): 1,900 units
Pot: Multi-ply maple rim with 11″ outside diameter (.580″ to .625″ thick below the flange), solid brass hoop tone ring, die-cast one-piece flange, notched die-cast stretcher band, all metal parts nickel-plated, single coordinator rod
Neck: Straight-grain maple, rosewood fingerboard, violin shaped peghead (2nd type) or "coke bottle" peghead, catalog specified "gull" pattern fingerboard inlays (but dots, diamonds and squares and even Bella Voce patterns have been seen), cream-colored ivoroid binding, Grover or Kluson brand tuners (usually two-tab type), mother-of-pearl "Gibson" script logo on peghead, has truss rod
Resonator: Removable "convex-back" type, straight-grain maple veneer over a laminated poplar core, mounted with three or four thumbscrews, cream-colored ivoroid binding (may be bound top and bottom or bottom only)
Finish: Nitro-cellulose lacquer over Sheraton brown stain
Serial Number: No serial number (1929-1937), die-stamped, two-letter prefix type serial number located on back of peghead (1938-1940 only)
Factory Order Number: Die-stamped on the interior rim wall, also copied in chalk at the center of resonator interior, and repeated in red paint to the right of the neck notch

Banjo: Style 11
Production Dates: 1931- in production at the start of World War II (last shipped 1944)
Total Estimated Production: Guitar neck (GB): 1 unit
Mandolin neck (MB): 120 units
Plectrum neck (PB): 80 units
Five-string neck (RB): 140 units
Tenor neck (TB): 700 units
Pot: Multi-ply maple rim with 11″ outside diameter (.580″ to .625″ thick below the flange), solid brass hoop tone ring (with reduced diameter post-1937 giving a "raised head" appearance), die-cast one-piece flange, notched die-cast stretcher band, all metal parts nickel-plated, single coordinator rod, rim painted dark blue
Neck: Straight-grain maple, celluloid fingerboard with stenciled floral pattern position markers, Kel Kroydon shaped peghead with celluloid overlay, cream-colored ivoroid binding, Grover or Kluson brand tuners (usually two-tab type), has truss rod
Resonator: Removable "convex-back" type, back covered in celluloid with stenciled floral pattern, mounted with three or four thumbscrews, cream-colored ivoroid binding (top and bottom)
Finish: Dark blue nitro-cellulose lacquer on neck, rim and resonator sides, transparent lacquer sunburst on resonator back, fingerboard and peghead overlay (may be brown, blue or gray)
Serial Number: Two-letter prefix type serial number located on back of peghead (1938-1940 only), no serial number used 1931-1937, 1941-1944
Factory Order Number: Single-letter prefix FON on back of peghead (1941-1943), no factory order numbers used (1931-1940)

Banjo: Style 2 (First Model)
Production Dates: 1920-1923
Total Estimated Production: Mandolin neck (MB): *data insufficient*
Tenor neck (TB): *data insufficient*
Note: This model does not appear in any catalog but has been reported to various lists.

Banjo: Style 2 (Second Model)
Production Dates: 1925 - 1926
Total Estimated Production: Mandolin neck (MB): 100 units
Plectrum neck (PB): 0 units
Five-string neck (RB): 0 units
Tenor neck (TB): 320 units
Pot: Multi-ply maple rim with 10.5″ outside diameter (.75″ thick below the flange), shoe and bracket hardware, tube type tone ring, serpentine flange, grooved stretcher band, all metal parts nickel-plated
Neck: Straight-grain maple, rosewood fingerboard, mother-of-pearl "Nick Lucas" pattern fingerboard inlays, cream-colored ivoroid binding, Grover brand tuners, mother-of-pearl "The Gibson" script logo on peghead, has truss rod
Resonator: Removable "convex-back" type, straight-grain maple veneer over a laminated poplar core, mounted with four hex-head screws, cream-colored ivoroid binding (bottom only)
Finish: Nitro-cellulose lacquer over Sheraton brown stain
Serial Numbers: No serial numbers used on this model
Factory Order Number: Die-stamped on the interior rim wall, also copied in chalk at the center of resonator interior, and repeated in red paint to the right of the neck notch

Banjo: Style 2 (Third Model)
Production Dates: 1926 - 1929 (except MB-2 model in production through 1931)
Total Estimated Production: Mandolin neck (MB): 100 units
Plectrum neck (PB): 0 units
Five-string neck (RB): 2 units
Tenor neck (TB): 1,480 units
Pot: Multi-ply maple rim with 11″ outside diameter (.75″ thick below the flange), shoe and bracket hardware, seen with tube type tone ring (1926) or cast "pyramid" tone ring (1927-1929), plate flange (diamond or hexagon pattern), grooved stretcher band, all metal parts nickel-plated
Neck: Straight-grain maple, rosewood fingerboard, mother-of-pearl "Nick Lucas" pattern fingerboard inlays, cream-colored ivoroid binding, Grover brand tuners, mother-of-pearl "The Gibson" script logo on peghead, has truss rod
Resonator: Removable "convex-back" type, straight-grain maple veneer over a laminated poplar core, mounted with four thumbscrews (or hex-head screws 1926 only), cream-colored ivoroid binding (bottom only)
Finish: Nitro-cellulose lacquer over Sheraton brown stain
Serial Numbers: No serial numbers used on this model
Factory Order Number: Die-stamped on the interior rim wall, also copied in chalk at the center of resonator interior, and repeated in red paint to the right of the neck notch

Banjo: Style 2 (Fourth Model)
Production Dates: 1929 - 1937
Total Estimated Production: Mandolin neck (MB): 10 units
Plectrum neck (PB): 20 units
Five-string neck (RB): 35 units
Tenor neck (TB): 600 units
Pot: Multi-ply maple rim with 11″ outside diameter (.580″ to .625″ thick below the flange), solid brass hoop type tone ring, die-cast one-piece flange, notched die-cast stretcher band, single coordinator rod, all metal parts nickel-plated
Neck: Walnut, violin shaped peghead (2nd type), celluloid fingerboard and peghead overlay (with engraved and painted patterns), cream-colored ivoroid binding, Grover brand tuners (usually two-tab type), has truss rod
Resonator: Removable "convex-back" type, figured walnut veneer over a laminated poplar core, mounted with three or four thumbscrews, cream-colored ivoroid binding (bound top and bottom)
Finish: Nitro-cellulose lacquer over natural walnut
Serial Numbers: No serial numbers used on this model
Factory Order Number: Die-stamped on the interior rim wall, also copied in chalk at the center of resonator interior, and repeated in red paint to the right of the neck notch

Banjo: Style 3 (First Model)
Production Dates: 1919 (MB's and TB's), 1920 (GB), 1923-1924 (PB's and RB's)
Total Estimated Production: Guitar neck (GB): *data insufficient*
Mandolin neck (MB): *data insufficient*
Plectrum neck (PB): *data insufficient*
Five-string neck (RB): *data insufficient*
Tenor neck (TB): *data insufficient*
Pot: Multi-ply ash rim with maple veneer of 10.5″ outside diameter (TB's, PB's and RB's), 9″ outside diameter (MB's), 14″ outside diameter (GB's), metal "tone tube"-type tone ring, simple tube flange, grooved stretcher band
Neck: Straight-grain maple, rosewood fingerboard, dot fingerboard inlays, mother-of-pearl "The Gibson" logo in peghead, no fingerboard binding, plate-mounted tuners, "pointed" peghead on TB models, "wavy" peghead on MB models, has truss rod after 1921
Resonator: Tone projector "trap-door" type on TB's (1918-19, 1921-24), Pyralin "Professional Special" concave type on TB's (1920), no resonator on MB's
Finish: Varnish over dark mahogany stain on rim and sunburst on neck
Serial Numbers: Die-stamped on wooden dowel rod (1919-1920 production only), no serial numbers used 1921-1924
Factory Order Number: Die-stamped on the interior rim wall or dowel stick (1921-1924)

Banjo: Style 3 (Second Model)
Production Dates: 1925 - 1926
Total Estimated Production: Guitar neck (GB): 60 units
Mandolin neck (MB): 220 units
Plectrum neck (PB): 125 units
Five-string neck (RB): 35 units
Tenor neck (TB): 1,860 units

Banjo: Style 3 (Second Model - continued)
Pot: Multi-ply maple of 11" outside diameter (except MB models with 10.5" outside diameter), .75" thick below the flange, Mastertone ball-bearing tone ring system (holes in exterior retaining skirt 1925 only), tube and plate flange (except MB models with shoe and bracket hardware), grooved stretcher band, metal parts nickel-plated, dual coordinator rod system, Mastertone guarantee decal inside rim
Neck: Straight-grain maple with "violin" peghead of the 1st type (except MB models), rosewood fingerboard, cream-colored ivoroid binding, mother-of-pearl "diamonds and squares" fingerboard inlays with "Gibson" script logo in peghead, "Mastertone" inlaid in peghead using small letters (usually 1925 only) or etched on mother-of-pearl block in fingerboard (1926), has truss rod
Resonator: Removable "convex-back" type, straight-grain maple veneer over a laminated poplar core, mounted with four thumbscrews (or hex-head screws, usually 1925 only), plain back, cream-colored ivoroid binding (bottom only)
Finish: Nitro-cellulose lacquer over red mahogany stain
Serial Numbers: No serial numbers used on this model
Factory Order Number: Die-stamped on the interior rim wall, also copied in chalk at the center of resonator interior, and repeated in red paint to the right of the neck notch

Banjo: Style 3 (Third Model)
Production Dates: 1927 - 1929
Total Estimated Production: Guitar neck (GB): 25 units
Mandolin neck (MB): 100 units
Plectrum neck (PB): 130 units
Five-string neck (RB): 45 units
Tenor neck (TB): 1,980 units
Pot: Multi-ply maple of 11" outside diameter, .75" thick below the flange, cast brass "raised head" tone ring (with no holes usually 1927 only, or with 40 holes 1927-1929), tube and plate flange, notched brass stretcher band, metal parts nickel-plated, dual coordinator rod system, Mastertone guarantee decal inside rim
Neck: Straight-grain maple with "violin" peghead of the 1st type (except MB models), rosewood fingerboard, cream-colored ivoroid binding, mother-of-pearl "diamonds and squares" fingerboard inlays with "Gibson" script logo in peghead, "Mastertone" etched on mother-of-pearl block in fingerboard, has truss rod
Resonator: Removable "convex-back" type, straight-grain maple veneer over a laminated poplar core, mounted with four thumbscrews, plain back, cream-colored ivoroid binding (top and bottom)
Finish: Nitro-cellulose lacquer over red or brown mahogany stain (brown mahogany is usually later)
Serial Numbers: No serial numbers used on this model
Factory Order Number: Die-stamped on the interior rim wall, also copied in chalk at the center of resonator interior, and repeated in red paint to the right of the neck notch

Banjo: Style 3 (Fourth Model)
Production Dates: 1929 - 1937
Total Estimated Production: Cello neck (CB): 5 units
Guitar neck (GB): 10 units
Mandolin neck (MB): 70 units
Plectrum neck (PB): 110 units
Five-string neck (RB): 53 units
Tenor neck (TB): 1,100 units
Pot: Multi-ply maple rim with 11″ outside diameter (.580″ to .625″ thick below the flange), cast brass "raised head" tone ring (MB's and TB's) or cast brass "flathead" tone ring (CB's, GB's, PB's and RB's), die-cast one-piece flange, notched die-cast stretcher band, dual coordinator rods, all metal parts nickel-plated, Mastertone guarantee decal inside rim
Neck: Mahogany with "scroll" (double-cut) peghead, rosewood fingerboard, cream-colored ivoroid binding, catalog specified mother-of-pearl "leaves and bows" fingerboard inlays (but many variants seen), "Gibson" script logo in peghead, "Mastertone" etched on mother-of-pearl block in fingerboard, has truss rod
Resonator: Removable "convex-back" type, mahogany veneer over a laminated poplar core, two white/black/white concentric rings inlaid on back, mounted with four thumbscrews, cream-colored ivoroid binding (top and bottom)
Finish: Nitro-cellulose lacquer over red mahogany stain
Serial Numbers: No serial numbers used on this model
Factory Order Number: Die-stamped on the interior rim wall, also copied in chalk at the center of resonator interior, and repeated in red paint to the right of the neck notch

Banjo: Style 4 (First Model)
Production Dates: 1919
Total Estimated Production: Cello neck (CB): *data insufficient*
Guitar neck (GB): *data insufficient*
Mandolin neck (MB): *data insufficient*
Tenor neck (TB): *data insufficient*
Pot: Multi-ply maple rim of 10.5″ outside diameter (TB's) or 9″ outside diameter (MB's) or 14″ outside diameter (CB's and GB's), metal "tone tube"-type tone ring, simple tube flange, grooved stretcher band, coordinator rods, metal parts silver-plated
Neck: Curly maple with rosewood center strip, extended ebony fingerboard, dot inlays, mother-of-pearl "The Gibson" logo and fleur-de-lis inlaid in peghead, cream-colored ivoroid binding, plate-mounted tuners, "pointed" peghead (CB's, GB's and TB's), "wavy" peghead (MB's), no truss rod
Resonator: Tone projector "trap-door" type
Finish: Varnish
Serial Numbers: Die-stamped on wooden dowel rod.
Factory Order Number: No factory order numbers used on this model

Banjo: Style 4 (Second Model)
Production Dates: 1920 - 1924
Total Estimated Production: Cello neck (CB): *data insufficient*
Guitar neck (GB): *data insufficient*
Mandolin neck (MB): *data insufficient*
Plectrum neck (PB): *data insufficient*
Five-string neck (RB): *data insufficient*
Tenor neck (TB): *data insufficient*
Pot: Multi-ply maple rim of 10.5″ outside diameter (MB's, RB's and TB's) or 14″ outside diameter (CB's and GB's), metal "tone tube"-type tone ring, simple tube flange, grooved stretcher band, coordinator rods, metal parts silver-plated
Neck: Curly maple with rosewood center strip, extended ebony fingerboard, dot inlays, mother-of-pearl "The Gibson" logo and fleur-de-lis inlaid in peghead, cream-colored ivoroid binding, plate-mounted tuners, "pointed" peghead (CB's, GB's and TB's), "wavy" peghead (MB's), no truss rod
Resonator: Tone projector "trap-door" type
Finish: Varnish over Cremona brown sunburst
Serial Numbers: Die-stamped on wooden dowel rod (1920 production only), no serial numbers used 1921-1924
Factory Order Number: Die-stamped on the interior rim wall or wooden dowel rod (1921-1924 production only)

Banjo: Style 4 (Third Model)
Production Dates: 1925 - 1926
Total Estimated Production: Plectrum neck (PB): 40 units
Five-string neck (RB): 20 units
Tenor neck (TB): 460 units
Pot: Multi-ply maple of 11″ outside diameter, .75″ thick below the flange, Mastertone ball-bearing tone ring system (holes in exterior retaining skirt 1925 only), tube and plate flange, grooved stretcher band, metal parts nickel-plated, dual coordinator rod system, Mastertone guarantee decal inside rim
Neck: Mahogany with "violin" peghead of the 1st type, rosewood fingerboard, white/black/white binding, mother-of-pearl "hearts and flowers" fingerboard inlays with "Gibson" script logo in peghead, "Mastertone" inlaid in peghead using small letters (usually 1925 only) or etched on mother-of-pearl block in fingerboard (1926), has truss rod
Resonator: Removable "convex-back" type, mahogany veneer over a laminated poplar core, mounted with four thumbscrews (or hex-head screws, usually 1925 only), two white/black/white concentric rings inlaid on back, white/black/white binding (top and bottom)
Finish: Nitro-cellulose lacquer over brown mahogany stain
Serial Numbers: No serial numbers used on this model
Factory Order Number: Die-stamped on the interior rim wall, also copied in chalk at the center of resonator interior, and repeated in red paint to the right of the neck notch

Banjo: Style 4 (Fourth Model)
Production Dates: 1927 - 1929
Total Estimated Production: Mandolin neck (MB): 1 unit
Plectrum neck (PB): 11 units
Five-string neck (RB): 3 units
Tenor neck (TB): 275 units
Pot: Multi-ply maple of 11″ outside diameter, .75″ thick below the flange, cast brass "raised head" tone ring (with no holes usually 1927 only, or with 40 holes 1927-1929), tube and plate flange, notched brass stretcher band, metal parts nickel or chrome-plated, dual coordinator rod system, Mastertone guarantee decal inside rim
Neck: Mahogany with "violin" peghead of the 1st type, rosewood fingerboard, white/black/white binding, mother-of-pearl "hearts and flowers" fingerboard inlays with "Gibson" script logo in peghead, "Mastertone" etched on mother-of-pearl block in fingerboard, has truss rod
Resonator: Removable "convex-back" type, mahogany veneer over a laminated poplar core, mounted with four thumbscrews, two white/black/white concentric rings inlaid on back, white/black/white binding (top and bottom)
Finish: Nitro-cellulose lacquer over brown mahogany stain
Serial Numbers: No serial numbers used on this model
Factory Order Number: Die-stamped on the interior rim wall, also copied in chalk at the center of resonator interior, and repeated in red paint to the right of the neck notch

Banjo: Style 4 (Fifth Model)
Production Dates: 1929 - 1936
Total Estimated Production: Plectrum neck (PB): 25 units
Five-string neck (RB): 16 units
Tenor neck (TB): 275 units
Pot: Multi-ply maple rim with 11″ outside diameter (.580″ to .625″ thick below the flange), cast brass "raised head" tone ring (TB's) or cast brass "flathead" tone ring (PB's and RB's), die-cast one-piece flange, notched die-cast stretcher band, dual coordinator rods, metal parts seen nickel or chrome-plated (catalog specified chrome), Mastertone guarantee decal inside rim
Neck: Walnut with "scroll" (double-cut) peghead, rosewood fingerboard, cream-colored ivoroid or white/black/white binding, catalog specified mother-of-pearl "flying eagle" fingerboard inlays (but many variants seen), "Gibson" script logo in peghead, "Mastertone" etched on mother-of-pearl block in fingerboard, has truss rod
Resonator: Removable "convex-back" type, walnut veneer over a laminated poplar core, two concentric rings of wood marquetry inlaid on back, mounted with four thumbscrews, cream-colored ivoroid or white/black/white binding (top and bottom)
Finish: Nitro-cellulose lacquer, no stain
Serial Numbers: No serial numbers used on this model
Factory Order Number: Die-stamped on the interior rim wall, also copied in chalk at the center of resonator interior, and repeated in red paint to the right of the neck notch

Banjo: Style Granada (First Model)
Production Dates: 1925 - 1926
Total Estimated Production: Plectrum neck (PB): 40 units
Tenor neck (TB): 320 units
Pot: Multi-ply maple of 11" outside diameter, .75" thick below the flange, Mastertone ball-bearing tone ring system (holes in exterior retaining skirt 1925 only), tube and plate flange, grooved stretcher band, dual coordinator rod system, metal parts gold plated, engraving on armrest, stretcher band and tailpiece, Mastertone guarantee decal inside rim
Neck: Curly maple, "violin" peghead of the 1st type with wood marquetry design inlaid on the back, rosewood fingerboard, fingerboard bound with wood marquetry in combination with white/black/white binding, mother-of-pearl "hearts and flowers" fingerboard inlays with "Gibson" script logo in peghead, "Mastertone" inlaid in peghead using small letters (usually 1925 only) or etched on mother-of-pearl block in fingerboard (1926), has truss rod
Resonator: Removable "convex-back" type, curly maple veneer over a laminated poplar core, mounted with four thumbscrews (or hex-head screws, usually 1925 only), two wood marquetry concentric rings inlaid on back, sides bound with wood marquetry, white/black/white binding (top and bottom)
Finish: Nitro-cellulose lacquer over dark brown stain
Serial Numbers: No serial numbers used on this model
Factory Order Number: Die-stamped on the interior rim wall, also copied in chalk at the center of resonator interior, and repeated in red paint to the right of the neck notch

Banjo: Style Granada (Second Model)
Production Dates: 1927 - 1929
Total Estimated Production: Guitar neck (GB): 2 units
Mandolin neck (MB): 1 unit
Plectrum neck (PB): 30 units
Five-string neck (RB): 10 units
Tenor neck (TB): 450 units
Pot: Multi-ply maple of 11" outside diameter, .75" thick below the flange, cast brass "raised head" tone ring (with no holes usually 1927 only, or with 40 holes 1927-1929), tube and plate flange, notched brass stretcher band, dual coordinator rods, metal parts gold plated, engraving on armrest, stretcher band and tailpiece, Mastertone guarantee decal inside rim
Neck: Curly maple, "violin" peghead of the 1st type, rosewood fingerboard, white/black/white binding, mother-of-pearl "hearts and flowers" fingerboard inlays with "Gibson" script logo in peghead, "Mastertone" etched on mother-of-pearl block in fingerboard, has truss rod
Resonator: Removable "convex-back" type, curly maple veneer over a laminated poplar core, mounted with four thumbscrews, two wood marquetry concentric rings inlaid on back, white/black/white binding (top and bottom)
Finish: Nitro-cellulose lacquer over dark brown stain
Serial Numbers: No serial numbers used on this model
Factory Order Number: Die-stamped on the interior rim wall, also copied in chalk at the center of resonator interior, and repeated in red paint to the right of the neck notch

Banjo: Style Granada (Third Model)
Production Dates: 1929 - 1936
Total Estimated Production: Plectrum neck (PB): 37 units
Five-string neck (RB): 17 units
Tenor neck (TB): 185 units
Pot: Multi-ply maple rim with 11″ outside diameter (.580″ to .625″ thick below the flange), cast brass "raised head" tone ring (TB's) or cast brass "flathead" tone ring (PB's and RB's), die-cast one-piece flange, notched brass or die-cast stretcher band, dual coordinator rods, metal parts gold plated, engraving on armrest and stretcher band, Mastertone guarantee decal inside rim
Neck: Curly maple with "scroll" (double-cut) peghead, rosewood fingerboard, white/black/white binding, catalog specified mother-of-pearl "flying eagle" fingerboard inlays (but other variants seen), "Gibson" script logo in peghead, "Mastertone" etched on mother-of-pearl block in fingerboard, has truss rod
Resonator: Removable "convex-back" type, curly maple veneer over a laminated poplar core, seen with two concentric rings of wood marquetry inlaid on back or no concentric rings, mounted with four thumbscrews, white/black/white binding (top and bottom)
Finish: Nitro-cellulose lacquer over dark brown stain on neck and Cremona sunburst on resonator
Serial Numbers: No serial numbers used on this model
Factory Order Number: Die-stamped on the interior rim wall, also copied in chalk at the center of resonator interior, and repeated in red paint to the right of the neck notch

Banjo: Style 5 (First Model)
Production Dates: 1920 - 1924
Total Estimated Production: Tenor neck (TB): *data insufficient*
Pot: Multi-ply maple rim of 10.5″ outside diameter with Pyralin veneer, metal "tone tube"-type tone ring, simple tube flange, grooved stretcher band, coordinator rods, metal parts gold plated, bottom of rim bound in cream-colored ivoroid
Neck: Curly maple with rosewood center strip, extended ebony fingerboard with "artist" inlays, mother-of-pearl "The Gibson" logo and vine inlaid in peghead, cream-colored ivoroid binding, plate-mounted tuners, "pointed" peghead, no truss rod
Resonator: Tone projector "trap-door" type
Finish: Varnish over Cremona brown sunburst
Serial Numbers: Die-stamped on wooden dowel rod (1920 production only), no serial numbers used 1921-1924
Factory Order Number: Die-stamped on the interior rim wall or wooden dowel rod (1921-1924 production only)

Banjo: Style 5 (Second Model)
Production Dates: 1925 - 1926
Total Estimated Production: Plectrum neck (PB): 10 units
Tenor neck (TB): 250 units
Pot: Multi-ply maple of 11″ outside diameter, .75″ thick below the flange, Mastertone ball-bearing tone ring system (holes in exterior retaining skirt 1925 only), tube and plate flange, grooved stretcher band, dual coordinator rod system, metal parts gold plated, engraving on armrest, stretcher band, tone ring skirt and tailpiece, interior and exterior of rim bottom edge

Banjo: Style 5 (Second Model - continued)
bound with wood marquetry and Pyralin, rim bottom finished in black, Mastertone guarantee decal inside rim
Neck: Walnut, "violin" peghead of the 1st type with wood marquetry design inlaid on the back, rosewood fingerboard bound with wood marquetry in combination with Pyralin binding, mother-of-pearl "wreath" fingerboard inlays with "Gibson" script logo in peghead, "Mastertone" inlaid in peghead using small letters (usually 1925 only) or etched on mother-of-pearl block in fingerboard (1926), Pyralin-capped heel, has truss rod
Resonator: Removable "convex-back" type, walnut veneer over a laminated poplar core, mounted with four thumbscrews (or hex-head screws, usually 1925 only), two wood marquetry concentric rings inlaid on back, sides bound with wood marquetry, Pyralin binding (top and bottom)
Finish: Nitro-cellulose lacquer over dark brown stain
Serial Numbers: No serial numbers used on this model
Factory Order Number: Die-stamped on the interior rim wall, also copied in chalk at the center of resonator interior, and repeated in red paint to the right of the neck notch

Banjo: Style 5 (Third Model)
Production Dates: 1927 - 1928
Total Estimated Production: Mandolin neck (MB) 1 unit
Plectrum neck (PB): 10 units
Regular neck (RB): 1 unit
Tenor neck (TB): 100 units
Pot: Multi-ply maple of 11" outside diameter, .75" thick below the flange, cast brass "raised head" tone ring (with no holes usually 1927 only, or with 40 holes 1928), tube and plate flange, notched brass stretcher band, dual coordinator rods, metal parts gold plated, engraving on armrest, stretcher band, tone ring and tailpiece, interior and exterior of rim bottom edge bound with wood marquetry and Pyralin, rim bottom finished in black, Mastertone guarantee decal inside rim
Neck: Walnut, "violin" peghead of the 1st type with wood marquetry design inlaid on the back, rosewood fingerboard bound with wood marquetry in combination with Pyralin binding, mother-of-pearl "wreath" fingerboard inlays with "Gibson" script logo in peghead, "Mastertone" etched on mother-of-pearl block in fingerboard, Pyralin capped heel, has truss rod
Resonator: Removable "convex-back" type, walnut veneer over a laminated poplar core, mounted with four thumbscrews, two wood marquetry concentric rings inlaid on back, sides bound with wood marquetry, Pyralin binding (top and bottom)
Finish: Nitro-cellulose lacquer over dark brown stain
Serial Numbers: No serial numbers used on this model
Factory Order Number: Die-stamped on the interior rim wall, also copied in chalk at the center of resonator interior, and repeated in red paint to the right of the neck notch

Banjo: Style 6 (First Model)
Production Dates: 1928-1930
Total Estimated Production: Plectrum neck (PB): 30 units
Regular neck (RB): 1 unit
Tenor neck (TB): 245 units
Pot: Multi-ply maple of 11" outside diameter, .75" thick below the flange, cast brass "raised head" or "flathead" tone ring, tube and plate flange, notched brass stretcher band, dual coordinator rods, metal parts gold plated, engraving on armrest, stretcher band, tone ring and tailpiece, Mastertone guarantee decal inside rim
Neck: Curly maple, modified "violin" peghead with checkerboard or gold-sparkle binding, ebony fingerboard, top and side-bound with checkerboard or gold-sparkle binding in combination with cream-colored ivoroid, mother-of-pearl fingerboard inlays in modified "hearts and flowers" pattern, "Gibson" script logo in peghead, no Mastertone block, heel capped in white and black stripes or gold-sparkle, has truss rod.
Resonator: Removable "convex-back" type, figured maple veneer over a laminated poplar core, mounted with four thumbscrews, no concentric rings inlaid on back, sides bound with checkerboard or gold-sparkle binding in combination with cream-colored ivoroid
Finish: Nitro-cellulose lacquer over Argentine Grey stain
Serial Numbers: No serial numbers used on this model
Factory Order Number: Die-stamped on the interior rim wall, also copied in chalk at the center of resonator interior, and repeated in red paint to the right of the neck notch

Banjo: Style 6 (Second Model)
Production Dates: 1934
Total Estimated Production: Plectrum neck (PB): 18 units
Tenor neck (TB): 2 units
Pot: Multi-ply maple of 11" outside diameter (.625" thick below the flange), cast brass "raised head" tone ring, die-cast one-piece flange, notched die-cast stretcher band, dual coordinator rods, metal parts gold plated, engraving on armrest, stretcher band, tone ring and tailpiece, Mastertone guarantee decal inside rim
Neck: Curly maple, modified "violin" peghead with checkerboard binding, ebony fingerboard, top and side-bound with checkerboard binding in combination with cream-colored ivoroid, mother-of-pearl fingerboard inlays in modified "hearts and flowers" pattern, "Gibson" script logo in peghead, no Mastertone block, heel capped in white and black stripes, has truss rod.
Resonator: Removable "convex-back" type, figured maple veneer over a laminated poplar core, mounted with four thumbscrews, no concentric rings inlaid on back, sides bound with checkerboard binding in combination with cream-colored ivoroid
Finish: Nitro-cellulose lacquer over Argentine Grey stain
Serial Numbers: No serial numbers used on this model
Factory Order Number: Die-stamped on the interior rim wall, also copied in chalk at the center of resonator interior, and repeated in red paint to the right of the neck notch

Banjo: Style "Royal P-T"
Production Dates: 1929
Total Estimated Production: Plectrum-Tenor neck (PT): 125 units
Pot: Multi-ply maple of 11" outside diameter (.75" thick below the flange), cast brass "flathead" tone ring, tube and plate flange, notched brass or die-cast stretcher band, dual coordinator rods, metal parts gold plated, engraving on armrest, stretcher band, tone ring and tailpiece, Mastertone guarantee decal inside rim
Neck: Curly maple, modified "violin" peghead with gold-sparkle binding, ebony fingerboard with 20 frets and extended "plectrum-tenor" scale length, top and side-bound with gold-sparkle binding in combination with cream-colored ivoroid, mother-of-pearl fingerboard inlays in modified "hearts and flowers" pattern, "Gibson" script logo in peghead, no Mastertone block, heel capped gold-sparkle, has truss rod.
Resonator: Removable "convex-back" type, figured maple veneer over a laminated poplar core, mounted with four thumbscrews, no concentric rings inlaid on back, sides bound with gold-sparkle binding in combination with cream-colored ivoroid
Finish: Nitro-cellulose lacquer over Argentine Grey stain
Serial Numbers: No serial numbers used on this model
Factory Order Number: Die-stamped on the interior rim wall, also copied in chalk at the center of resonator interior, and repeated in red paint to the right of the neck notch

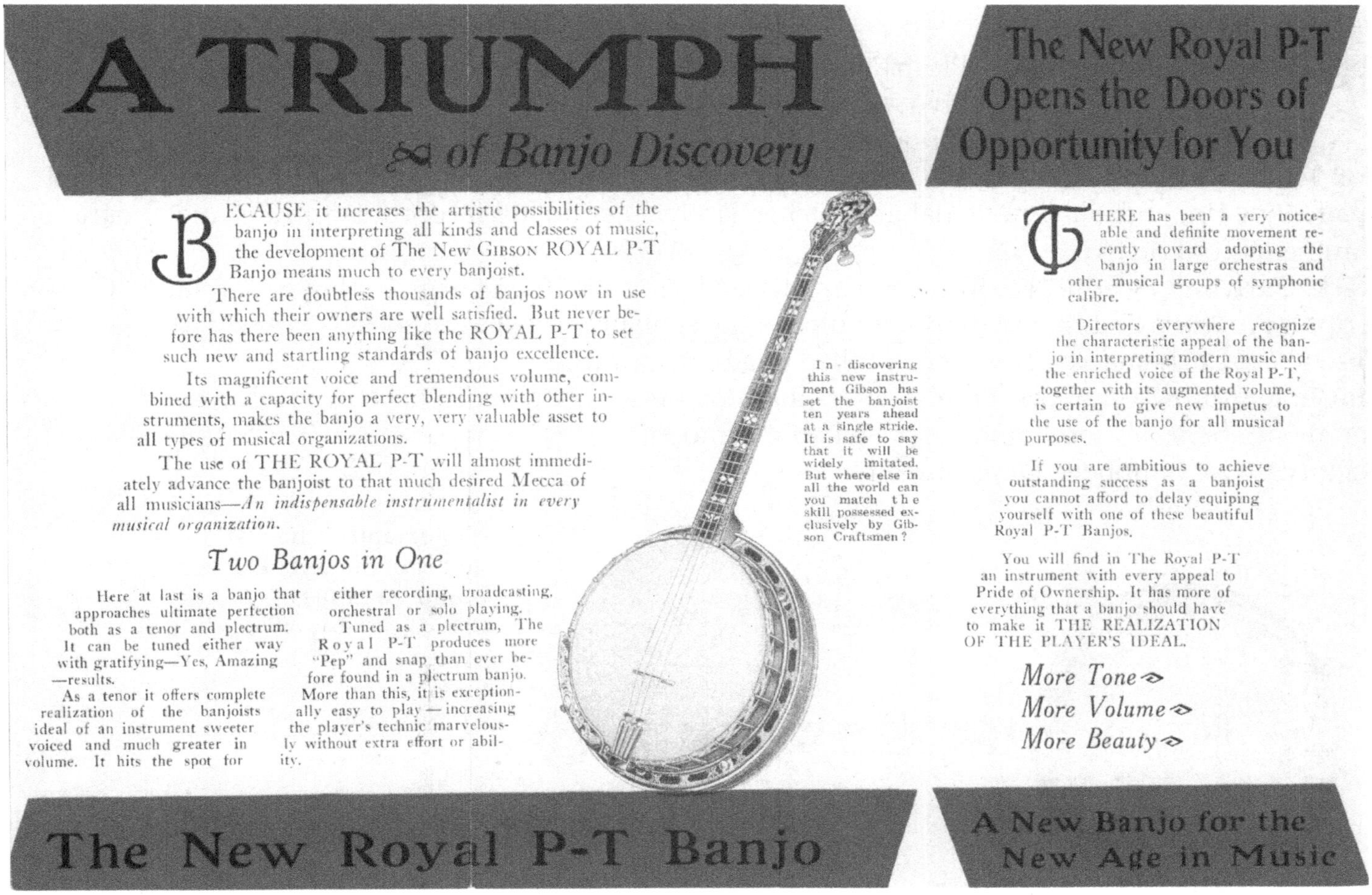

A TRIUMPH

of Banjo Discovery

BECAUSE it increases the artistic possibilities of the banjo in interpreting all kinds and classes of music, the development of The New GIBSON ROYAL P-T Banjo means much to every banjoist.

There are doubtless thousands of banjos now in use with which their owners are well satisfied. But never before has there been anything like the ROYAL P-T to set such new and startling standards of banjo excellence.

Its magnificent voice and tremendous volume, combined with a capacity for perfect blending with other instruments, makes the banjo a very, very valuable asset to all types of musical organizations.

The use of THE ROYAL P-T will almost immediately advance the banjoist to that much desired Mecca of all musicians—*An indispensable instrumentalist in every musical organization.*

Two Banjos in One

Here at last is a banjo that approaches ultimate perfection both as a tenor and plectrum. It can be tuned either way with gratifying—Yes, Amazing—results.

As a tenor it offers complete realization of the banjoists ideal of an instrument sweeter voiced and much greater in volume. It hits the spot for either recording, broadcasting, orchestral or solo playing.

Tuned as a plectrum, The Royal P-T produces more "Pep" and snap than ever before found in a plectrum banjo. More than this, it is exceptionally easy to play—increasing the player's technic marvelously without extra effort or ability.

In discovering this new instrument Gibson has set the banjoist ten years ahead at a single stride. It is safe to say that it will be widely imitated. But where else in all the world can you match the skill possessed exclusively by Gibson Craftsmen?

The New Royal P-T Opens the Doors of Opportunity for You

THERE has been a very noticeable and definite movement recently toward adopting the banjo in large orchestras and other musical groups of symphonic calibre.

Directors everywhere recognize the characteristic appeal of the banjo in interpreting modern music and the enriched voice of the Royal P-T, together with its augmented volume, is certain to give new impetus to the use of the banjo for all musical purposes.

If you are ambitious to achieve outstanding success as a banjoist you cannot afford to delay equiping yourself with one of these beautiful Royal P-T Banjos.

You will find in The Royal P-T an instrument with every appeal to Pride of Ownership. It has more of everything that a banjo should have to make it THE REALIZATION OF THE PLAYER'S IDEAL.

More Tone
More Volume
More Beauty

The New Royal P-T Banjo

A New Banjo for the New Age in Music

The "Royal P-T" never appeared in any catalog. This 1929 pamphlet documents the model.
Steve Huber Collection

Banjo: Style 7
Production Dates: 1937- in production at the start of World War II (last shipped 1944)
Total Estimated Production: Plectrum neck (PB): 21 units
Five-string neck (RB): 36 units
Tenor neck (TB): 67 units
Pot: Multi-ply maple rim with 11" outside diameter (.580" to .625" thick below the flange), cast brass "flathead" tone ring, die-cast one-piece threaded flange, die-cast top-tension stretcher band, dual coordinator rods, metal parts nickel-plated, Mastertone guarantee decal inside rim
Neck: Maple, "art-deco" guitar-type peghead with cream-colored ivoroid binding, radiused rosewood fingerboard with cream-colored ivoroid binding, "slashed-bowtie" fingerboard inlays (but other variants seen), "Gibson" script logo in peghead, has truss rod
Resonator: Removable lathe-turned type with solid maple back and matching sidewall veneer, no concentric rings, mounted with four thumbscrews, cream-colored ivoroid binding (top and bottom)
Finish: Nitro-cellulose lacquer over dark brown stain
Serial Numbers: Die-stamped, two-letter prefix type serial number located on back of peghead (1939-1940 ONLY), no serial number (1941-1944)
Factory Order Number: Die-stamped in rim also copied in chalk at the center of resonator interior (1937-1938) or single-letter prefix type die-stamped on back of peghead (1941-1944)

Banjo: Style 12 (First Model - NOT top tension)
Production Dates: 1933 only
Total Estimated Production: Plectrum neck (PB): 1
Five string neck (RB): 1
Tenor neck (TB): 1
Pot: Multi-ply maple rim with 12" outside diameter (.75" thick below the flange), cast brass "raised head" tone ring, tube and plate flange, notched stretcher band, dual coordinator rods, metal parts chrome or gold plated
Neck: Curly maple with "scroll" (double-cut) peghead with "flying eagle" inlay pattern and "Gibson" script logo, rosewood fingerboard with block inlays, no binding, has truss rod
Resonator: Curly maple back veneer, rolled edges, no binding
Finish: Red-brown sunburst on resonator, Sheraton brown stain on neck, black finish on rim
Serial Numbers: No serial numbers used on this model
Factory Order Numbers: Die-stamped in rim

Photograph of the first model of the style 12 banjo, produced in 1933.
Collection of the author

Banjo: Style 12 (Second Model)
Production Dates: 1937- 1939, 1941
Total Estimated Production: Plectrum neck (PB): 4 units
Five-string neck (RB): 4 units
Tenor neck (TB): 19 units
Pot: Multi-ply maple rim with 11" outside diameter (.580" to .625" thick below the flange), cast brass "flathead" tone ring, die-cast one-piece threaded flange, die-cast top-tension stretcher band, dual coordinator rods, metal parts chrome-plated, Mastertone guarantee decal inside rim
Neck: Walnut, "art-deco" guitar-type peghead with white/black/white binding, radiused rosewood fingerboard with white/black/white triple binding, "stepped block" fingerboard inlays (but other variants seen), "Gibson" script logo in peghead, has truss rod
Resonator: Removable lathe-turned type with solid walnut back and matching sidewall veneer, no concentric rings, mounted with four thumbscrews, white/black/white triple binding (top and bottom)
Finish: Nitro-cellulose lacquer over brown sunburst (but other variants seen)
Serial Numbers: Die-stamped, two-letter prefix type serial number located on back of peghead (1939 ONLY), no serial number 1937-1938, 1941
Factory Order Number: Die-stamped in rim also copied in chalk at the center of resonator interior (1937-1938) or single-letter prefix type die-stamped on back of peghead (1941)

Banjo: Style 18
Production Dates: 1937- in production at the start of World War II (last shipped 1943)
Total Estimated Production: Plectrum neck (PB): 13 units
Five-string neck (RB): 7 units
Tenor neck (TB): 27 units
Pot: Multi-ply maple rim with 11" outside diameter (.580" to .625" thick below the flange), cast brass "flathead" tone ring, die-cast one-piece threaded flange, die-cast top-tension stretcher band, dual coordinator rods, metal parts gold plated, engraving on stretcher band, tone ring, arm rest and tailpiece, Mastertone guarantee decal inside rim
Neck: Curly maple, "art-deco" guitar-type peghead with white/black/white triple binding, radiused rosewood fingerboard with white/black/white binding, "stepped block" fingerboard inlays (but other variants seen), "Gibson" script logo in peghead, has truss rod
Resonator: Removable lathe-turned type with solid curly maple (or birds-eye maple) back and matching sidewall veneer, no concentric rings, mounted with four thumbscrews, white/black/white triple binding (top and bottom)
Finish: Nitro-cellulose lacquer red-brown sunburst stain
Serial Numbers: Die-stamped, two-letter prefix type serial number located on back of peghead (1939-1940 ONLY), no serial number (1941-1943)
Factory Order Number: Die-stamped in rim also copied in chalk at the center of resonator interior (1937-1938) or single-letter prefix type die-stamped on back of peghead (1941-1943)

Banjo: Style 75
Production Dates: 1937 – in production at the start of World War II (last shipped 1944)
Total Estimated Production: Plectrum neck (PB): 11 units
Five-string neck (RB): 72 units
Tenor neck (TB): 121 units
Pot: Multi-ply maple rim with 11" outside diameter (.580" to .625" thick below the flange), cast brass "raised head" tone ring (TB) or cast brass "flathead" tone ring (PB's and RB's), die-cast one-piece flange, notched die-cast stretcher band, dual coordinator rods, all metal parts nickel-plated, Mastertone guarantee decal inside rim
Neck: Mahogany or straight-grain maple with "scroll" (double-cut) peghead, rosewood fingerboard, cream-colored ivoroid binding, catalog specified mother-of-pearl "leaves and bows" fingerboard inlays (but many variants seen), "Gibson" script logo in peghead, "Mastertone" etched on mother-of-pearl block in fingerboard, has truss rod
Resonator: Removable "convex-back" type, mahogany veneer over a laminated poplar core (usually 1937) or laminated maple core (usually later), two white/black/white concentric rings inlaid on back, mounted with four thumbscrews, cream-colored ivoroid binding (top and bottom)
Finish: Nitro-cellulose lacquer over red mahogany stain
Serial Numbers: Two-letter prefix serial number stamped on back of peghead (1939-1940)
Factory Order Number: Die-stamped on the interior rim wall, also copied in chalk at the center of resonator interior, and repeated in red paint to the right of the neck notch (1937-1938), single-letter prefix FON die-stamped on back of peghead (1940-1943), also seen with no FON

Banjo: Style "All-American"
Production Dates: 1930-1931 (last shipped 1941)
Total Estimated Production: Five-string neck (RB): 1 unit
Tenor neck (TB): 24 units
Pot: Multi-ply maple rim with 11" outside diameter (625" or .75" thick below the flange), cast brass "raised head" or "flathead" tone ring, seen with either tube and plate flange or die-cast one-piece flange, notched brass or die-cast stretcher band, dual coordinator rods, all metal parts gold plated, engraved stretcher band, tone ring, armrest and tailpiece, interior and exterior bottom edge of rim bound with wooden marquetry, Mastertone guarantee decal inside rim
Neck: "White holly" (painted maple) or burled walnut with carved and painted "American Eagle" peghead, celluloid fingerboard with etched and painted scenes of American history, white/black/white triple binding, carved and painted heel
Resonator: Removable "convex-back" type, "white holly" (painted maple) or burled walnut veneer over a laminated poplar core, embossed and painted American eagle on back, embossed and painted sidewalls, white/black/white triple binding, mounted with four thumbscrews
Finish: Nitro-cellulose lacquer.
Serial Numbers: No serial numbers used on this model
Factory Order Number: Die-stamped on the interior rim wall, also copied in chalk or grease pencil at the center of resonator interior, and repeated in red paint to the right of the neck notch, also seen with no FON

Banjo: Style "Bella Voce"
Production Dates: 1927-1929
Total Estimated Production: Guitar neck (GB): 1 unit
Mandolin neck (MB): 1 unit
Plectrum neck (PB): 7 units
Five-string neck (RB): 2 units
Tenor neck (TB): 175 units
Pot: Multi-ply maple rim with 11" outside diameter (.75" thick below the flange), cast brass "raised head" or "flathead" tone ring, tube and plate flange, notched brass stretcher band, dual coordinator rods, all metal parts gold plated, engraved stretcher band, tone ring, armrest and tailpiece, interior and exterior bottom edge of rim bound with a custom selected decorative binding, Mastertone guarantee decal inside rim
Neck: Available in "White holly" (painted maple), burled walnut, curly maple or rosewood, carved and painted peghead, usually rosewood fingerboard with mother-of-pearl inlays but also seen with celluloid Florentine style fingerboard, double side-bound with a custom selected decorative binding and cream-colored ivoroid, carved and painted heel
Resonator: Removable "convex-back" type, "white holly" (painted maple), burled walnut, curly maple or rosewood veneer over a laminated poplar core, embossed and painted back with floral scene containing a banjo, lute and harp, embossed and painted sidewalls, side-bound with a custom selected decorative binding and cream-colored ivoroid, mounted with four thumbscrews
Finish: Nitro-cellulose lacquer.
Serial Numbers: No serial numbers used on this model
Factory Order Number: Die-stamped on the interior rim wall, also copied in chalk or grease pencil at the center of resonator interior, and repeated in red paint to the right of the neck notch

Banjo: Style "Florentine"
Production Dates: 1927-1937 (last shipped 1942)
Total Estimated Production: Plectrum neck (PB): 30 units
Five-string neck (RB): 1 unit
Tenor neck (TB): 100 units
Pot: Multi-ply maple rim with 11" outside diameter (.625" or .75" thick below the flange), cast brass "raised head" or "flathead" tone ring, seen with either tube and plate or die-cast one-piece flange, notched brass stretcher band, dual coordinator rods, all metal parts gold plated, engraved stretcher band, tone ring, armrest and tailpiece, interior and exterior bottom edge of rim bound with a custom selected decorative binding, Mastertone guarantee decal inside rim
Neck: Available in "White holly" (painted maple), burled walnut, curly maple or rosewood, carved and painted peghead, celluloid peghead veneer with rhinestones, celluloid fingerboard with etched and painted Venetian scenes, double side-bound with a custom selected decorative binding and cream-colored ivoroid, carved and painted heel
Resonator: Removable "convex-back" type, "white holly" (painted maple), burled walnut, curly maple or rosewood veneer over a laminated poplar core, embossed and painted faux coat-of-arms on back, embossed and painted sidewalls, double side-bound with a custom selected decorative binding and cream-colored ivoroid, mounted with four thumbscrews
Finish: Nitro-cellulose lacquer.
Serial Numbers: No serial numbers used on this model
Factory Order Number: Die-stamped on the interior rim wall, also copied in chalk or grease pencil at the center of resonator interior, and repeated in red paint to the right of the neck notch

Banjo: Style X
Production Dates: 1935-1936
Total Estimated Production: Tenor neck (TB): 40 units
Pot: Multi-ply maple rim with 11″ outside diameter (.580″ to .625″ thick below the flange), unique tone ring with exterior holes and vertical cuts, die-cast one-piece flange, notched die-cast stretcher band, single coordinator rod, all metal parts nickel or chrome-plated
Neck: Maple or mahogany, "scroll" (double-cut) type peghead, usually seen with radiused rosewood fingerboard and mother-of-pearl "leaves and bows" inlay
Resonator: Removable "convex-back" type, alternating white/black pattern on back (1935) or Cremona sunburst on curly maple veneer (1936), laminated poplar core, painted sidewalls
Finish: Seen in dark blue or black nitro-cellulose lacquer
Serial numbers: No serial numbers used on this model
Factory Order Number: Die-stamped on the interior rim wall, also copied in chalk at the center of resonator interior

Bass Banjo
Production Dates: 1930-1932
Total Estimated Production: 1 unit
Pot: Multi-ply maple rim with 22″ outside diameter, tube and plate flange, notched stretcher band, metal parts all gun metal finish
Neck: Three-piece maple with guitar "open book" style peghead, celluloid peghead veneer with rhinestones
Resonator: Removable "convex-back" type, straight-grain maple veneer over a laminated poplar core, mounted with four thumbscrews, dark binding (bottom only)
Finish: Nitro-cellulose lacquer in a natural finish
Serial Numbers: No serial numbers used on this model
Factory Order Number: Die-stamped on the interior rim wall

Electric Banjo: Style 150
Production Dates: 1938-1941
Total Estimated Production: Plectrum neck (ETB): 34 units
Five-string neck (ERB): 3 units
Tenor Neck (ETB): 66 units
Body: Figured maple, 11″ outside diameter, single bar pickup, volume and tone controls are mounted on the side of the body, "firestripe" pickguard, rosewood armrest, all metal parts nickel-plated
Neck: Figured maple (one-piece), rosewood fingerboard with white/black/white "triple" binding, mother-of-pearl "slashed bowtie" inlays, "art-deco" guitar-type peghead with white/black/white "triple" binding
Finish: Nitro-cellulose lacquer (dark sunburst)
Serial Numbers: Die-stamped, two-letter prefix type serial number located on back of peghead (1938-1940)
Factory Order Number: single-letter prefix type (1941 only)

Appendix B – Production Totals

Overview

The following table summarizes *actual* production totals taken from Gibson's surviving financial records and corporate income tax returns. The original documents are part of the Steve Huber Collection.

Instrument Type	1925	1926	1927	1928	1931	1935	1937	1939
Banjos	5,693	6,223	4,828	3,626	1,704	4,703	1,502	586
Banjo-Ukes	1,555	7,569	4,338	1,730				
Guitars	615	1,433	1,885	2,785	4,509	20,575	22,358	12,327
Mandolins	1,279	1,372	1,194	1,195	714	2,294	2,171	1,194
Mandolas & Mando-Cellos	115	91	103	66				
Mando-Bass & Harp Guitars	26	14	22	11				
Violins, Violas, Cellos & Bass								787
Ukuleles	2,556	6,705	4,338	1,730	776	197	208	178

"A shipment of Guitars, Banjos and Mandolins arrive in New Zealand"
A music store in New Zealand sent in this photograph for the June-July 1937 issue of the "Mastertone"
Gibson's most distant representative
Centerstream Archives

Appendix C – 1941 Production Costs

Overview

The following table summarizes *actual* 1941 production costs as calculated by Gibson's accounting department. The original document is part of the Steve Huber Collection.

Model	Materials	Labor	Overhead	Total Cost	Retail Price
L-0	$2.300	$2.626	$2.626	$7.55	$29.00
L-00 "Regular finish"	$2.300	$2.664	$2.664	$7.63	$36.75
L-00 "Natural finish"	$2.300	$2.630	$2.630	$7.56	$42.00
HG-00	$2.225	$2.601	$2.601	$7.43	$36.75
TG-00	$2.386	$2.660	$2.660	$7.71	$36.75
TG-50	$4.920	$4.820	$4.820	$14.56	$68.25
Special # 3	$3.360	$4.010	$4.010	$11.38	
Special # 5	$3.446	$4.242	$4.242	$11.91	
L-50	$5.642	$4.824	$4.824	$15.29	$68.25
L-4 "Regular finish"	$7.645	$6.266	$6.266	$20.18	$99.75
L-4 "Natural finish"	$6.984	$5.959	$5.959	$18.90	$105.00
L-4 "Converted natural"	$6.984	$6.019	$6.019	$19.02	
L-5 "Regular finish"	$23.620	$17.590	$17.590	$58.80	$288.75
L-5 "Natural finish"	$23.620	$17.430	$17.430	$58.48	$299.25
Super 400 "Regular finish"	$25.870	$22.970	$22.970	$71.81	$325.50
Super 400 "Natural finish"	$25.870	$22.380	$22.380	$70.63	$336.00
Smeck Hawaiian	$2.380	$3.120	$3.120	$8.62	$63.00
TB-11	$8.880	$4.580	$4.580	$18.04	$68.25
PB-11	$8.560	$4.620	$4.620	$17.80	$68.25
RB-11	$9.360	$4.820	$4.820	$19.00	$68.25
MB-11	$8.030	$4.540	$4.540	$17.11	$68.75
A-00 "Regular finish"	$1.760	$3.120	$3.120	$8.00	$31.50
A-00 "Natural finish"	$1.760	$3.030	$3.030	$7.82	$36.75
Uke-1	$0.840	$1.910	$1.910	$4.66	$14.25
Tenor Uke	$0.900	$2.150	$2.150	$5.20	$18.50

Appendix D – Gibson Ephemera

Overview

Gibson scholar Steve Huber has amassed a large assortment of rare, pre-World War II Gibson ephemera. He has generously allowed many of these items to be photographed and included in this book. The photographs on these pages show a portion of his collection.

Gibson dealer items, including promotional banners, string displays, pick boxes and polish kits
Steve Huber Collection

Additional promotional items, including an extremely rare artist endorsement in a rotating frame.
Steve Huber Collection

A hand-colored and professionally-framed poster for Gibson endorser Tommy Davis
Steve Huber Collection

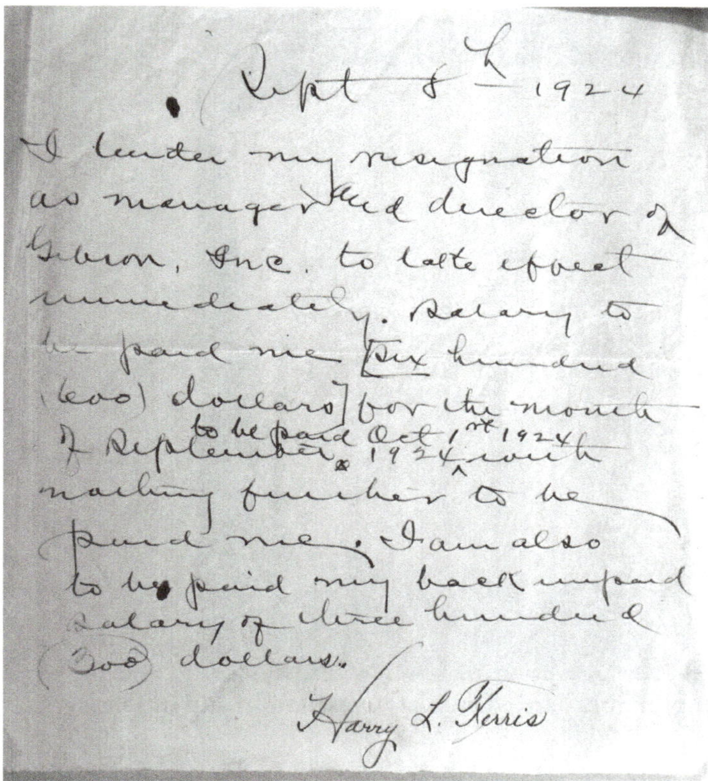

Sept 8th 1924

I tender my resignation as manager and director of Gibson, Inc. to take effect immediately. Salary to be paid me [Six hundred (600) dollars] for the month of September 1924 to be paid Oct 1st 1924 with nothing further to be paid me. I am also to be paid my back unpaid salary of three hundred (300) dollars.

Harry L. Ferris

The original resignation of general manager Harry L. Ferris from 1924. The body of the document is in the handwriting of Judge John Adams, President of Gibson, Ferris merely signed at the bottom.
Steve Huber Collection

A re-creation of the Gibson shipping clerk's desk, showing several of the ledgers
Steve Huber Collection

This is an original pre-war Gibson cardboard shipping box. It probably carried an F-style mandolin and hard case.
Steve Huber Collection

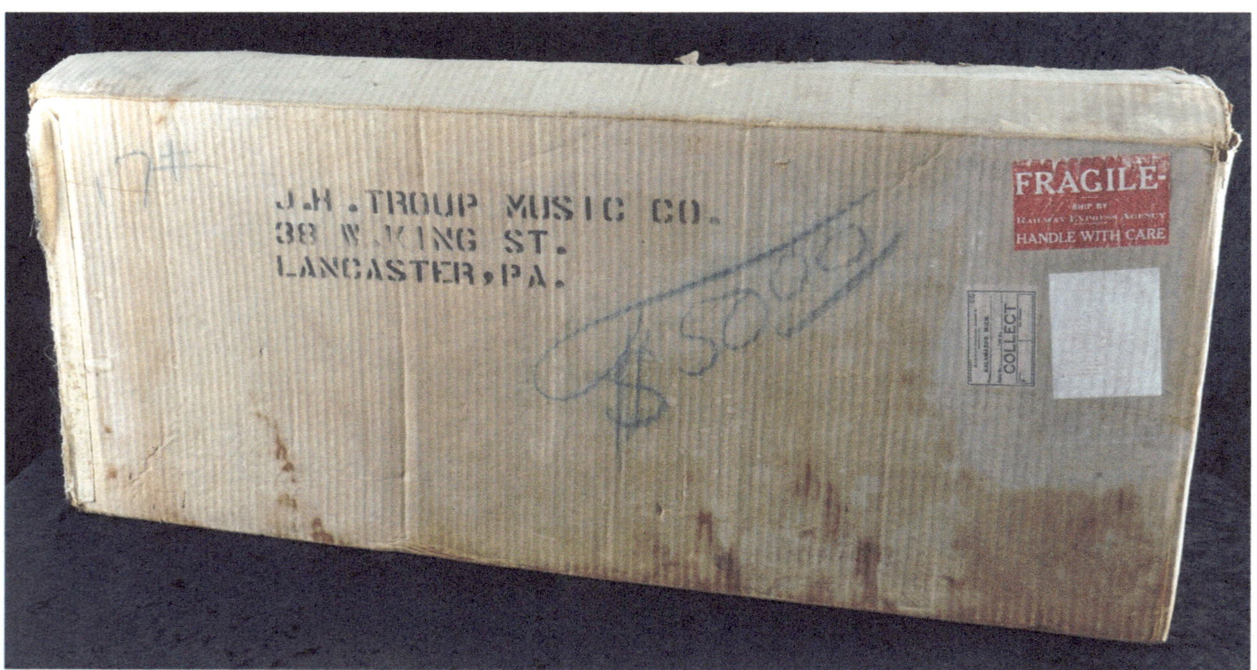

Reverse side of above.
Steve Huber Collection

Gibson stock certificate filled out by Lloyd A. Loar for himself. His well-known signature appears in three places. The printed version of his name in the center may also be from his hand.

Steve Huber Collection

Various pre-war Gibson pamphlets (above) and catalogs (below)
Steve Huber Collection

Pre-war Gibson catalogs
Steve Huber Collection

Very rare pre-war catalog mailing envelopes
Steve Huber Collection

A variety of original Gibson dealer price lists.
Steve Huber Collection

Promotional brochures promising that the "Road to Happiness" is a Gibson instrument. Many of us would agree.
Steve Huber Collection

Source List

Internet

Beimborn, Dan. *The Mandolin Archive*. Website. http://www.mandolinarchive.com : 2008-2010.

Earnest, Greg. *Prewar Gibson Banjos*. Website. http://www.earnestbanjo.com : 2008-2010.

International Arcade Museum (Pasadena, CA). *International Arcade Museum*. Website. http://www.arcade-museum.com : 2008-2010.

Michigan. Kalamazoo County. 1900 U.S. census. Digital images. *Ancestry.com* http://ancestry.com : 2008-2010.

Michigan. Kalamazoo County. 1910 U.S. census. Digital images. *Ancestry.com* http://ancestry.com : 2008-2010.

Michigan. Kalamazoo County. 1920 U.S. census. Digital images. *Ancestry.com* http://ancestry.com : 2008-2010.

Michigan. Kalamazoo County. 1930 U.S. census. Digital images. *Ancestry.com* http://ancestry.com : 2008-2010.

Michigan. "Kalamazoo Cemetery List 1831-1941." Database. *Kalamazoogenealogy.org* http://www.kalamazoogenealogy.org : 2008-2010.

Michigan. "Kalamazoo County Marriage Records 1831-1941." Digital images. *Kalamazoogenealogy.org* http://www.kalamazoogenealogy.org : 2008-2010.

Michigan. "Index to Obituaries: Kalamazoo Gazette." Database. Kalamazoo Public Library – Local History Collection http://www.kpl.gov/genealogy/obituary-requests : 2008-2010.

Polk, R.L., compiler. Kalamazoo, Michigan, City Directory. Richmond: R.L. Polk Directory Co, 1905, 1915, 1926, 1935. Digital images. *Kalamazoogenealogy.org* http://www.kalamazoogenealogy.org : 2008-2010.

Polk, .L., compiler. Kalamazoo, Michigan, City Directory. Richmond: R.L. Polk Directory Co, 1927, 1939, 1943, 1945. Digital images. *Ancestry.com* http://ancestry.com : 2008-2010.

Interviews

Bergeon, John. Interviews by Joe Spann. 2009. Transcripts. Privately held by Spann, Winter Haven, Florida. 2011.

Bettencourt, Glen. Interviews by Joe Spann. 2009. Transcripts. Privately held by Spann, Winter Haven, Florida. 2011.

Blaisdell, Lewis J. Interview by Joe Spann. 1 April 2008. Transcript. Privately held by Spann, Winter Haven, Florida. 2011.

Branch, Dave. Interviews by Joe Spann. 2009. Transcripts. Privately held by Spann, Winter Haven, Florida. 2011.

Chittenden, Edward. Interviews by Joe Spann. 2009. Transcripts. Privately held by Spann, Winter Haven, Florida. 2011.

Cook, Jack. Interviews by Joe Spann. 2009. Transcripts. Privately held by Spann, Winter Haven, Florida. 2011.

Curtis, Jack. Interview by Joe Spann. 20 April 2009. Transcript. Privately held by Spann, Winter Haven, Florida. 2011.

French, Jack. Interviews by Joe Spann. 2009. Transcripts. Privately held by Spann, Winter Haven, Florida. 2011.

Glerum Jr., Adrian. Interviews by Joe Spann. 2009. Transcripts. Privately held by Spann, Winter Haven, Florida. 2011.

Glover, Ruth McMichaels. Interviews by Joe Spann. 2010. Transcripts. Privately held by Spann, Winter Haven, Florida. 2011.

Grossman, Pat Abrams. Interview by Joe Spann. 27 March 2009. Transcript. Privately held by Spann, Winter Haven, Florida. 2011.

Hart, Robert Lamb. Interviews by Joe Spann. 2009. Transcripts. Privately held by Spann, Winter Haven, Florida. 2011.

Hutchens, Jim. Interviews by Joe Spann. 2009. Transcripts. Privately held by Spann, Winter Haven, Florida. 2011.

Kennedy, Davis. Interview by Joe Spann. 31 July 2009. Transcript. Privately held by Spann, Winter Haven, Florida. 2011.

Kievit, Donald. Interviews by Joe Spann. 2009. Transcripts. Privately held by Spann, Winter Haven, Florida. 2011.

Musselman, Joy. Interviews by Joe Spann. 2010. Transcripts. Privately held by Spann, Winter Haven, Florida. 2011.

Nolting, William. Interviews by Joe Spann. 2010. Transcripts. Privately held by Spann, Winter Haven, Florida. 2011.

Post, Gerald R. Interviews by Joe Spann. 2010. Transcripts. Privately held by Spann, Winter Haven, Florida. 2011.

Post, John A. Interviews by Joe Spann. 2010. Transcripts. Privately held by Spann, Winter Haven, Florida. 2011.

Stadler, Carl. Interviews by Joe Spann. 2009. Transcripts. Privately held by Spann, Winter Haven, Florida. 2011.

Veen, Phillip. Interviews by Joe Spann. 2009. Transcripts. Privately held by Spann, Winter Haven, Florida. 2011.

Published

Bellson, Julius. *The Gibson Story*. Kalamazoo, Michigan: Julius Bellson, 1973.

Carter, Walter. *Gibson Guitars – 100 Years of an American Icon*. Los Angeles: General Publishing Group, 1994.

Duchossoir, Andre R., *Gibson Electrics – Volume 1*. Winona, MN: Hal Leonard Publishing Corporation, 1981.

Gibson Inc. (Kalamazoo, Michigan). *Catalog J*. Kalamazoo: n.pub., 1917.

Gibson Inc. (Kalamazoo, Michigan). *Catalog K*. Kalamazoo: n.pub., 1918.

Gibson Inc. (Kalamazoo, Michigan). *Catalog L*. Kalamazoo: n.pub., 1920.

Gibson Inc. (Kalamazoo, Michigan). *Catalog M*. Kalamazoo: n.pub., 1921.

Gibson Inc. (Kalamazoo, Michigan). *Catalog N*. Kalamazoo: n.pub., 1923.

Gibson Inc. (Kalamazoo, Michigan). *Catalog P*. Kalamazoo: n.pub., 1926.

Gibson Inc. (Kalamazoo, Michigan). *Catalog R*. Kalamazoo: n.pub., 1929.

Gibson Inc. (Kalamazoo, Michigan). *Catalog S?*. Kalamazoo: n.pub., 1930.

Gibson Inc. (Kalamazoo, Michigan). *Catalog U*. Kalamazoo: n.pub., 1932.

Gibson Inc. (Kalamazoo, Michigan). *Catalog W*. Kalamazoo: n.pub., 1934.

Gibson Inc. (Kalamazoo, Michigan). *Catalog W*. Kalamazoo: n.pub., 1935.

Gibson Inc. (Kalamazoo, Michigan). *Catalog X*. Kalamazoo: n.pub., 1936.

Gibson Inc. (Kalamazoo, Michigan). *Catalog Y*. Kalamazoo: n.pub., 1937.

Gibson Inc. (Kalamazoo, Michigan). *Catalog AA*. Kalamazoo: n.pub., 1939.

Gibson Inc. (Kalamazoo, Michigan). *Catalog BB*. Kalamazoo: n.pub., 1942.

Gibson Inc. (Kalamazoo, Michigan). *Gibson Mastertone Banjos*. Kalamazoo: n.pub., 1926.

Gibson Inc. *Mastertone Magazine* (August 1928).

Gibson Inc. *Mastertone Magazine* (September 1929).

Gibson Inc. *Mastertone Magazine* (October 1929).

Gibson Inc. *Mastertone Magazine* (November 1929).

Gibson Inc. *Mastertone Magazine* (June 1930).

Gruhn, George, and Walter Carter, *Gruhn's Guide to Vintage Guitars*. San Francisco: Backbeat Books, 1999.

Whitford, Eldon, David Vinopal, and Dan Erlewine, *Gibson's Fabulous Flat-Top Guitars*. San Francisco: Backbeat Books, 1994.

Miscellaneous

Collected Documents of Gibson Inc. 1902-1941. Steve Huber. Hendersonville, Tennessee.